Come Collect With Me

Musings on Collecting
and
American Antiques

Baron Perlman

CKBooks

Names: Perlman, Baron, 1946- author.

Title: Come collect with me: musings on collecting and American antiques / Baron Perlman.

Description: New Glarus, WI : CKBooks Publishing, [2019] | Includes index.

Identifiers: ISBN 9781949085082 (paperback) | ISBN 9781949085099 (hardcover) | ISBN 9781949085129 (ebook)

Subjects: LCSH: Antiques--Collection and preservation--United States. | Antiques--United States. | Collectors and collecting--United States.

Classification: LCC NK1105 .P47 2019 (print) | LCC NK1105 (ebook) | DDC 745.10973--dc23

LCCN: 2019930248

CKBooks Publishing
P.O. Box 214
New Glarus, WI
53574
ckbookspublishing.com

Dedication

To the people who first lent me their passions
for collecting

◆

Charlie and Betty, Bernice and Jim

Table of Contents

Items Pictured

Image Page Number

Preface

My wife and I have collected antiques for more than 40 years. Over that whole period, my profession (teacher, researcher, and clinical psychologist) intervened in what might have been little more than a hobby: It drove me to closely observe and try to fathom the collectors' passion. I added to that analysis endless talks with dealers and individuals – some successful, others not. Put together, those streams provided the fountainhead for this book.

Surely some of you are already muttering, "Oh God, he's a psychologist; will professional babble inundate us?" I can only reply, "Not if I have anything to do with it." *Come Collect with Me* is intended to offer insights for collectors of anything from cigar bands to fine art, but particularly those who collect American antiques, casually or seriously. My goals are simple ones: To tell you what I have learned in my many years as a collector (some arising from mistakes I or others have made) and in doing so to allow you to be better prepared to pursue your collecting passion. Along the way, I hope to provide both insights and wry commentary on an activity that to many people seems alien.

Is the notion of a sane collector an oxymoron? I have yet to decide. Close friends who now shake their heads at your collecting will understand you better by reading this book. And for the prospective collector of antiques I hope this little volume will open your mind to what can be an enduring and fascinating pastime.

My classroom for learning about collecting and antiques embraces back roads, dealers' shops, auction houses, antique shows, fellow collectors, books and publications, and a heap of websites. I decided early on I did not know enough (and still do not) to purchase anything of much value at open-air markets (think acres of antiques, collectibles, and – let's be candid – junk), unless I was working with dealers I already knew. What I have found in this wandering is pertinent to collectors of classic cars, Star

Wars toys, stamps, or coins, but I have restricted my focus to American antiques, the area I know best.

Rarely do books come into being without the assistance of, and a debt of gratitude to, many midwives. One person in particular, Clayton Pennington, Editor of *Maine Antique Digest,* extended his support and gave me the chance to share my observations on collecting and American antiques as a columnist. *MAD*'s staff seamlessly put my writing into print. Versions of the section, *Why Collect?* and Chapters 11, 12, 13, 19, 20, and 21 previously appeared in *Maine Antique Digest.*

I thank my dear friend Tom Herzing for his creativity and helping me transition from academic to a more informal writing style. His honesty in what was good and less so never wavered. My sister Judith's queries (she is not a collector) about what the heck I was talking about, and what non- or new collectors would want to know, aided my thinking. My good friend Tricia Keith-Spiegel urged me to write this book and I appreciate her support. Countless, nameless dealers, collectors, and museum staff answered questions, corroborated my opinions, or politely offered their viewpoints. Ken Cravillion did a remarkable job taking the photographs that appear in the book and I am grateful for his wonderful eye.

Several antique dealers helped me sharpen my language and understanding in accurately describing pictured pieces. Arnold Frenzel, a retired economics professor, offered insights into collecting, and money and the collector. Helaine Fendelman, author, appraiser, and columnist, inspired me to think seriously about style and connoisseurship, giving the book structure and depth. George Witman, Vice-President of the Pewter Collectors Club of America, suggested readings about his love. Frank Gaglio, antique dealer and show promoter helped me understand the chaos that becomes an antique show.

I have purposely omitted dealers' name, not because they are biased or incorrect but because they generally are self-effacing and more interested in the hobby than personal publicity. I make one exception: Bernice and Jim Miller, now both deceased, who started the two of us on the path of serious collecting. If it were not for the inspiration and friendship offered by two of them, this book would not be possible. Most of all, I owe thanks to my collecting partner – my wife Sandy – who encouraged, questioned and tolerated both my successes and mistakes. I am persuaded my successes outnumber my mistakes, a fault endemic to all collectors.

I avoid issues of what antiques should and do cost. Markets for antiques fluctuate over time, just as do those for houses, gold and tulip bulbs. The insights in this book are intended to be more general and timeless. Any mistakes in facts or conclusion in writing this book are mine alone.

Any fledgling author (and I certainly put myself in that category) feels he sends his newborn child into a cold and unappreciative world. At the same time, no one writes for the sake of writing alone. At the end of all that effort, all I have to fall back on is Chaucer's plea – *go lyttle booke* and high hopes for you, the reader. Welcome to the world of collecting

Baron Perlman
Oshkosh, WI
December 2018

P.S. If you enjoy this book, reviews are greatly appreciated. Connect with me at comecollectwithme.com and facebook.com/baron.perlman.

Introduction

Collecting involves, to use an old-fashioned word, *taste*. People pursue things that appeal to them, though it is difficult at times to explain why that attraction exists. A collector may own five Picassos or wind-up toys or Rookwood vases, but each one has its own story and touches some wellspring of feeling. The questions are, what makes a collector a collector? and why is collecting so common? Neither yields an easy answer.

Some of us become collectors by accident; we inherit a table that Uncle George said was made in 18th century New England. Curiosity compels us to track down its history and in the process we develop some expertise regarding antiques from that era. The expertise generates an interest in pieces from the same period, in the same style. Beyond our will, we are launched on a coherent collection. In contrast, Uncle George leaves his ugly knickknack to Dick, who groans, puts it in the attic and – years later – gives it to a resale shop. So ends history. The crucial difference in these cases is the presence or absence of curiosity. Some people truly care about the past and see themselves as caretakers for its objects and history. Others live in the present. Both sorts can collect: Personally, I study and buy American antiques, but Dick or Dick's wife may have a closet full of souvenirs from recent British royal weddings. I, of course, see my collection as more justified, noble, and superior the piffle of modern Elizabethan tchotchkes, but the fact is that we are both collectors.

Those who pursue antiques vary in every dimension of human attributes and frailty. Collectors can be extroverts or introverts, the nicest persons you ever met or curmudgeons, revolutionary or loyalist, rich or poor. Antique dealers vary just as much. Nonetheless collectors and dealers have their common traits. They almost always love to show their treasures to others. Most of them constantly upgrade, add to, and cull what they own. All make – and often do not admit – mistakes. As you will find, collectors make countless decisions over time. And coping with the imbalance between passion on the one hand and available funds on the other is an endless balancing act.

What follows looks at collectors and the universe of American antique collecting. They are involved in an endless quest: searching for, longing for, purchasing objects to make the perfect collection. Beyond this fascination with stuff there glimmers of course the cosmos where it is sold. Its denizens are dealers, auctioneers, other collectors, pickers, financial institutions, consignment shops, counterfeiters, craftsmen, caterers, show promoters, museums, appraisers, historical societies, publishers, editors, writers, reporters, and of course gossips.

I have often wondered about becoming a "collector whisperer" or "American antique whisperer." Collectors could get in touch and we could talk through a decision they face, which way they lean, and other concerns. More than once such a whisperer would have been most helpful for me. This book serves as a whisperer for its readers.

Let's take a look.

Chapter 1

℮

The Story of a Collector and a Painting

Circa mid-19ᵗʰ Century Hudson River School Washington Head-quarters rare polychrome sandpaper painting. Under glass. Original frame. 21½" x 24" framed, painting is 18¼" x 21". Superb condition. Painted in the manner of Jasper Francis Cropsey (1823-1900). Although his paintings were often copied, it is extremely unusual to see one done using this technique

Collectors of Americana knew the auctioneer: He owned a reputable auction house in New England that regularly handled antique furniture, rugs (old furniture and Oriental rugs have an affinity for each other), silver, clocks, painted boxes, pewter, candlesticks, and paintings. He started by reading the auction rules, made a joke or two, and soon the first item crossed the block. From the outset, prices seemed strong.

Our protagonists, Julia and Robert Jones had begun collecting when in their 20s, and became deeply involved in antiques after a year or two. Julia had long since given away or packed up most of the early items she had once thought would be her collection. After all, how many baskets can one person own? (For those who collect baskets, the answer is "never enough.") She had no black wrought iron rack in the kitchen to hang them from, they collected dust, and they were more fragile than she expected. Once a basket got a break or two in its structure, its value

1

fell. She still used one of them for magazines, another to hold rolled up blankets. As for Robert, he had been drawn to pewter but his interest in it had sagged over time.

Slick, modern furnishings had never struck the couple as something that fit their style, so they continued to accumulate older pieces. At first they had an apartment to furnish and then a house. Slowly their decent pieces grew in number – beds, chairs, tables, an old settee. Then the need arose for smalls – candlesticks, a box or two, redware plates (Julia liked them small with interesting slip decoration), even lamps made out of new stoneware jugs (functional, even though they looked old).

So she was smitten, bitten by the collecting bug. Robert enjoyed her fervor but evidently had a bit less enthusiasm for antiques. Old, well cared for things connected Julia to the past. She had always loved history. Robert just liked their ambiance; they felt relaxed and unpretentious.

Robert and Julia had come late to considering collecting works of art, but their unadorned walls called out for things to catch the eye and pique interest. Paintings of anonymous – and likely undistinguished – dead people seemed a silly way to go, so they found a gifted artist who painted portraits of their children and themselves in early 19th century styles. They (Julia actually) had added to these family pictures over the years with a few small landscapes in a nice grouping and a couple of samplers. For some time, they had been looking for a piece of art that would catch their eye and hearts, and had been captured by several paintings of ships. Unfortunately, they had not found an affordable one that they loved. At one shop, they had passed on a farm scene, mid-19th century, and regretted it to this day.

Then the on-line catalogue for this auction had appeared and Julia took a look. One particular painting caught her attention. Soft to the eye, it had two figures in the foreground and she adored its folk art feel (no expert painterly touches: the boat was far too small, the perspective a bit off, the artist sort of tentative on the forms of trees). Given her love of history, the fact that Washington's headquarters on the Hudson during one winter of the Revolutionary War appeared in the piece fascinated her. She decided to learn more.

First Julia looked at the painting's price estimate. Unless it skyrocketed in cost, (i.e., was a real sleeper and far more valuable than anyone realized) they could afford it. She had looked up similar paintings on the Internet but had never found many painted in color, as this one was. Robert and she budgeted for antiques, after all. If someone loved the piece more than they, and drove the price too high, they would keep looking. It would be a loss but they had suffered such disappointments before. So money was not a stumbling block.

Julia had contacted a dealer they had purchased pieces from previously, who agreed to meet them at the auction preview and look at the painting with her. He had planned to attend anyway. Julia asked the dealer his fee for his expertise, and it seemed affordable and fair. Julia would do her own bidding so there would be no charge for that. She knew "Buyer beware" is the first rule of any auction. Julia had made enough mistakes to be wise about the pitfalls of antique buying. A piece of furniture she bid on turned out to be "married" (top and bottom had started life separately). And once she won a blanket chest that turned out to have been repainted at some time in its life. That explained its low price, and she should have grasped the problem well before raising her paddle. Yes, she would bid but having wise counsel was nothing more than common sense.

As expected, crowds thronged the preview. The auction house's reputation stemmed in part from its summer sale offering high quality items. A buzz filled the air and muted voices muttered polite "excuse me's" time after time. The dealer assisting them informed Julia that the painting looked right to him. "Can you explain that?" she asked. "It looks undisturbed," he said, magnifying glass in hand, spending almost more time looking at the back than the front. There were no auction house labels, artist signatures, or descriptions of the scene. But the frame looked original and the painting seemed undisturbed. It lacked signs of condition problems – foxing, inpainting, or paint loss. The expert asked an auction house staff person to take the painting off the wall, bringing it to the best natural light in the room. He had a magnifying glass with him. "Excellent condition," he murmured.

Julia had told her advisor how the muted colors of the piece appealed to her. He explained a sandpaper painting's characteristics and how unusual it was to find one in color. From him, Julia learned that women had painted many sandpaper works of art. However he could offer no firm opinion as to whether the painting had been done by a female or male hand. He smilingly observed that the artist painted Washington's headquarters on the wrong side of the Hudson, which amused Julia. The painting now appealed to her even more.

Julia asked him, "What would make the painting even better?" "Aside from perhaps another sailboat or two," he said, "or more than the two figures you can readily see pictured, it's a gem." That was exactly what she felt. Aesthetically, the painting appealed to her and she knew they would enjoy it hanging on a wall in their home. It suddenly struck her that at one point the dealer had implied that there were three figures depicted, not just the two in the foreground. When she scanned the piece with his magnifying glass, she saw a third person on the edge of the field, looking almost like a scarecrow. A few lines delineated the person (He? She? Impossible to tell).

She asked about attribution, and he said that artists rarely signed such paintings. But some might argue it was painted in the style of Jasper Francis Cropsey; trained as an architect, he became a painter of some renown, known for his use of color and precise arrangement and outline of forms. Julia owned a book with color plates of Hudson River school artists. (She had once found a work for sale painted by the well-known Thomas Chambers on a dealer's website and she had loved the piece. Alas, the price was one they could not afford.) While Cropsey probably had not painted this particular piece, the artist – "whoever she was," Julia thought definately – had done a good job. The dealer understood why Julia liked it and approved of her eye and choice. "Go for it," he said. He respected Julia's effort in becoming educated about such artwork.

The two of them had ventured out East a day or two prior to the auction, to attend the preview and look more closely at the painting, go to a museum she loved, and get some great seafood. Robert wanted to wander around and soak up the urban culture. The auction was tomorrow. Julia was excited.

At shortly after noon (the auction had begun precisely at 10:00 am) the auctioneer laughingly told the auction crowd that he had competition. Apparently the local historic society's women group had underestimated auction attendance, as had the local firemen. The latter's chili now sold for $12/bowl. There were hungry customers and a rapidly diminishing

4

supply. But the ladies clam chowder had climbed even higher in price. The auctioneer offered to help them move the last of it but they reported doing fine on their own. Prices were indeed strong.

The painting crossed the block right around 1 p.m. (the auctioneer was motoring along at 65 items per hour). "Am I bid. . . " the auctioneer intoned from the block. Front and center, a runner held the painting for all to see. Julia waited. Robert waited. Robert sat stiffly. While it was completely irrational, he always worried if he rubbed his nose or shifted in his chair, the auctioneer would interpret the movement as an offer. He feared owning something in which he had no interest and embarrassing himself to boot.

Robert and Julia waited. The auctioneer began with a somewhat low "left" bid (a bid by someone not attending the auction), and then as several people in the audience signaled their intent he raised the figure using other left bids that he had at hand. Two assistants stood to the side, telephone receivers in hand; each had a bidder interested in the painting with whom they were talking, relaying their current offer or telling them what their next bid had to be if they wanted to continue.

The auction house, as do so many nowadays, also accepted bids via Internet, using one of the familiar sites that offered such services across the country. And some interested collectors like Julia and Robert actually sat in the hall. The couple had agreed Julia actually would do the bidding, so Robert was still as a statue.

The price climbed by increments but stayed reasonable. Julia wondered why they said she 'won' if she had the highest bid. She didn't really win, she thought to herself; she paid. She had fixed a dollar amount in her head she would not exceed, although she knew from experience she wouldn't really know her limit until the auctioneer reached it. Unknown to Robert, what she was willing to offer exceeded what they had agreed on. Every antique collector needs a secret now and then.

Finally she raised her biding card, not subtly but not waving her card to and fro, either. The auctioneer acknowledged it. The final step had begun. After only a few seconds, only two bidders remained, the other on the phone. She hesitated and bid again. The telephone assistant shook her head: her phone bidder would go no higher. "Going once, going twice. . ." and suddenly a new bidder from the floor jumped in. Julia bid again, for a bit more than she and Robert had discussed. He threw her a glance. No secrets now. Heck, she'd take the difference out of her own funds if they won the piece. Up the price climbed and then the bidding stalled. "Going once, going twice, fair warning, sold!" and the auctioneer hammered the item home. Julia had purchased the painting. Love had won out over financial sense.

ℰ

An Exercise in Style and Connoisseurship

In this chapter, unlike those that follow, I weave the object (painting) and the stylistic criteria together in commenting. Artists made sandpaper paintings by coating a thin layer of paint on paper and while the paint was still tacky, sprinkling on a thin coat of marble dust to create a dimensional painting. Julia's eye serves her well. This painting contains wonderful detail and proportion.

Compromises. While I love this piece, I still continue to seek a Hudson Valley painting with West Point pictured (typically on the bluff in the background) and sailboats on the Hudson. They become available now and then. We knew nothing about sandpaper paintings before purchasing this one. Its market value priced the painting affordably. We snapped it up and have not regretted it.

Ƹ

Julia paid up at the auction house desk and arranged to have the painting shipped home. The cost included a 23 percent buyer's premium that Julia had entered into her calculations of the painting's final cost when she was bidding. Almost all auction houses charged similar buyer's fees and there was no avoiding them.

Several people congratulated her on her successful bid; it would seem the painting had more fans than bidders, as is so often the case. The camaraderie felt good to her. The painting had cost what she had offered; her desire and the marketplace had decided its worth. Its value, however, was another matter: it would lie in the pleasure it pro-vided Robert and her over the years. The painting would be a new addition to the family collection alongside their own portraits, and who knew what other artworks yet waited to be acquired and displayed. It had been a very good day indeed. Still, having committed herself to the painting, the pricey chili and clam chowder now exceeded their financial reach. Time for a late lunch somewhere else.

Julia reflected that evening. She and Robert had slowly, over time, purchased some artwork they both enjoyed. So far they had had no regrets. Their patience had been rewarded. Their due diligence completed, they knew the auction house accurately represented the painting. Julia really had wanted the painting and even though it had required some sacrifice (and an apology to her spouse) she was delighted to have purchased it.

Why the story of Julia and Robert? It lets you shadow some not unusual, long-time collectors. Their trip east and success at auction anticipates many of the themes you will find in the chapters that await you. In other words, Julia and Robert are prologue and at the same time exemplars. Buying seems so simple on the surface, yet years of personal study lay behind the 30 seconds or so it took for the Julia's triumphant bid. She and Robert were well along the collecting pathway and had learned many lessons over the years. Right now we are at the beginning of the journey that they have already taken: What follows in this book will examine the complexities, motivations and pitfalls that confront the collector. Their purchase of the sandpaper painting sets the scene for what awaits you in *Come Collect with Me. Bon appetite!*

Chapter 2

℮

Style and Connoisseurship

*Circa 1770-1800 cherry drop front desk. 36"w, 40½"h, 17½"d,
30" writing height, New England or Massachusetts origin. Interior
with drawers, scalloped decorated document compartments.
Possible replacement to one of eight scalloped-carved valances.
Band inlay prospect door. Fan carved center interior drawer.
Exterior with four graduated lipped drawers. Applied bracket
base. Minor lip repair to top drawer, old knot repair on second
drawer, hinge repair on lid, two missing glue blocks on rear
feet, two drawer runners built up. Brasses replaced, original
escutcheon. Old finish.*

This chapter, particularly after our introduction to Julia and Robert
at auction and preceding all else, is the most logical and important place
to talk about the elements of style. One of the recurring themes of *Come
Collect with Me* emphasizes developing and learning as a collector –
"understandings" I call them. Collectors need to know what aesthetically
pleases them and why. They need to develop their taste. We revere some
collectors – great ones – for their seemingly unfailing ability to separate the
so-so from the marvelous. The fact we are impressed implies, in a devilish
way, that some of us are born with an indefatigable sense of what is right
and wrong, good and evil, socially acceptable and taboo. Tastemakers tend
to be people who lead the parade: They see the merits of an object – say

a Faberge perfume bottle – before everyone else does, those who who simply see a piece of bluish glass. It does not matter what genre of objects you love. Whether your passion is pricey artwork or affordable painted wooden round storage boxes, a collection, if it is to shine, calls on your developed taste and having done your homework.

Some believe that taste is no more than personal preference, but I do not. No matter what you collect, you need to be aware that criteria exist for what is worth desiring: Knowledge of criteria for style and connoisseurship, carefully considered provenance (certain creators, historical association and previous owners), passion and beauty, nostalgia (objects that once seemed part of our identity), and rarity (sometimes) all add up. When one or more of the elements is missing, the piece begins a slow slide down the scale. At some point, the experts weigh in to assess an antique, some alive and some long deceased. A museum show may redefine a really good antique's characteristics in a certain area, the curators using treasures in the archives to put together a show that wows. (I lament the millions of articles not on display in museums' archives that I would love to see, having once visited Colonial Williamsburg's warehouse-size storage building.)

Standards – some mathematical, some historical (need I point to the passion for ormolu decoration in the 18th century?), some that have evolved over time – define the most desirable proportions for a William and Mary desk or a Windsor chair. As a collector, you need to be sensitive to what suits your mood, your developing sense of style and your personal preference. But a knowledge and command of the elements of connoisseurship will help you buy antiques that reflect who you are. Yes, the particular Victorian desk evidences massive proportions, is made of lovely woods, shows excellent craftsmanship . . . and fits in you study the way, perhaps, a stuffed rhinoceros might. Its proportions, its livability, its placement in the room, its beauty fail to make it much more than what it unquestionably is – a white elephant. Considering all that, what can you do? Someone with taste would simply say, "I pass."

I learned long ago when looking at antiques that in order to judge their quality I needed "pegs" to hang my hat on. Think of these pegs as criteria defining a particular style, a vocabulary that allows you to describe what you see. No matter what stage of collecting you are in, you need to scrutinize closely and then see more. Observation and knowledge of a few rules (some objective, some personal) allow you to make sense of what you are seeing.

In this and the next chapter I explore some of the basics. Passionate (collectors never stop developing and learning,) and while the basics may be especially useful for a relatively new collector, someone who has been collecting for some time still ought to be open to learning.

In this chapter I ponder the different characteristics and design elements that collectors need to master. Think of them as the building blocks of an object. In the next chapter I turn to "questioning and listening," looking both to others and inside ourselves. As important as knowing the character of an object is learning what questions to ask. Preparation is everything if you want to collect antiques with a degree of seriousness.

Why start with the basics? Part of the joy of collecting resides in building [expertise] and efficacy (the ability to act on the world effectively). Add to that the inescapable truth: You do not want to waste your time and money. You want the outcome of your efforts to be a thoughtful collection with which you want to live and that makes you and others smile. The truth is, collecting is a nexus of objectivity and passion – a difficult high wire act. A caution whispers in my ear: I thought that as I grew older I would become wiser and instead [there is always more to know] The same will be true as you master the basics, truly a life-long endeavor. Surely you will know a good deal more but you will be aware of how much still remains unfathomed. Humbling.

What do the basics of collecting embrace? After some reading and contemplation I offer the following.

Many of the books in the recommended readings have informative photographs. Take a look at Eversmann's *The Winterthur Guide to Recognizing Styles in Your Collection*, and Lanmon's *Evaluating Your Collection: The 14 Points of Connoisseurship*, for example. Lanmon brings to light Charles Montgomery's connoisseurship criteria that had previously only appeared in a little known and less-read 1961 work: the *Walpole Society Notebook*. A leading expert in American decorative arts, Montgomery (as channeled by Lanmon) deserves our careful attention. He held the directorship at the Henry Francis du Pont Winterthur Museum, in Winterthur, Delaware. According to his obituary, while at the Winterthur he started the first master's program in the country for training museum curators. A spinoff grew into a highly successful course for art conservators.

Eversmann's work will help you learn about 17th Century, William and Mary, Queen Anne, Chippendale, Federal, and other periods of American decorative arts. More important for our purposes, you will begin to learn what makes an object from that period beautiful. Using examples in color, she teaches us how to see and appreciate visual characteristics (design elements). She gives us, as she intends, a short course in "aesthetics' analysis." Eversmann emphasizes that beauty resides within an antique in the complex interaction of line, proportion, volume, ornamentation, material, color, texture and scale.

Lanmon, building on Montgomery's work, emphasizes connoisseurship, "taste" if you will. He asks us to be conscious and appreciative of the fact that the design elements of objects do not exist in isolation. Queen Anne pad feet on both a chair and a table relate to a particular period. The vibrant paint surface on a piece may identify it as *American Fancy*, a movement of exuberance in American according to Priddy (see Recommended Readings). An eagle weathervane from the 1870s and an inlaid eagle on a piece of 1790 furniture both may reflect differing periods and understandings of American history and patriotism. Wonderfully, he teaches us not to mistake connoisseurship for elitism: Lanmon's first example in his book, when talking about condition, is a Honus Wagner (Pittsburgh Pirates) baseball card.

Everyone, myself included, implores you to "recognize the best." Still, even when we know and laud what is of the first water (as they say of jewels) few of us can afford to purchase such objects. My point is subtle but critically important: Once you can recognize the best, you know what objects are better than others, and why. You can then play with the design elements. Thus, you can intentionally compromise as necessary as you add antiques to your collection – good or great surface, good or great craftsmanship, proportion, signed or unsigned, for example. What enters your calculus depends on your pocketbook, taste and preference. I cannot emphasize enough how significant this ability is.

These authors provide a list of criteria by which to judge an antique the list may take a lifetime to knowledgeably use but we have to learn to hang our hat on its pegs sooner or later. You can disagree with any particular elements but not the main thrust of their arguments. What then do we need to know? To borrow from the masters:

Form/Lines: Border, angles and curves. Outline of an object and lines within it.

Proportion: How the various dimensions and size relate one to another.

Volume: How an object takes up space.

Ornamentation: Decorative elements. Is the piece better for them? Are they well executed?

Texture and Finish: Roughness or smoothness of the object's material, to the eye or touch. How original or aged?

Material: What the object and its parts are made of.

Color: Hue and how intense and vivid.

Scale: Short or tall, sturdy or delicate, and how the object relates to others.

Craft Techniques: How constructed? Quality, practices employed, idiosyncrasies.

Trade Practices: Commonly labeled, part of a set?

Function: Why was it made, what was it used for, what was the intent of the craftsman?

Attribution: Labels, signatures, forgery?

History of Ownership: Documentation from families, dealers, auction houses.

Condition: Wear, tear, originality, aging, softening, fading.

Overall Appearance: Especially useful in comparing two objects. Does it work?

Proportions: Do they add or subtract? Is ornamentation expected? Did the draftsman do a good job?

Evaluation: Overall assessment of the object. Is it rare? Is it beautiful? Is it worthy of purchase? At what price? Your preference.

As we proceed, these basic questions will keep cropping up and being considered. Except for the most advanced collectors I do not believe everyone is inclined to – perhaps is capable of – systematically applying every one of these criteria to an antique they are viewing or are interested in. But familiarity with each of them is needed. For each piece you consider purchasing, one, two or more of these aesthetic elements may be especially applicable. Being knowledgeable regarding the criteria also assists you in your discussions with other collectors, dealers, and auctioneers. In sum, these elements of design not only give you benchmarks that allow you to evaluate the quality of what you are collecting, they allow you to share what you know, even those who lack your level of expertise and interest. It is hardly less important to appreciate that a thorough knowledge of a piece encourages us to be better guardians of the antiques we own.

An Exercise in Style and Connoisseurship

Practice allows a collector to become familiar with aesthetic criteria and to use them more proficiently. Remember, the quality of a collection depends on such expertise. To assist the reader in gaining such mastery – "understandings" – *An Exercise is Style and Connoisseurship* may be found in all chapters except the two (Chapters 1 and 22) depicting paintings. Let's begin by applying the criteria to the desk described at the beginning of this chapter. No wood analysis or other fancy scientific investigations have been carried out. It is not a museum piece, but it is a nice antique my wife and I have lived with for decades. What do we make of it? What do you make of it?

The piece is a rectangular chest with four drawers, with a drop front lid that serves as the desk's surface. It was made in New England or Massachusetts (the latter perhaps because of the thickness of the drawer sides I was told). I lean toward New England. The proportions work: The overall height, depth, and writing height go well with its 36-inch width. Making a sturdy functional desk, the craftsman accomplished his goal. The understated ornamentation elements soften the somewhat boxy desk and simply emphasize that this was everyday furniture, meant to be used rather than merely displayed. A dealer once informed me that you are best off inspecting a desk from the inside out. This one's interior contains a carved fan, document door and curves (scallops) on the cubbyhole valances. The desk takes up space with a bit of flair. The craftsman made a document door with banding (inlayed top and bottom, and on both sides). By Lanmon's standard, the ornamentation accomplishes its purpose, presenting a nice counterpoint to the rest of the desk. We will come to that document door again later.

The desk is cherry, one of the woods from which they were often made (they are also found in maple, walnut and birch . . . and mahogany for more sophisticated big-city types). The texture looks and feels smooth to the eye and touch. While not an old crackly finish the cherry wood has a deep patina. The bracket base is good height. The "rounded spurs" to the left and right of the two feet, and on the sides, add an understated flair. All of these elements, plus the dovetails reflect good craftsmanship. It came without documentation or history of ownership. Usually none would be expected for a country desk.

I rate the desk's condition as "good." The replaced valance and various repairs are acceptable, likely reflecting the piece's age and utility, rather than being marks of deficiency.

I do not believe the document (prospect) door is original to the desk, primarily because the door's color is a bit different from other parts of the piece. Bracket bases were crafted from about 1770 to 1800. They were popular and profitable and thus cabinetmakers kept making them. A desk in the latter part of the 18th century might have banding or inlay on the prospect door as this one does. Also the bottom document door hinge sticks out and is sharp to the touch. I would have expected the craftsman to cut the metal so it was flush but two dealers with whom I spoke were unconcerned about this feature. What I see as a deficit might be a sign of country craftsmanship.

The desk's overall style is good but not great. It is true to what it was meant to be, a workable object for daily use. It probably would rank *7* on a *1* to *10* scale. It cost more in the early 1980s when we purchased it than it would be worth today. Such desks cannot be used for a desktop computer but their utility grows as laptops and tablets gain popularity. Function aside; it suits our taste and environment.

Compromises. Did we want to wait for a nicer base (ogee bracket for example? See the photo of the blanket chest in Chapter 25 for a picture of this base)? The craftsman-carved fan is nice ornamentation but hardly exquisitely sculpted. Did we want to find a desk with a better fan or multiple fans? Surely they would be out of our price range back then. The surface represented the biggest compromise. Maybe sometime we will want to find a desk with a more original finish. However, the desk pleases the eye (scale, color). Balancing price versus waiting, we purchased it and felt it had a lot to recommend it . . . and still do.

Lest you believe every object in a collection has to be a blue ribbon winner, I would like to disabuse you of the notion. Why, you may ask, after spending years and years mastering as best we can the points of style and connoisseurship, would collectors purchase something that is just average? Fact is; it happens all of the time and really should. The several small tables beside our beds in our home are just that – simple tables (two are pictured in Chapter 21). They have four legs and a drawer or two. As you would expect they get a lot of use (a lamp sits on each, and they bear phones, Kleenex, pens, books, and cats that jump on and off). I have never lusted after a classy bedside table. When such antiques are still used for the purpose for which they were crafted, each collector has to make a decision: Should this be an item that can be "used and endure" (a piece not terrible in its aesthetics but with no pretentions) or a purchase where only the best will do? If the latter, knowledge of the style and connoisseurship criteria assists us in purchasing the quality we seek. For these tables my wife and I have been happy with a choice based on "use and endure."

Are we born with a sense of style and aesthetics? Probably not. I hope this chapter yields insights into how such a sense develops. If someone like me – who my wife will tell you has no real sense of fashion, cannot dance worth a dang (don't feel the music), and does not have much of a sense of how best to arrange, display, and decorate our home – at this point in my life can identify and assess wonderful American antiques, then connoisseurship is surely within your grasp as well.

Chapter 3

ॐ

Collector Preparation – Becoming Knowledgeable

Circa 1780 pair of Tracy brace-back Windsor side chairs. Black. Gold decoration from 1840s (pin-striping and tear drops on spindles). One stamped Tracy. Seat height 17½", seat width 16", 20"deep, full height 37". Completely original.

When Arthur Conan Doyle first introduces Sherlock Holmes in *A Study in Scarlet* (1877) Holmes is already a full-blown detective. He needed no learning and development. Holmes gathers the clues, has all of the scientific knowledge he requires, and Dr. Watson documents his solutions with amaze. Oh, if collecting were only so simple.

You purchase the second iteration of something – a classic car, Americana, Coca Cola memorabilia – and, *voila*, you are suddenly more than an owner, you are a collector. Unlike Sherlock Holmes, you are hardly in command of the subject. The quests for background knowledge and the development of expertise become ongoing challenges. Being an informed collector proves anything but *elementary* (and I'd add "my dear Watson," but Holmes never said exactly that.)

What makes a collected item really good and how can you know it is? Many have attempted to answer those questions, knowing just how frequently they crop up.

There is no single, simple answer. Collecting is a sort of detective work. First, reason has to guide the collector always, just as it does Sherlock.

19

Remember, though, that he also counts on intuition, which is nothing more than instinct built on endless experience. Science – footprints, tobaccos, fingerprints, ciphers, hand writing – gives Holmes a foundation for his solutions. At the same time, Holmes is almost preternaturally conscious of what should be and wasn't: The dog did not bark. Finally, he has the help of others – Dr. Watson and his group of boys in London, the Baker Street Irregulars, who often gather information for him. We can learn a great deal from this.

Being a little less literary, we should remember than none of these aids is foreign to the collector: accumulated knowledge and taste, attention to the little (seemingly inconsequential) details, borrowed wisdom and dug-up expertise. The last only comes over time, of course, but it is a lynchpin of the collector's art.

How in the world do you develop expertise? Who can you trust to make you a more knowledgeable collector? The queries plague us because (1) it takes time (and caution) to find real experts, (2) more time to learn from them (assuming they are willing to teach us), and (3) even longer before we feel we have a solid grasp on the subject we are studying.

Connoisseurship – How does one become a connoisseur?

Here is a beginning point: As a collector, whatever you buy or pursue must suit you in some manner and that means understanding not only *what* it is but *why*. Sounds simple: This is a table and it is meant to hold a light. Only it is also a specific sort of a table, from a certain era, in a catalogued style. And "hold a light" is not the whole story; it might be a particular height because the lamp or candle (which may depend on the era it came from) is meant to illuminate the book great grandma was reading or the stew meat she was cutting up. Becoming an expert starts with asking good questions, often of people who know what they are talking about.

For the collector, reaching the goal of extensive (no, never infallible) understanding is progressive. The path Montgomery traces in *A History of American Pewter* mirrors my development and that of other collectors.

> The primary personal attribute of the connoisseur is a good visual memory stocked with infinite images of ordinary, fine, and superior objects. The connoisseur remembers especially those

objects he has personally examined, but he also has in his mind published photographs and the facts connected with them. . . . Anyone who aspires to become a connoisseur must first learn to see, then he must look and look, and remember what he sees. . . .

During the first flush of excitement over a new discovery, the true collector is off on a cloud, his senses hazy. This is the time when the spirit of inquiry is a major asset; the true connoisseur instead of leaping to conclusions will proceed cautiously. He will ask questions and consider the answers carefully. Objectivity on the part of the connoisseur becomes all important as he attempts to evaluate his prize. To do this, he must establish certain facts . . . The connoisseur judges the excellence of workmanship, the condition, and the effect of wear and tear. Historical evidence will be less important to the 'object collector' than to the cultural historian. . . .

Each connoisseur consciously or unconsciously, looks at an object from many points of view. (pp. 42-43)

Becoming a connoisseur is, in a word, difficult. At some point collectors have to get off the couch and act.

Genre – **What do I want to collect?**

The choices seem (and probably are) endless – American or European antiques, foreign coins or sports cars, ceramics or silver? The central question is, what fascinates you? After visiting our first mentors' home, a reproduction Deerfield saltbox, the temptation to collect anything other than Americana vanished. Its ambiance sealed the deal.

Are you drawn to furniture, or is it less compelling than textiles, metalware, weathervanes, clocks, redware, or painted boxes? Only after much exposure to New England antiques did I learn the answer to that question for me. For whatever reason furniture is my first love, clocks are second (wooden works, but how many tall case clocks can you put in an average sized home? The answer for us in three.), textiles (blankets, love them), Hudson Valley paintings, maritime paintings (small-size examples), and a variety of accessories. As I write this I am drawn to silver, go figure. Your answer will differ from mine, but you will want to find your answer.

Consider that the first baby step.

Years later a dealer told me that I would not truly understand the history or meaning of American decorative arts from New England unless I traveled its back roads and visited small towns. So I did. In Wiscasset, Maine, I saw relatively undisturbed homes almost 300 years old. Some were still without central heating. They gave me a context, the realization that everything collectible once had a purpose, sometimes utile and sometimes aesthetic (and surprisingly often, both). If you bathe in the original well, you will come out changed.

Learn is an overused word, particularly among us members of the academic community. Nonetheless, fixing in our heads why different sorts of antiques attract dealers and collectors is the only way to begin to be serious about this hobby. Collectors never stop going to school, something you once thought the least desirable thing you might ever do. It is not.

Aesthetics and Beauty – **What is the aesthetically best piece or two in your booth (collection)?**

Ask dealers and collectors what makes a piece good or great. Ask a dealer what he has on sale for sale that he would most like to keep for himself, and why. Continual looking and reading will help you learn what makes a truly beautiful piece of furniture, hooked rug, or pair of candlesticks. When a dealer is proud of his wares, it affirms both the genre and builds your aesthetic knowledge.

Whenever you judge a potential purchase, remember that lots of craftsmen made average or mediocre objects. A label such as "From the era of Rembrandt" does not mean a thing. Your goal: recognizing a gem from the era, something exceptional. Exceptional can be the best coin silver spoon, though its price is trivial, or the 18th century pie crust table with a cost that makes you gasp. "Exceptional" can be applied to country furniture's simplicity and craftsmanship, not just the fine woods and famed handwork of a recognized artisan. Almost everyone agrees, the proportion, lines, color, materials and that indefinable genius of a craftsman make an item great. Eventually these criteria unite to create a gestalt, an antique that is greater than the sum of its parts – a masterpiece, a marvel, or just something you enjoy owning.

Deepening the Discussion – **What else should I be asking you?**

Informed discussions deepen and bring to the fore assumptions or missed issues, and that often means pushing again clichés and glib replies. Experts don't overlook the details but they often assume we know more than we do – what is the significance of extra nail holes, patina, replaced hinges or brasses, loving wear where it should be on a chair's stretcher? Let your chosen victim (eh, expert) know what pieces you are drawn to, and try to explain why. Such conversations repeated again and again assists collectors develop appreciation for beautiful objects. And always close with the query, "what else should I be asking you?"

Price/Cost – **How do I navigate buying something?**

Money is an important consideration for collectors. It is so central that I devote an entire section in this book to it. Collectors need to learn, within a genre, what affordable *Good, Better,* and *Best* look like. If you do not like the aesthetics of *Good*, and cannot afford *Better* or *Best* then you need more disposable income or to divert your attention to a genre where affordable objects still make you smile. I concluded long ago there is no point in tilting at windmills.

Some collectors love to find a bargain, to visit places where unlikely gems may be discovered once in a while – what I call the "bottom of the food chain" approach. Kirk (1979) seems to value this. I prefer to sleep well at night, so I would rather pay a bit more and buy from a dealer who knows his stuff. Yes, I am disclosing my insecurities as a collector: Despite the time I have put into learning, I still do not trust myself to judge the trueness of many antiques. Still, good buys can be found at prestigious shows, not just in back alleys. I attended the New Hampshire Dealer's Show and found a piece of redware most reasonably priced. The dealer who I like had bought it well and was willing to sell it for a fair price. Don't get me wrong. If a piece's price is too good to be true, regardless of where it is being shown, something is probably wrong with it.

Condition is central to collectors. It is nigh impossible to make sense of the cost of an antique shown in a print periodical, auction results, magazine, or on-line if its condition is not fully described. Condition drives price. I ask for condition reports from prestigious auction houses for furniture and still am not told whether the paint is original, a crucial piece of information. But within broad parameters prices listed in auction results, articles on shows, and prices in dealers' booths point the way to valuing an antique.

Never be fearful of asking dealers about pricing. Almost all antiques in a dealer's booth at a show or his shop carry a price tag. Now and then objects on dealer's websites tell you to consult the dealer for price, *POQ* (price on request, think expensive).

You will not be thrown out of a show if you ask a dealer about a better price. He may huff, but I can assure you it will not be the first or thousandth time he has heard the question. "How much?" (If the piece lacks a price tag) "How much out the door?" "Can you do better?" "Can you come down?" If you are reaching a bit above your height and still want the piece, many dealers offer payment plans.

Learning – Where are the best places and methods?

Sellers best serve their own interests when they market their goods in a variety of different venues where collectors and other dealers buzz about. Ask potential buyers and sellers who handles items you are looking for. They will send you to people who have been helpful to them in the past. Once in a while you will learn of a dealer new to you or an auction house that regularly has your sort of antiques cross its block.

And there are other worthwhile resources:

The Dealer's Forum. A few dealers now and then invite people to attend a class – actually a couple of hours looking at certain types of furniture, clocks, paintings. Such classes allow you to meet fellow collectors and deepen your knowledge.

Auctions. Auction previews furnish an opportunity to look, touch, and learn. Have someone knowledgeable accompany you if you can, though an auction can be an education (not always in what you want to know) all by itself. I remember an auction preview where several dealers studied and minutely analyzed a tiger maple desk and bookcase. On their hands and knees with lights and magnifying glasses, the piece received the closest of inspections. I stood nearby and watched. The paramount question was: Did the top and bottom start life together? I talked with a dealer I know after they were done. He thought they conclusion they reached was valid, the piece was not a "marriage," and we talked for a few minutes as to how they arrived at that conclusion. An education for me.

Good Shows. Good shows are amazingly crowded their first few hours. Bring a small notebook with you, and if you see pieces you like or want to learn more about, write down the dealer's name and a brief description of the piece. Later in the day or day two of the show is the time to talk. Even if the piece sold, the dealer will remember it. Dealers have incredible memories for their own wares. Better yet, the piece may still be there, waiting for you to fall in love.

Dealers' Shops. Unfortunately, many dealers do not keep regular hours. I (and many other collectors) lament this state of affairs. Nothing is better than a leisurely stroll through a dealers' shop to look, learn, and spend money. No offense, but I do not find group shops where multiple dealers have areas for their wares as attractive or helpful.

Museums. You look at beautiful antiques when you visit Winterthur, Historical Deerfield, Sturbridge Village, historical houses, Colonial Williamsburg, or other museums. Some styles and individual pieces will call to you, others not, but you can be sure – and train your eye for – top quality.

Periodicals. Periodicals are a convenient and important source for a great mass of objects of varying quality, pricing and the rhythm of the market. (I have listed several in the Recommended Reading.) All are available on-line as well as on paper. Their websites list auctions, their wares, dates of shows and dealers.

Dealer and collector associations' websites. All of these highlight dealers, upcoming shows, and links to sellers and their wares. Collector clubs exist for just about any genre you covet ranging from silver and pewter to Star War toys.

Getting Advice – **If you were me, what would you do?**

Asking knowledgeable others "what do you think?" "If I were your dad, your brother, your son, what advice would you give me?" Learn what alternatives exist. An honest opinion about what you are looking to add to your collection is priceless. But "what do you think?" can be ticklish if the selected respondent is a dealer. Dare he be honest and risk hurting your feelings or lose a sale? Should she simply agree with you? When seeking advice, hope for consensus, with several collectors and dealers pointing you in the same direction after voicing reasons that make sense. Dare I say, good luck?

It is Your Collection – **Can I collect what I like, experts be danged?**

Yes, you can pursue or scorn whatever you want. Many collectors specialize quite narrowly: their antique must have horses, flowers, or birds painted on. Some settle for nothing but the few superb pieces with such a motif. I once saw a small painting, perhaps three inches in diameter that had sold with a woman holding a cat. Had I known the piece was on the market I would have snapped it up because it struck my fancy. But it slipped by and disappeared into someone else's hallway or bedroom (by the way, cats in paintings add to their value).

Consider "Make-Dos" and "Fragments" – **What gives a collection a bit of panache?**

Some collectors love the fine lines of a single bulbous stretcher from a chair, so they buy the stretcher (a fragment, no chair comes with it). Others love the history of how someone salvaged an object and kept it useful. Imagine a glass pitcher that at one time broke and is now held together with an iron band (a make-do). Or consider an early 18th century door latch or beautiful strap hinges not attached to a door. Display a few those fragments together and they look beautiful.

Learn Your Display Style – **How do I learn my style of display?**

Look at museums and dealers' booths or fellow collectors' or dealers' homes to learn their decorating tastes. Once you own some pieces, display them, rearranging until you are happy with the effect. Personally, I like to group several similar objects: had my wife agreed with me (collecting as a couple is so interesting I devote an entire chapter to the topic) I would have added a second, a third . . . to our one print of a 4th of July celebration. She thought one good example could and should stand by itself.

Will I Get it? – **Will I become more proficient in identifying good style and connoisseurship?**

I cannot find anyone who talks about what percentage of collectors fail to learn aesthetics, history, or develop a sense of preservation. Getting any of these takes time and is a learned skill. Let me offer an example. My wife and I occasionally participate in a local *Learning in Retirement* by opening our house to about 10 guests and teaching them about antiques. I will never forget putting several Windsor chairs side by side. One was average, one better, and one pair really exceptional. I talked about form, bulbous turnings, saddle seats, paint layers and splayed legs. To me it was clear. One pair of chairs (described at this chapter's opening and pictured below) epitomized Windsor design and aesthetics. Of course I had seen hundreds of such chairs. These may be the first Windsor chairs my audience ever laid its eyes on. Initially they could not feel or see why the Tracy Windsors were *better* than the others. The successful teaching moment (or learning moment) took a while, and then a few of them got it. Every collector has similar experiences.

An Exercise in Style and Connoisseurship

Ebenezer Tracy had a shop in Lisbon Connecticut and his fine Windsor chairs are pictured in any book about collecting American furniture. Do our chairs measure up to the definition of fine craftsmanship? Their lines draw the eye. The splay to the legs, the bending of the spindles to fit within the bow back, the two extra spindles because they are brace-back Windsors, the curve to the saddle seat create a sturdy chair on which to sit, but one that looks light, as if it were dancing on the floor. Their proportions approach the perfect – the height of legs, the seat height, the back height, the splay. They occupy space gracefully. Different woods (some easier to bend) make up a Windsor. These have the original black paint with wear from use. The gold teardrops on the spindles added in the 1830s or 1840s delight me. They might bother a purist. I love the whimsy. They make the chair more interesting as "material culture," providing an additional storyline to the chairs not there when they were crafted.

Their overall appearance pleases the eye. The craftsmanship is outstanding and one of the two has Tracy's name stamped in the bottom (makers sometimes marked their Windsor chairs, I found, but not always). Their history of ownership is unknown, common for a pair of brace-back Windsors.

In summary, they are really nice. One has a break to the hoop at the very top that seems old. If the desk described in Chapter 2 were a 7, I would rate these chairs a *9 or* 10. They were priced fairly but were not inexpensive. I would steal them from 221b Baker Street Marylebone, London. Think Holmes would miss them?

Compromises. Few if any. Maybe a paint color other than black, Windsor green perhaps?

Be Open to What You Feel: Good Judgment and Intuition – **What if I like something but cannot put into words why?**

The process of collecting involves more than your brain and eyes. It does not take much to recognize a bulbous turning, compare a 39-inch wide chest to one that is 35½ inches wide, or recognize a Queen Anne pad foot. But after you have looked at hundreds of examples of these and other elements, thought translates into instinct (that foot is the right style but somehow . . . clumsy). Once you have mastered a form (table, chair, desk), you can look at others in the category and refine your aesthetics. It takes time before your feelings will talk to you and for you to trust them.

I recall looking at a small, carved folk art wooden bird at a prestigious show in 2017. I had never thought of owning one, immediately loved it, definitely could not afford it. The dealer bought it because he felt the piece was great. No rulers. No scales. The research came next and confirmed the maker.

Start the process by staring at and meditating on a piece. Visit a dealer's shop when few people are around and find an antique that speaks to you. If after some practice you cannot lose yourself in a piece I believe you will feel it is not beautiful. I look at the walnut drop leaf Queen Anne table in our living room pictured in Chapter 13 and am conscious of its small size, its dark walnut color, the curves of its legs, the cutouts on the side. To step back and use Eversmann's language I am "lost" in it – its curved cabriole leg; lack of ornamentation, proportion, and color.

Critically, and I cannot emphasize this enough, after you have intuited the quality of a piece, crucial and rational work remains.

Avoid Common Mistakes

Every collector makes mistakes. But some are avoidable. First of all, you have to accept that more is not better when it comes to antique collecting. Too many objects detract from the few special items you really love. Keep in mind that one good reason to own a piece trumps several rationalizations to possess its poor, crippled cousins.

Buying objects you cannot live with – chairs too fragile to sit on, a couch so uncomfortable even the cat sleeps somewhere else, lighting that really doesn't light – is almost always a mistake. Remember that some of the best decisions you make are to pass – leaving an item in a dealer's booth for someone else to purchase, not bidding on something at auction.

Never spend your money because you believe an object will appreciate in value. I can almost guarantee you are wrong. Yes, the best of the best typically holds its value, but few collectors have many such pieces.

29

And there is always the phenomenon of the one-off: people will want that 1805 silver dollar until, some time, somehow, a gunny sack full of them shows up in some dude's chicken coop. What we purchase should delight us, not be part of a retirement portfolio. We live with what we purchase and hope to pass it down to the next generation. When we sell something for less than we paid for it, the loss is the rent on the cost of pleasure. I will not know which of my better antiques have appreciated in value unless I live long enough and sufficiently avoid dementia to see them sold by one means or another. I keep receipts for our antiques. One of my sons will have to visit my gravesite someday and inform me what pieces the market favored.

Being ignorant creates mistakes. At present having original finish on American furniture is the only way to go. Did you pass on a nice candlestand because you thought it needed refinishing? Currently an "ended out" chair leg (the lower inch or two is new) can be acceptable. Did you purchase a chair with two legs totally replaced because you thought it made no difference? How do you account for a tall case clock that sold for six figures in 2018 with replaced fretwork, finials, and feet? The answer: a famous maker, extravagant design, iconic. At the same auction a candlestand's replaced foot kept the price down but it still sold at about twice its high estimate. Each of these examples prove that what we think we know is not necessarily a good guide for what others or we do.

There is No One Way to Collect – **Is there no true path?**

Style and connoisseurship criteria are the doorway to sound purchases. Once there, however, you can travel whatever byway you want. There is no one right way to collect. We have returned where we began: Your collection must suit you and can reflect whom you are in any way you so choose.

Let me offer an example. As I write this, a well-known dealer has for sale a highboy. It meets all of the aesthetic criteria except one. The price is affordable because, and this is important, it does not have its original or old finish. Another dealer has a similar highboy. It is nice, nothing wrong with it at all. It is not quite as pleasing as the first. Still it has its original finish. Which should you prefer? Do you gravitate towards the piece telling a story through its nicks and worn surface (where they are expected, e.g., the drawer pull area on the drawer fronts), or are those less important to you than a highboy that would be a *10* except for its surface? It comes down to the fact that the choice is yours. You may not know, by the way, until you begin to develop your collection, and discover in looking at it one day whether you are a "surface collector" or a "surface is less important collector." Is one better than the other? No.

A cautionary tale: In early 2018 a Chippendale chest (with ball and claw feet and serpentine drawer fronts – not flat but curved – and a center fan drop) was auctioned. It was refinished and relatively shiny. Three bidders chased it to over five times its high estimate. The "form collectors" made themselves known.

In contrast, I had looked for a Windsor bench for some time. I found one with wonderful form, nice small size, and a known maker. It was everything I had hoped for. But the bench had been stripped of paint. Paint and its history are important parts of Windsor furniture to me. I thought the grain in the seat strident. I wanted finish and form. I passed on it. Yet the bench sold almost immediately. Somewhere a form collector is happy.

Voltaire once said that we should judge a man by his questions, rather than his answers. He may as well have been talking to collectors. Questioning assist any collector develop or improve a collection. As for listening, who knew that Ernest Hemingway was such a good role model for collectors? "I like to listen. I have learned a great deal from listening carefully. Most people never listen."

Will collecting ever be *elementary* as Sherlock Holmes said? Not all of the time. But Holmes proved both an eccentric and profoundly flawed genius. So while we may not use cocaine, smoke a pipe, or play the violin, collectors come to have many attributes similar to Sherlock Holmes. Prepare yourself carefully and after some time you will look to aspiring collectors like Holmes when we first meet him – knowledgeable, ready, and enjoying the game that "is afoot." Being prepared is the best way to enter the collecting world.

This is perhaps the time to move onward and follow a fascinating classroom give and take between professor and student about antique collectors and collecting. All sorts of education can be instructive, as you shall see.

Chapter 4

ℰ

Antique Collectors

Circa 1840 American coin silver FIDDLE style handle mustard ladle. 5"l. Excellent condition. Retailed by John A. Cole (4 Little Green Street) with pseudomarks Monarch-lion-D; monogrammed "PAW" in period script with flourishes, heavier than the average piece of coin silver. NY: Manufacturer was probably Marquand, a prominent firm that changed to Ball Black & Co. then Black Starr & Frost.

"Collecting antiques is the product of elevated passion, refined aesthetics and informed judgment," intoned J. Cadwallader Brock III from the lectern at Bates College. A gaggle of undergraduates sat in various stages of boredom, none taking notes.

"It's a hobby like any other" came a none-too-respectful voice.

J.C., as he preferred to be known, was appalled. The lower-level classes at Bates were noted for their sheep-like tranquility. The notion of challenging a professor (well, an assistant professor but just for now, J.C. hoped) was as out-of-sorts as a Saturday morning without a massive hangover.

"Who said that?" he said in his strictest voice. He thought of his collection of political ephemera. He would not let it be dismissed. (For more on ephemera, see the 'Devil's Dictionary of American Antiques,' Chapter 21).

A string bean chap idly raised a hand and said, "It was I."

Sheer disrespect and snarky to boot. Discipline in the classroom was going to hell. "And what, my dear sir (*count on sarcasm to straighten things out*, J.C. thought), do you know about it?"

"Oh, I come from a long line of antique collectors. Aunts. That sort of thing. Dad was a bit on a nut about coin silver pieces. Mom collected old costume jewelry. For a while, I was into coins and then stamps. Bosh, mostly."

"So, Bosh collector, what are you called?"

℀

Exercise in Style and Connoisseurship

Functional, pretty, bright and shiny, this somewhat heavier-than-usual coin silver mustard ladle in excellent condition curves and swoops. (Sterling silver is 92 percent silver with 7.5 percent copper or other metals. Coin silver is 90 percent silver and 10 percent copper or other metals. It is more pliable. It supposedly was originally made from melted silver coins, thus the name.)

In proportion to other silver set on a table, it provides the pleasure of using serious silver to get a dab of mustard from an elegant mustard pot. Few decorative flourishes are here – mainly the monogram. Oh, if we only knew *PAW*'s identity. Silversmiths labeled their products in the era. Coin silver remains affordable, sometimes selling for no more than it's worth if melted down. Amazing how it fits in your hand when picked up, like it started life there. It usually sits with five or six others in a small glass pitcher on a shelf in our kitchen.

According to a Ruby Lane blog (http://rubylane.com) posted in 2008

In England hallmarks have been applied to silver articles since the 14th century. The English marking system for identification has always been comprehensive and is overseen by the Guild of London Goldsmiths.

For sterling silver items, along with the symbol that indicates sterling quality, in an English silver hallmark, symbols also identify the city where the item was made, the date it was made and who made it. When comparing the marks on a piece to those recorded for the purposes of making proper identification a symbol must exactly match in both the way a shape or letter is formed and also in the shape of the cartouche in which it is contained.

In Colonial America silversmiths frequently created and applied their own hallmarks to silver articles, too, and in such a way as to have them resemble English registered hallmarks of the time. Many of these items were made of 'Coin' silver, which was a 90 percent silver content standard lower than .925. Sometimes items made of Coin silver (which originated literally from the use of melted coins) are marked 'Coin' for accuracy.

In other words, pseudo hallmarks were used to fool the buying public into thinking the piece was English. I have never investigated this particular piece but I am told I should be able to determine exactly who made it based on the mark. Interestingly, there are collectors who specialize in silver pieces with these faked hallmarks.

The mustard ladle provides an avenue to regional collecting. It is not unusual for collectors of silver and coin silver to specialize in a particular geographical area of manufacture. The practice of regional specialization is also common for art, furniture, and other American pieces.

Compromises. None. Since it cost little we decided this piece well worth purchasing. We use it still.

ॐ

"Swell, my name is Sam White." No middle initial. No number behind his name. *What sort of collector might this be? He had said, 'coin silver' as if he knew something about the subject. But better yet here was a sign of life. Somebody had actually been listening. Maybe this was one of those 'learning moments' the department chair was so fond of categorizing.*

"Well, Mr. White, I gather we have somewhat divergent views on the matter of antique collecting. This being a history class, I merely touched on the topic *en passant*, but this might deserve a bit of our attention. Are you willing to share your wisdom (*every teacher knows this is the sort of question guaranteed to put a student in his place*)?"

And then the darned kid stood up and actually walked to stand beside him as if he had the right. He made a little bow.

J.C. looked at Sam and continued as if he had never been interrupted. "The early collectors in this country were attached to antiques because of their ties to famous people. In other words, their associations. But also their patriotism, a romantic view of the past, and finally their aesthetics – design, finish and construction. Eventually American antiques were to be appreciated as art. The last acknowledgement came much later, of course. With the rise of aesthetics came the accumulation of Americana in museums to educate and be enjoyed. An American silver exhibit in Boston at the Museum of Fine Arts in 1906 comes to mind. It was the first major American museum exhibition of American decorative arts with a printed catalogue." J.C. was flying now. How he so enjoyed the feeling.

"While typically wealthy, these early collectors often rode horse and buggy or automobile into the countryside to look for antiques themselves and were quite well informed about the objects they sought. One person's rubbish was another person's treasure, which still is true I guess. These early collectors authored some of the seminal works on American silver, ceramics and antique furniture. They owned two or three homes and often named them, and the product of their collections grace important museums to this day. Collecting began in New England and eventually spread elsewhere. Oh, there were disagreements. Did one value the appearance of a piece despite extensive restoration or did one value its originality? George Dudley Seymour and Horace Eugene Bolles, well-known early collectors, favored the latter. Eventually George Francis Dow, another early collector, became interested in everyday objects that showed something about life as it was lived by common citizens, not just the upper classes. I have found that among collectors today that attraction thrives. Dow set the stage for Colonial Williamsburg's approach, for example. Those early collectors also liked the distinctive look American antiques gave their homes, as do collectors today.

"Prior to the turn of the century, the 20th that is, furniture groupings became popular, and eventually in 1909 the famous, well probably not to you (J.C. swept his arm towards the class) Hudson-Fulton Celebration took place at the Metropolitan Museum, the first comprehensive well-organized exhibit of American antiques." *Thank you Elizabeth Stillinger,* J.C. thought to himself. *What a lode of information her book was.* "That's the *Metropolitan Museum* in New York City. One more comment," J.C., said. "The objects were displayed by period, not all the tables in one room and desks in another. Its American Wing opened in 1924 and the rest is history as they say.

Stillinger says that collectors could be found in all walks of life then but offers no examples. A pity. Just prior to the creation of the museum's American Wing, the magazine to which I subscribe, *The Magazine Antiques* was born. That is how much interest there was."

J.C. had suddenly come to life. Something to say, someone to listen! "When one looks at the black and white photos in Stillinger's book, the furniture is brown and shiny. That was the preferred style up to... up to . . ." *Darn it, he didn't know when original surface and paint became important. He'd have to find out.* "Never mind."

"So tell us" – J.C. gestured toward the slouched undergrad standing next to him, who suddenly seemed to have come awake – "about antique collecting."

Sam White didn't even take a deep breath. "Collecting began in earnest in Europe in the 16th century. Collections acquired great prestige."

"And your source?" *Dang it, this was a college setting, let's keep it academic* J.C. thought to himself.

Sam was up to the task. "Philipp's Blom's book, *To Have and to Hold: An Intimate History of Collectors and Collecting.* Published in 2002, I believe. And your source about the early collectors in America?"

Well, that was nervy, J. C thought to himself. "Elizabeth's Stillinger's, *The Antiquers,* written in 1980. As I understand her, there was little collecting of American-made objects prior to 1850 and she ends her history with the Great Depression. I would love to learn when folks like you and me - not the wealthy – began collecting in earnest. And your knowledge of the collecting of bosh?"

"Well, what about the sanitary fairs?"

J.C. blinked and blinked again. *This young man was informed.* "Can you tell the class to what you refer?" he asked.

Sam was happy to do so. "During the Civil War fairs were held to raise money for the sick and wounded. The Sanitary Commission was in charge, an early version of the Red Cross, thus their names. Those fairs often sold early objects. "But," and he didn't wait for J.C.'s permission, "let me return to where we were. Those who collect what you consider nonsense would disagree, they most certainly would. Many folks collect what is known as 'kitsch,' dare I say what an advanced a collector such as you might call crap." He paused.

"Go on," J.C. intoned. *The fellow couldn't be all bad. He recognized J.C.'s collecting connoisseurship. Apparently he knew about the collecting craze of such trash as Princess DI wedding souvenirs and McDonald's toys or Superman collectibles.*

"Those objects may be junk to you, but to the collectors of tea towels, commemorative coins or mugs, mass produced stuffed animals, Christmas decorations of a wide variety, the generally available, the loveable, dare I suggest even the cuddly – these objects give them the same sense of search and accomplishment as your collection, sir."

So he was 'sir' now, was he? That wasn't too bad or was he being damned with faint praise? J.C. couldn't tell. So once again, he said, "go on."

Sam went on. "I imagine someone wants every Star Wars toy every made and sold, or someone already has them all. To a collector, that time long ago in a galaxy far, far away is important. People who pursue these things need knowledge, too, just of a different kind. What is rare and what common? What are the signs that unopened box has been fiddled with? Is China making fakes even if they manufactured the originals? What is the fair market price? Where is the market going? Such collectors may view what traditional collectors of American antiques pursue as unimaginable. Old Stuff for big money. Imagine that.

"People collecting that stuff may or may not need the finely honed aesthetic, informed judgment you promote, but they do possess some judgment. Perhaps what you collect demands working knowledge that is years in the making, but perhaps the same is true of Barbie dolls? I cannot say." Sam paused, apparently having said enough for the moment.

"Well, you agree, Mr. White, that the best antique collectors are basically historians, passionate students of the past and cultures, finely tuned judges of beauty and significance. And we do not collect the mass-produced."

"But there are so few 'best' antique collectors," Sam replied. "It sounds like Stillinger refers to just them in her book. You're correct, though: Most seem to value what they collect, and some tie it to the age when the antiques were new. Others just like the graphics, looks, or have a house to furnish. And again I beg to differ. Wooden works clocks were mass-produced before the mid-1800s but not many survive in superb condition or desirable form today. Truly sir (*there was the sir again*), what is difference between a shrine to stoneware and one to paperweights all made post-World War II?"

My, he was subtle, J.C. thought. *Was he agreeing or disagreeing? To heck with the goals of today's class. This is fun.* He hadn't had fun teaching in quite some time. "So," he asked, "what do antique collectors do? What in the heck is a collector?"

Sam smiled. The soapbox was his. "I come from a long line of predecessors, so don't look at me funny. The library at Alexandria, VA is one example. If you have ever visited Monticello you know that Jefferson was a collector of many things – his theme I believe was one of 'objects about which he was curious.' FDR and Queen Elizabeth II collected stamps. J. P. Morgan was an art collector. DuPont and Ford pursued American history but in very different ways. Today collectors differ in age, income, and interests. Our personalities differ widely. I await your rebuttal, professor."

"So your pedigree is good," J. C. said. "There has to be more to it than that."

"There is," Sam replied. "People like me devote our time to collecting antiques – old or not so old objects of all sizes and types – and as a hobby it gives us pleasure – well at least most of the time – and it usually provides a diversion from our everyday work world. And whatever we collect, we like how it feels and looks. It is important to us.

One more point, we have to learn what pieces are worth. As do most folks when they have a hobby, we spend time at it. The amount of time we devote to collecting depends on other responsibilities and wears on our attention, piques our obsessiveness and feeds our craziness. Yet most collectors seem to lead normal lives. For some the pursuit of collecting is an uncontrolled passion, a restlessness that drives a person to scour catalogues at three in the morning. Others have achieved more balance in their lives."

J.C. was deep in thought. *Stillinger had referred to the 'power of environment' in talking about the early collectors but he wished she had been clearer about what she meant.* His reverie ended. "Ah, you finally arrive at the idea of value. Can you expound just a little on value, if you will? We are almost out of time."

And expound Sam did, but briefly. "The Star Wars collector and others like him decide the toys' value. Collectors and fans create a market. They decide what is to be ignored and what attended to, which toys are special and which prosaic, which therefore are worth more or less. You or I may not understand the value or market, but those collectors do. Your collection, whatever it is, and I would guess it is Americana of one sort or another given your knowledge in that area, is a bridge to the past, the Star Wars toys to that galaxy in the future, no matter how distant. Dealers in stoneware let me know when they have found a jug they think I will like.

They teach me what is special. Kenner had it easier. It simply produced special edition Star Wars toys in limited supply."

J.C. cleared his throat. *Having done a bit of collecting himself – focused on New England political races back to 1900 or before, he didn't want to veer into the stereotype of collectors as loonies.* "Let's save abnormal psychology for another time. What makes a collection then?"

"Rather than merely amass or hoard our old objects, as collectors mature they tend to arrive at an overarching theme. And typically they live with and display their antiques. My mom had several shelves of small, carved decoys. Some collectors' antiques are spread throughout their homes as they copy a late 18th century or early 19th century style of decor. Some are more diehard *(again, the term 'crazy' came to mind but since professor J.C. wanted to avoid that terrain, Sam would also)*. Appliances are hidden behind wooden panels that replicate 18th century paneling. The stereo and television are out sight as well. Such folks do not abandon modern comforts – their homes have bathrooms, washers and dryers, and the Internet. But modern accouterments are not the showpiece – the home with its antiques is. No stainless appliances or granite or quartz countertops to be proudly displayed."

My, the kid was a born orator, thought J.C. *And students were paying attention.* "Any other way of defining an American antique collection's theme?" he queried.

"Some collectors mix their genres. They often have superb examples of this or that, say, artwork, weathervanes, or furniture, but sparsely intermixed with other forms and genres. Really good antiques go well with anything. The theme here may be antiques from several nations or periods, or simply exquisite taste. The latter is where you started."

J.C. knew the answer to his next question but he wanted to learn if Sam was the real deal; was he truly a collector? "But antiques don't walk up to your front door and knock. How do you find them?"

Sam was up to the task again. "Antique collectors search for and locate their pieces. They do this by reading trade journals such as *Maine Antique Digest* or the *Bee*, or magazines such as *The Magazine Antiques* or *Antique Toy World*. They use the Internet to locate dealers and communicate with them, as well as viewing their inventories. They talk with dealers at their shops or at shows. They also seek out auction notices and spend some time looking at dealer inventories on-line. They attend shows, flea markets, use EBay and other on-line sites. They may go to museum symposia or those held by auction houses. Vacations may be spent tramping fields or waiting in line at shows. They may not be drinking margaritas in Mexico in winter but walking NYC or hailing cabs in January for Americana month."

J.C. had left history far behind. *I wonder if this kid could help me with my collection?* "But what about education?" This was a fair question in a college class.

"The antique collectors I know," Sam said, "know something about what they love and are always studying. They do this not only to know whether they are getting a fair deal for their hard-earned dollars but also because many are intellectually curious and want to know about what they are purchasing – about the locations where they were made, like the Connecticut Valley, periods such as Queen Anne, makers such as Paul Revere or Ebenezer Tracy, and how good an example it is that they have just added to their collection. Their bookshelves often are a library that is read and revisited over time."

My goodness, J.C. said to himself. *Talk about intellectual discovery,* said with some excitement. *He hadn't heard that from a student for at least a year.* "But you spend money, don't you?"

"Not as much as I would like. Tuition here is expensive, you know. But how often collectors acquire things and what they acquire varies. Many antique collectors have a budget for the year; some are blessed with greater disposable wealth but it is the rare collector who can buy whatever and whenever he wants."

Again, J.C. tested Sam. "I started by mentioning passion. You agree?"

Sam looked amused "Not totally. Passion is just one emotion of many that antique collectors experience. There's also obsession, envy, elation, satisfaction, happiness, despair, curiosity – you get the point. Pride and love. Collectors are proud of having their antiques, may even love their antiques. But collecting antiques is not always safe from everyday stresses. Not all emotions are positive. Frustration, madness, and sadness are not uncommon. The consumption of good alcohol, Irish whiskey for example, is sometimes required to deal with the stress. Some of the people you encounter in the pursuit of antiques are difficult."

J.C. was dumbfounded. *How did this undergraduate even know about the mysteries and pleasures of good Irish whiskey, let alone being able to afford it? But life wasn't fair*, J.C. knew that. "Any use of skills you learn in college when you collect antiques?" was his next question.

Sam hesitated. "I don't know if this is what you mean but yeah, critical thinking, writing, organization. Antique collectors catalogue what they own. I can describe each one of my pieces of stoneware if you want. Many collectors have appraisal lists where their antiques are kept with photos, each showing a value and sometimes from whom and when the antique was bought. Antique collectors are systematic."

Sam added one more comment. "And there is manual labor as well. Antique collectors maintain their antiques, dusting, lugging, lighting, providing humidity control."

J.C. knew about humidity. He had to be careful at home or his valued political pieces would suffer grievously. "I see we are out of time today," he announced. "Mr. White, if I may talk with you for a moment please." As students filed out of class Sam turned to Professor Cadwallader Brock III. "Mr. White," J.C. said. "Do you have time for a cup of coffee? While I didn't mention it in class I collect political ephemera. I thought we could compare notes. And I am especially interested in why you collect, a fascinating subject and one too little written about."

"Sure," Sam replied.

Chapter 5

Our Fascination With Objects

Circa 1820. Mid-Atlantic (Pennsylvania, New Jersey, Maryland, Delaware – probably Pennsylvania) walnut corner cupboard in old dry finish. 87" tall. 28" corner. Top is 34"w with an additional 3" on the returns (to the side). Bottom is 35"w with 3¼" additional angling to side. Glazed top door with 12 panes, all glass original. Paneled lower door. Strong upper cornice, nice cutout to base, fine waist molding. Concave French feet. Old hinges/locks with key. Escutcheons on bottom doors. No repairs or replacements.

Saying collectors collect "things" or "stuff" states the obvious, but sometimes looking at the obvious provides a good starting place. Once we recognize objects are the currency of the collectors' life, a deeper and more interesting question arises: What motivates this compulsion? Put another way, why are people – not just collectors – plagued with this odd preoccupation? Moreover, the magical attraction of objects lies not only in old stuff, but also in "collectibles" (broadly defined: anything eccentric or rare), and even in new things.

My wife and I have friends with two sons who live next door. One boy would own every Lego set ever made if he could. The attraction of these tiny plastic bricks has little to with what they are but more so with the infinitude of things they could be. They provide him with an extension of his self and his overactive imagination. There is also the fascination

45

of the new: Each year a children's toy or two appears that must be under the Christmas tree. Parents scour far and wide. The future well-being of their son or daughter depends on that very toy. Ralphie in the movie *The Christmas Story* had to have a BB gun, a Red Ryder to be exact. Put simply it seems built into our genes to lust after and covet things.

But collecting involves owning more than one of something, and the things cannot be *doppelgangers*. They may have a kinship but may not have an identity. If we were to meet Ralphie today (as an adult) I would not be surprised if he had a grand Red Ryder collection, one varied in age, form, materials, whatever. It would evoke a remembrance of and testify to his childhood. And no doubt the Red Ryders would carry him back to that very Christmas when his parents met his most passionate wish by giving him his first.

Ralphie would not have a "bunch" of BB guns. He would have deliberately selected each for his collection and would be able to differentiate them: when each was made, how many were sold, differences in how they loaded and fired, financial value. Collections have organization. Collectors assign characteristics and meaning to items they display, are proud of, love. To think of such objects as "things" is to miss the point.

My wife has a cousin who every holiday season fills a room with small houses that light up. She regularly searches for more. My wife's mother, who grew up in the Depression and was a salt-of-the-earth woman as ever lived and breathed, adored her collection of beanie babies. Collections are as varied as people. And we take a certain personal pleasure in being surrounded by things that fulfill us; being able to personally choose the examples makes it even better.

As a psychologist I could try to explain why people collect using language about sublimation and substituting objects for love and the like. Who knows, some of those explanations (musings) may actually be true. But it does not matter. At the 4th of July parade in many towns across the country you see antique tractors some guys (yes, they are mostly guys) lovingly restored. Perhaps they date back to the day his dad sat him in his lap, put his hands on the steering wheel and taught him to plow a furrow. The now like-new tractor is putting and belching nostalgia, the past brought back. On the other hand, perhaps he just likes to tinker or simply gets a kick out of riding in parades. We may be over-reading if we assign his motives.

One cannot dismiss either personal pride or perfectionism as powerful motives behind the instinct to collect, and in few places is it as evident in the addiction for cars and trucks. One can watch auctions of collectible vehicles on television most any day. They gleam, they twinkle, they emit sounds that set hearts aflutter. A few look original. Others sport seams and paint jobs better than anything that ever came out of the factory. It is not unreasonable to say that these wheeled icons are extensions of the egos and hearts of the people who have spent so much (take your pick: time or money, or both) on them. Personally, the owner may be overweight and overage, scarred and dumpy, but this absolutely perfect 1989 BWM 633csi is the "real" him or her.

No matter what they are – clothing, hats, cars, or jewelry – the things we have and show define us. You read about men who have hundreds of pairs of first-release gym shoes. Women collect high heels and need large walk-in closets to store them appropriately. Objects do more than that, of course. Collecting gives us purpose. To a collector of license plates from a specific state, all displayed in chronological order on the wall of a workshop or garage, filling the last empty space makes the world seem complete, right and good. I remember when I was a teen and I would paste the last United States stamp from an early series in a Scott album. The sense of accomplishment was marvelous.

Even people who do not collect much or at all seem enthralled by objects. The televisions show *Antiques Roadshow* and its appraisers and experts have thousands of objects over its lifetime, but the people who watch – ogling and exclaiming, "I could not imagine it was worth that much!" – may have absolutely no desire to possess these artifacts (the money is a different matter). The BBC version predated the PBS program, but both educate fans about the monetary and – oftentimes more important – historical value and history of antiques or collectibles. One result is that owners may keep pieces for posterity they might otherwise have tossed. And the discussions (factual information mostly) regarding objects shown can both illuminate history and sensitize us. Though we are a relatively young nation, the American *Antiques Roadshow* reinforces the historical and social framework for what the average person has in his possession.

"It allows us to believe in the eternal worth of everything" (Petrusich, *What Antiques Roadshow Taught Us, The New Yorker*, December 4, 2017). Frankly I like Petrusich's emphasis on measuring value by more than dollars and cents. Worth resides in a thing's history and meaning. These objects tell tales worth knowing and saving, preserving community and family lore for future generations.

One's initial response to watching one of these shows is pure amazement: How in the heck did something that fragile survive all these years? How in the heck did something that fragile and ugly survive all of these years without being tossed in the bin? How in the heck did something that fragile and ugly survive all these years and be worth so much? I find myself asking those very questions almost every time I watch. Of course the marketplace sets the monetary value, which means at least one other person and no doubt more (unbelievably) want to own great-great grannie's perfume bottle, coffee grinder or corset.

The matter of winning and losing strongly appeals to our humanity, too. The antique may not be quite right; it may have been enhanced or turn out to be an outright fake. The proud owner who believed the family's treasured fountain pen (no; there is nothing too outlandish for credibility) was used to sign the Declaration learns its age is only two score, and isn't even American or British to boot. Throughout history, a good story has almost always been more appreciated than facts. Antique collectors are not beyond this temptation. Of course, some *Antique Roadshow* visitors do win; they have to or we would stop watching. So Granddad, stationed overseas, had a good eye and made a good buy when he brought grandmother back that piece of sculpture. Or that $5 spent on a painting at a rummage sale was a surprisingly good investment. Hence we sometimes see the pallid-faced owner who realizes insurance on her suddenly precious antique is a budget-buster.

Money isn't everything, as my mother used to say. It tugs at my heartstrings to see antique owners who truly do not care what their heirloom is worth; they will keep it in the family and pass it down to the next generation simply because if its associations, the feelings it inspires, the memories it invokes. To them, what they know about the artifact is its most important attribute and is its value. After being apprised of why it is such a wonder, they know why it deserved such a prominent place in their homes. Perhaps the antique darn well better occupy a more prominent place. Such a treasure – an antique corner cupboard my wife and I own – will belong to one of our sons someday. We assume it will be precious to him because of what it means to us.

An Exercise in Style and Connoisseurship

The lines of the piece are angular but softened by the cornice and the cupboard's smaller size. The top and bottom are in proportion as are the glass panes, and the cupboard is well suited to the room in which it sits. Decorative elements are limited to escutcheons and a painted interior. I view walnut, the primary wood, as a step-up from pine or cherry. Its dark color gleams from an old, untouched surface.

It was made to display objects on the top and store them on the bottom. Such cupboards are usually not signed. The history of ownership is unknown. It wears its years well with a softening of interior color, the patina, and its originality, including the bubbled glass. It is not rare but it is beautiful. Its value lies in its size and originality. We had looked some time for a cupboard in this size and purchased it with no hesitation as it had an affordable price.

Compromises. We never could locate a painted cupboard we liked as much. Sitting as it does in front of off-white walls and having an original blue interior show through the top half's glass panes offset what could be a dark presence. Happily, other pieces we own add even more color in the room.

I also often mutter to myself "what luck!" when watching one of the *Roadshows*. How come I don't have an attic with something like that tucked away? When my mother moved some time ago, her mid-century modern furniture fetched little. Today it brings a pretty penny. And I have never had a friend give me something as a token of his good will, or been listed in his will to receive a really nice antique. My father's parents, who emigrated from Russia, brought with them a pair of silver candlesticks, covered in ash, with one bent (both done deliberately to make them look more like junk so a custom's official would not take them) that I would now kill to own. But I do not know what became of them. And I could display in my home the family samovar from Russia that somehow survived and made it to this country but it never appealed to me (just my luck, I know; how dumb). My brother enjoys it immensely. It pleases me that it is still in the family. But collecting is not all luck, though I hardly dismiss it. As pointed out before, being knowledgeable and having sharp instincts are more likely to contribute to an admirable collection than, say, poisoning your aunt so you can inherit her rocking chair.

I also find myself captivated by the range of antiques and collectibles on an average *Roadshow*. People save things. We do. And we keep objects with obscure functions. The silver my wife and I inherited contains a multitude of different spoons – for stirring coffee, eating ice cream or shoving peas around our Spode. But the details on some of the antique toys bring wonderment, as does some of the antique jewelry (gigantic, awkward, weird, extravagant, gorgeous). The craftsmanship of furniture, the details in the quilts hand cut and stitched, the old photographs, all call up an earlier time and sometimes inspire awe.

Nostalgia and fantasy are also powerful draws. The objects and stories about them take us back in time. Perhaps deep down we want to live in another, simpler time, or least visit for a while (via a time machine or a sojourn to Colonial Williamsburg). Of course if the objects I now collect were expensive and belonged in a stately home, I would have been the servant downstairs cleaning or polishing them, not one of the masters upstairs enjoying their look and utility. But still, one can dream, and antiques are avenues to dreams. My wife and I visited a viewing of the clothes from the PBS television show *Downton Abbey*. Sandy is much more a clothes maven than I, but oh my goodness! The clothing buoyed my wife's spirits by their beauty. She showed me the women's clothes' fabrics and details in their tailoring, especially the stitching. She would love to wear such couture today. Of course then it was expected one would wear well-designed, intricately designed clothes on a daily basis; although donning them (of course with maids' assistance for the ladies and valets for the men) took hours and different outfits were required for each of the day's activities. All I could think was "Men never went outdoors without a hat; what a pain in the neck that would be." But at the same time, "how classy."

The good old days were old. Period. The "good" is little more than wishful thinking. *Downton Abbey* lingers at the cusp of what we now call WWI and the government would soon start taxing the daylights out of these sprawling manses, not totally impoverishing the upper classes – the Great Depression would take care of that – but leaving them like us, worrying about money and the fickleness of governors and the future. Yet we dream.

We, like Ralphie with his BB gun collection, keep the past alive. When my maternal grandmother died, the only object in her house I asked for was a print of a Chinese emperor with a cat's snout and whiskers appearing

51

in several places. It was hardly a notable antiquity. Still, it reminds me of her home and more importantly of her. That, finally, may explain our inclination to get and keep things, whether precious, reminiscent, evocative or part of what we imagine to be our real selves.

Yes, I am drawn to objects with a good sense of design and that are pleasing to the eye. Many antiques radiate beauty, each in its own way, and I like to imagine aesthetics alone are sufficient justification for having or getting something. Of course someone looking at my wife's collection of antique toy airplanes, none with a wingspan surpassing five inches, might very well shake his head and wonder why in the blazes she would be drawn to those darned things. One could ask the same question about a woman on BBC's *Roadshow* who had a collection of over 400 toast racks. Antiques and collecting make the world go round. As we have seen, this is not all a matter of differing tastes. Our motives for amassing stuff and things are complex, varied, sometimes even baffling to ourselves; c'mon, acknowledge that there have been occasional "impulse buys," even of such things as autos or jewelry.

Collecting, getting and accumulating are human traits. They need not be dismissed as beyond explanation; in fact they activities may help us understand ourselves.

Chapter 6

ℓ

Some Well-known Collectors

Circa 1830-1850 Ink and Penholder. Grain painted wood. New England. Made by S. Silliman & Co., Chester, Connecticut. *3⅜"d, 1⅞"h.*

The Unitarian pastor George Washington Burnap once wrote that three things were necessary for happiness in life: "something to do, something to love and something to hope for." Collecting anything from coins, to art, to antiques touches all three – ambition, passion and anticipation. Still, those of us who are infected with the collecting bug are a source of endless fascination for those who lack the impulse . . . and, to be honest, to ourselves.

Charles Spencer Curb, quite an accomplished writer, made bold to insist in 2010 (*Why We Collect: A Historical and Psychological Perspective, Silver Society of Canada Journal, 13,* 30-43) that collecting is a "sensible and proper" thing to do, a sentiment I share. But the central question is, why? First, why is it proper and sensible? Second, why do we collect? We began to explore the second question in the previous chapter and will probe it in some depth in this chapter and those that follow. Frankly, we antiquers (along with those seeking to emulate us, and family, and friends) need to understand the impulse better (or at least understand it to a degree), be more fully conscious of what the hobby involves and have some insight into why in heaven we have been afflicted with this malady. The answers, even when we manage to hunt them down, prove to be dauntingly complex. Nothing proves the truth of that assertion like the writings put forth to explain collecting.

For instance, Mr. Curb acknowledges (though hardly comprehensively) the sundry varieties of collectors: those who boast of and cherish bargain prices, those proud of owning things of great rarity, and those who think of themselves as investors. James Barron, author of *The One Cent Magenta* (2017, NY: Workman) broadly portrayed collectors of stamps as victims of a disease only other philatelists fully appreciate and sympathize with. He was wrong: Postal fanatics do not suffer alone.

Kazuo Kawabata, when writing about the collector and his motives (*Asian Art: A Collector's Selection* (Young, M. W., [1973], Ithaca, NY: Herbert F. Johnson Museum of Art, pp. 21-33), notes how many American children collect "something." I was one of them, having caught the collecting bug for stamps (my father had collected stamps many years before), baseball cards, coins, and comic books. They all held fascination, especially stamps. I remember the packages of them arriving in the glassine envelopes when I began and as my knowledge and collection grew I graduated to purchasing specific stamps at a Marshall Fields in downtown Chicago. My fantasy was to fill my Scott's album of United States stamps, though and it remained no more than a hope (some stamps were simply too rare or too costly), but even in its flawed state the colorful panoply yielded me much satisfaction. For the first time in my life I recognized that to buy stamps I had to sacrifice comic books, gum or other delights. Even then I had a passion, despite the sacrifices it entailed.

At the other end of the fiscal universe, I have met a man who collects nothing but 16 cylinder cars; Cadillac, Marmon, Duisenberg and Peerless autos from the 30s sported these mechanical marvels. If the cost of buying one made the tycoon's eyes water then, he would have gone blind at the six figures one costs today. Oh, and the collector had 20 of them in his barn. He also had a full-time mechanic; just to make sure the one he took to church that Sunday would start right up. Even the poor souls and fellow parishioners not afflicted with the collecting bug were awed and fascinated by his – and the cars' – over-the-top commitment.

What makes collecting so intriguing is that you don't have to go overboard, although many collectors do. You can collect salt and pepper shakers, as does someone a friend of mine knows: She has more than 900 sets. Even then, in order to really collect you have to be selective. Choose a theme – critters, kids, buildings, trains. Then spend years and years hunting them down, even though you realize you can never own one of every model made. So collecting stuff does not necessarily require having a great deal of money, but it always necessitates some expertise. You have to know what you are doing even if you collect cigar bands (now that no one smokes cigars, these have become pricey items to own), matchbook covers (ditto), bubble gum cards (dare I even mention that?), Beanie Babies (suddenly dirt cheap; everybody collected them), *National Geographic* (you can buy boxes of them at every garage sale for pennies), soap (mostly stolen from hotel and motel rooms), pencils (apparently unsharpened ones are more valuable), decks of cards, and – latest of all – whiskey. Why one would collect bottles of costly bourbon and never take a sip baffles me, but collecting fever is apparently more potent than common sense. But I digress.

Kawabasta talks of collecting themes with which I agree: competition, aesthetics, seeing objects as trophies, collecting as a way of life, emotions such as anticipation, pleasure, and love. He labels the means, i.e., money, as a more mundane matter. Why collectors collect what they do may be related to childhood, even an exposure to art or other influences (your aunt's ormolu clock, for example), but as you will find reasons for collecting are more involved than merely understanding one's past. In my case, I collect, in part, because I like surrounding myself with objects I consider beautiful, but whether and how that motivation applies to those who surround themselves with Barbie Dolls and Beanie Babies occupies a universe beyond my ken.

I admit I start with a prejudice: I accept the passion for collecting uncritically, whether the folio contains stamps, rocking chairs, paintings or farm tractors. I recognized the catholicity of the hobby. Some cherish things from all eras. Others focus narrowly on one category or craftsman. Still others simply appreciate the old, the rare, the beautiful. And yes, there are those excited by the odd, the eccentric and the grotesque (ancient baseballs, Depression era carvings, so-called ugly pots). I accept and embrace them all because I am a collector myself. What I see in others explains a great deal about why I do what I do.

I am hardly alone in putting collectors under the microscope, of course. People at the heart of major collections display equal curiosity about how they came to where they are and what it signifies to any of us (with the small accumulations we command). They have written about their motivations and the feelings attached to collecting, and their observations provided insights into our central question of why we collect and keep at it. Three such collectors provide the grist for the mill we are slowly turning: self-examination.

Jane Katcher (*Expressions of Innocence and Eloquence: Selections from the Jane Katcher Collection of Americana*, 2011) emphasizes the power of visual art and the thrill of owning superb examples of it. Yet she honestly states she has no ready answer for this gradual change from the delight of looking at visual art to the action of purchasing it. Having no ready answer is a recurring theme in why we collect, unfortunately.

Clearly, something resonates within her, something powerful and important related to the aesthetic – an appreciation of the nobility, economy of means, power, grace, spirit, and unique vision of the artist or craftsman. Her collecting is based on a need to experience feelings not found in day-to-day life. The objects she is drawn to, their innocence and eloquence elicit these feelings. Part of her emotional attraction is keeping alive feelings and appreciation for beautiful art she first experienced as a teenager.

Katcher reminds us that collecting is a quest, but not merely for objects, a fact that may surprise non-collectors a great deal. In this she has company. I see it as a quest for our past, our futures, and for satisfying our souls, among other factors. Henry Wood Erving, one of the *Antiquers* Stillinger writes about in her book by the same name, "believed in the goodness of American things" (p. 79). He championed the craftsmen, delighting in their skills. Katcher also enjoyed the hunt - the seeking, looking, searching, and finding. Additionally she enjoyed learning and education, sating her curiosity, as many collectors do – satisfying her need to know and understand.

Collecting has given Katcher's life meaning and purpose; it has been fulfilling. Goodness knows we treasure those satisfactions in our own lives. Is she alone in these discoveries as a collector? Not at all. I can identify with what she writes and I imagine you may also. But for more understanding of "Why Collect?" let's turn to another well-known collector.

Ralph Esmerian made a wonderful contribution to our historical understanding. *American Radiance: The Ralph Esmerian Gift to the American Folk Art Museum* (2001) pictures and describes the collection. Esmerian's history goes back some years – collectors seem to look to their pasts to explain the present and future – and he writes of a female friend who collected early American pieces. In the process of purchasing a birthday gift for her (a colorful coverlet) he also saw and bought for himself a Pennsylvania German slipware dish. Something about handling it and its appearance connected in his psyche to the spiritual and physical awakening he had experienced during two years in Greece.

Stacy Hollander calls Esmerian an unrepentant romantic who loved American folk art. I can identify with that feeling: a love for what I collect, the emotional factor. The need to collect is so strong it motivated his behavior over decades. Is this true for you or someone you know? It certainly is for me. I have fond memories of when I began collecting. Does my continued collecting help me hang on to them? I believe it does – a notion worth thinking about: The present is a capturing or recapturing of the past, even if idealized at times.

In Esmerian's case, Hollander tells us, collecting also kept him connected to his father. Thus we have a new theme in Esmerian's collecting: relationships. Esmerian's father helped his son develop his aesthetic discernment. His father also was a collector, in his case of world-class rare bookbindings. Still, neither Katcher nor Esmerian seem to have been collectors as children. Perhaps collectors emulate behaviors modeled for them – mom or dad, grandpa or grandma – love for the arts, music, or even antiques? "Does a collector of barbed wire talk of aesthetics?" I don't know for certain but I bet he does.

Yet, collecting entails even more than I have discussed thus far. Not surprisingly both Katcher and Esmerian had a calculated plan for their collection. They were drawn to and purchased pieces that met their criteria of eloquence, innocence, quality, beauty, rarity and creativity. What remains unexplored? Identity. The identity for each collector as a collector. A powerful thing, identity, and we will talk more about it in a subsequent chapter.

Still yet another theme is the willingness and ability to shoulder responsibility for America's craftsmen and tradesmen, and the objects they produced. The books detailing Katcher and Esmerian's collections bear witness to that caretaker responsibility. Collectors preserve the past. But while doing so, we also are competitors.

In *A Yachtsman Eye* (Granby, A., 2004) we learn about Glen S. Foster, a marine painting aficionado with a knowledgeable eye who looked for paintings with quality. The idea of quality is a repetitive theme, codified in the adage, "buy the best you can afford." As a yachtsman Foster had a keen eye with which to assess marine art. At the same time he lived to compete. He transferred this competitive racing spirit to collecting marine art. Collecting is competitive. I probably downplay the importance of competition if my readings on collectors and their collections are at all valid. It may be a more important motivator than I acknowledge. Like Katcher and Esmerian, Foster also did his research. And friendships matter. John Carter and Alan Granby, who wrote the book's Foreword and Introduction, respectively, focus again on their thought that the reason for collecting is interpersonal. Both were friends with Foster, he their mentor. Competition, the intellectual (research), and relationships also are all the focus of my attention.

Immortality as a motivation to collect is difficult to argue with. For the three noted collectors I chose, the pieces they assembled not only reflected their taste but also will live on after them, even if dispersed. This legacy may be important to some collectors. The joy they experienced and the pieces that contributed to it, can be shared with others, as can their research.

As for myself, my collection is a humble one; no coffee tables need apply for the tome picturing my collection to be placed upon them. No immortality for me. A series of largely unplanned events led me to become a collector of Americana. In brief, it resulted from Sandy's interest and acceptance of collecting; friends who tutored us; dealers who became friends and mentored us; enjoying the time spent driving back roads antiquing; and an affinity for Colonial Williamsburg. I discovered that I possess a love for history largely unrecognized earlier in my life; a fascination antique collecting allows me to explore and deepen. As to why my wife and I are comfortable with antiques, I must again plead I have no ready answer. What does it mean to "like the look?" or to like "living with antiques?" I believe the answers to those questions are as complicated and nuanced as they are to why we collect.

My parents loved music, collected art, and visited museums regularly. Perhaps my reflection of their aesthetic appreciation popped up in the world of antiques. I dream of the softness of a well-worn painted surface, the lines and mystery of a wooden works tall case clock, the look of a pottery mug on a darkened walnut Queen Anne table top, the sense of motion and beauty in a schooner at full sail, a surface that somehow should be inlaid on a candle stand but is instead paint, a simple painted quill penholder. The appreciation for the beauty that can be seen, touched and felt is somehow archetypically powerful. At least it is for me.

℮

An Exercise in Style and Connoisseurship

This is a simple, everyday object from long ago Connecticut. Pens (sharpened quills) needed an easily accessible place to rest. Every desk held such a penholder of one size or another. It is low enough to easily slip a quill in and out, of sufficient diameter to hold several of them. The *faux* painted surface mimics a more expensive wood and offers a wonderful example of the widespread desire to make a simple, utilitarian object into something aesthetically pleasing. Paint was of course less expensive than crafting the penholder out of a fancier wood, though it demanded some exquisite skill to pull off. It was readily affordable: We liked its appearance on a desk and purchased it.

Items like this holder are really interesting in terms of material culture and you find them all over the east coast, not just New England. Silliman did pretty well for himself and it was a very popular design. How do we know Silliman manufactured this quill penholder? Luckily, a dealer I know had an exact duplicate with a paper label on it. The website of the Chester (Connecticut) Historical Society (Chester Museum at the Mill) informs us:

> Before there were computers, before typewriters and ballpoint pens and even fountain pens, there was the inkstand. In the 1800s, the S. Silliman Company in Chester made itself known nationwide for its wooden inkstands and inkwells. Indeed, it is said that Abraham Lincoln had a Silliman inkwell in his Springfield, Illinois, law office, and in 1837 a Silliman inkwell was gifted to President Martin Van Buren.

Compromises. None. Looking at it closely made me wonder if several of them presented as a grouping, all with painted surfaces, might not make an interesting display. But the piece speaks for itself well and loudly.

ε

As an academic and a collector, I feel like iron filings being pulled toward a magnet; there is a new world to research and learn about. Taking my training and transferring it into a hobby nourishes me. And I know for myself that colleting antiques provided me with new meaning. Before I began collecting and deliberating (musing) on what was going on I had few other distractions, so perhaps unconsciously I needed something outside of work to attach myself to. To put it another way, a new theme emerges: Collecting was compelling because it something new and meaningful to do.

Oh, many reasons demand our scrutiny as to why we collect. Barron asks if we do so in order to touch the past and thereby escape the present, thus making collecting a form of nostalgia. I believe that we do. Do we collect because we want to know the world, or because we enjoy pretty things? Do we collect, quite simply because the things, pretty or not, are begging to be collected? (Bryant, J., in Barron,). "Absolutely," I reply.

Returning to where we began – Charles S. Curb's insights on the collecting of silver – we learn that important people have collected silver for centuries. And we know many other genres precious and quotidian have been assembled for a long, long time. We need to delve deeper into the themes touched upon here, so that we may begin to know ourselves as collectors better, or to know others as collectors. Why Collect? There is still much to discover, uncover, and talk about regarding Curb's "sensible and proper thing to do." I want to turn to what I believe may be the most important reason that people collect – the stories that collecting allows them to tell.

Chapter 7

ౌ

Stories

Circa early 20th Century, probably New England black doll. 22"h. Folk art, no clothes. Excellent condition. Probably one-of-a-kind. Specially made.

"Some of these things are true, and some of them lies. But they are all good stories." (Hilary Mantel, *Wolf Hall*)

For us to understand why people collect, we need to look at the telling of tales. Mantel's phrase, " . . . they are all good stories," captures one of the most basic reasons that people collect and love antique collecting so. The world of antique collectors is overflowing with stories. Narratives are a currency we cannot do without. "Explaining ourselves to ourselves by means of stories is as fundamental as eating and breathing" (Russo, *The Destiny Thief, 2018)* and telling them is perhaps even as primal as the urge to collect. Stories become myth, carrying truths important to remember. That is also why tales of accomplishments, encounters and mistakes permeate this book (as you shall see in the chapter "Memorable Moments,"· not all collecting adventures are impermeably positive and uplifting. The same might be said for life, I suppose).

A Native American proverb says, "Tell me a fact and I'll learn. Tell me a truth and I'll believe. But tell me a story and it will live in my heart forever." It is in stories where the emotions, truth, and the lasting importance of antiques lie. Narratives embed our love for these old things in our psyche, and when talking with others our stories help them understand why we collect. To paraphrase Rudyard Kipling, if antiques were taught in the form of stories, they would never be forgotten.

We humans need stories. They are the fabric of our souls – powerful, magical, and insightful: stories told around campfires so long ago, epic tales like the *Iliad*; those with morals such as Aesop fables; tributes to one's ancestors such as Chablon's *Moonglow*. Narratives true and false illuminate, fascinate, and educate. We seem hardwired to attend to narratives, to listen and appreciate stories and learn from them. They come in all shapes and sizes: fairy tales (at times unsuited to children), ghost stories, detective narratives, biographies, histories, legends. All cultures have stories that try to explain the presence of good and evil, interactions between gods and mortal men, the origins of our yearnings and the pitfalls of getting what we most desire (Midas, Helen of Troy to mention two).

We convey what we have experienced and observed through stories. They entertain and preserve a culture's values. Lingering behind them all is the sense that there is a right order in the world, the belief in both the cherished past and hoped for future, gloating about triumphs and sorrow over failures.

Surely the average antique collector is no stranger to any of these themes and feelings. It is hardly unfair to suggest that people revel in the uplifting and even enjoy the *frisson* generated by failure . . . as long as it is not theirs. The capture of a legendary painting purchased from a grand collection circulates in hushed tones, and over time it becomes the piece's story. The original estimate and final price, who bid, the tussles on the floor and on phones, and the applause are all elements of a good plot.

Collectors love these narratives, even collect them. With a little gasp in her voice she begins: "It was the last day of the show and I am sure hundreds of collectors had seen it but there it was." I am not exaggerating, by the way. The quote is stolen from a true story during Manchester's Antiques Week years ago, when at all its shows the best Windsor for sale (according to the author of a highly respected tome on such furniture) remained unsold. Unsold, though it was priced fairly. A tragedy, no? Now if an astute customer had bought it in the very last hour of the very last day that would a great story. "The wise owls had flown over, blind, and I –

little old me - snatched up the treasure" sayeth she. And sayeth a thousand times over the coming years.

Or take as a more modest example a tale my wife and I have told repeatedly over the years. We were looking for a roll top desk and found one for sale by a private party. We tootled off to his home, liked it, and agreed on a price. He said he would deliver it to us, which he did . . . in many pieces, on a winter night with the snow flying. The seller had great confidence we would be able to put it together and off he drove, chuckling I suppose. No instruction booklet, mind you, although we can probably do without those written in a foreign land and then translated for the tricycle or other children's toy that gives us such heartaches now. Who knew IKEA would follow in our desk's footstep? Yes, we did assemble it through trial and error and enjoy it to this day. But Sandy and I will never forget that winter night. As an aside, the desk is newer that most of our collection, circa 1910 or so. But its functionality is unsurpassed, and the story such a good one that we cannot part with it.

Collectors cherish fables like that and share them more than anything else as they trade dialogue, waiting for a show to open. One hears about how nicely their piece fit into a collection, how lucky the collector was to be in the right place at the right time. "It was in a barn." "The dealer waited fifteen years for a chance to purchase it." "I found it a feed store in a town that was literally a wide spot on the back road." Collectors glow when they get to tell their tales. These riffs are magic to them, glowing spots in their own lives, little miracles. We covet the stories sometimes even more than the antiques themselves. They are graphic, involving and a marvelous way to have a transaction with people who you may barely know but who love a well-told tale, even if some of it is slightly dramatized or fabricated.

Narratives are magical, but romantic ones are special. "Romantic" embraces the biography of the famed collector or notorious dealer from whom the piece was purchased. "Did you know that . . ." he begins, and the painting's current owner dominates the conversation with his version of the multiple marriages, tragedies, life trajectory of his predecessor's career, deaf to the irony that someday his own faults and failures may be laid bare by yet another generation. Sometimes the romance lies in the curse that hovered about the antique or its past owners. Think of the manifold treasures stolen from the pyramids, the signature masterpiece rescued from the trash, the gold bar casually used as a doorstop. To many antiquers, the building of their collection is the plot line of saga, preferably historical tragedy rather than light comedy. The characters, the history, the aura are the heart of ownership, and the collection and its collectors are shrouded in a supernal mist. Collectors and dealers are by nature fabulists and their audiences love nothing more than the arising of the improbable, the unexpected and the mysterious.

James Barron in *The One-Cent Magenta* (2017) provides readers with the captivating story of the world's rarest stamp, the only British issued postal piece not in the Queen's collection! He describes its journey since 1856 when it was issued, and probes the motives of the collectors who coveted it: investment, its importance in a collection, its uniqueness, or perhaps just personal satisfaction. But no one pursued it for its appearance interestingly enough, for it is not good-looking. Aesthetics aside, Barron is less interested in the stamp itself than he is in its cast of characters.

I pulled a few tomes from a bookshelf at home and let the pages fall open at random. In Leigh and Leslie Keno's *Hidden Treasures* (2000) I read about Sotheby's American Furniture Department in October, 1998 and Keno's story of a magnificent pier table with a ". . . gray-veined marble slab top and a trim mahogany cabriole-legged frame" (p. 217). After a paragraph describing the table Leslie immediately asked a colleague, "What's the story?" Out pops a dramatic tale of a west coast antique dealer finding the table in a consignment shop. Leigh uses this fact as his motivation for a lecture regarding the sixth sense needed to determine if a piece is genuine and how important it is to view antiques firsthand. We learn of the table's owner, more about the table itself when inspected in person, its misrepresentation as a 19th century English piece, that it had a mate, possibilities of selling it, whether it was stolen, and finally its sale. Altogether, we are given a grand story in which the piece itself is merely another plot element, not the center.

Thatcher Freund's well-written and fascinating *Objects of Desire: The Lives of Antiques and Those Who Pursue Them* (1993) provides another example of a collector's narrative skill, offering the stories of three pieces of antique furniture. The most interesting is of "a pine blanket chest made for a farmer in the 1750s and still wearing its original coat of robin's egg blue paint. The asking price is $250,000." He describes the craftsman's love for the chest when constructing it, its original state – lacking brasses, and its journey from owner to owner, including some well-known old-time dealers. We learn that pieces of furniture such as this one "want to belong," which somehow shrouds the thing with character and emotion, though that wanting surely dwells in whoever owns it. Freund writes about buyers who first fret about the price but then allow their appreciation of its form and their realization it is the finest of its period to win out. As the story ends, Fred Giampietro has the blanket chest in his booth at the Winter Antiques Show, where it does not sell. (I briefly talked with Fred a few years after reading the book and he told me the table was snapped up soon after the show ended.) Its story is over, but only for the moment, and the fable sticks in our minds far better than any memory of the chest itself. If the object gave us fleeting pleasure, the tale gave us more.

Our third book of stories is Harold Sack's *American Treasure Hunt: The Legacy of Israel Sack* (1966), in great measure his testament to his father. The story is one of a Boston gentleman – Colonel Fearing in the 1920s – and a sideboard. The Colonel purchases three pieces from Israel Sack, including a $7,500 sideboard, a most impressive price even then ($91,351.13 in 2018 dollars). It was a good sale and we are made aware that even in those bygone days sideboards were difficult to sell. I conclude, also, that being married has not changed one iota, for it is Colonel Fearing's wife who calls Mr. Sack, upset that he had sold those pieces to her husband, asserting she is the buyer in the family. Israel explains he did not sell his beloved pieces at all: He simply named a price and the Colonel agreed to pay it. The Colonel comes back and Mr. Sack fears the deal is off. The Colonel, however, apparently does not care where his wife will put the piece, even the woodshed. In love with them, he will cough up. Fifty years later the Colonel calls Israel's son, Harold, from California and Harold Sack talks with him, never having forgotten his father's story. As a result, the famed sideboard is once again shipped East and sold about a year later. Story *finis*, . . . for now.

The telling of stories in the antique world seems endless. In 2017 the exhibit at the Winter Antique Show featured folk art collected by Abby Aldrich Rockefeller and now in the Colonial Williamsburg collection. The loan exhibition commemorated the 60th anniversary of the Abby Aldrich Folk Art Museum. On display were featured pieces of ceramics, furniture, sculpture, drawings, paintings, *fraktur*, weathervanes, and such. The items are without exception exemplars of their forms.

The occasion prompted numerous articles about Mrs. Rockefeller, almost all stories, in publications such as *The Magazine Antiques*. They tell how she, one of the earliest female folk art collectors, began gathering outstanding pieces of Americana in the 1920s. We learn what others thought about her buying "those things" that few at the time saw beauty or merit in. Though she was one of the founders of the Museum of Modern Art, I find a certain wry satisfaction in the fact she pursued its antithesis, folk art, much to her husband's dismay. I can only surmise Mr. Rockefeller did not share her ardor. There must be a story in that, I thought. And of course there was.

Mrs. Rockefeller began collecting folk art not merely because she thought she should do so but because her modern art was its progeny; the parent was thus central to contemporary American art. That was her intellect at work. Her appreciation for folk art was based also on the emotions of a true fan. She loved it. Better yet, she had the means, a discerning eye, and the reputation for taste and wealth needed so that dealers give her first choice of the best pieces, "The lure and intrigue of Folk Art delighted Abby Rockefeller." (*I Collect, Abby Aldrich Rockefeller and her Folk Art Museum*, January 11, 2017 website). The seminal folk art collection in the United States is the consequence of her broader passion for the arts. Folk art stopped being mere historical precedent and became a genre in its own right.

As for my stories, I have but a few. My favorite story involves one of my wife's beloved black dolls. We had done a quick walk-through of the Mid-Week Show in Manchester years ago and then reversed our course. And then Sandy saw it: love at first sight (cue orchestra). She walked to the dealer telling her that she had to have it, all this before asking if the price was firm . . . a lesson in how not to negotiate. The dealer told her the price was set in concrete (cue orchestra in a minor chord). Despite all that, the doll now sits on our sofa in the living room sporting a shawl made from a napkin from United Airlines first class, but even that is part of the doll's legend: Coming home, we were grounded in Boston for 10 hours because of storms. Midwest Express – known then for its chocolate chip cookies and now but a fading memory – transferred us to United and we left Boston about 11 p.m. We were offered dinner but were too tired to eat. The flight attendant gave my wife a bottle of wine as we deplaned wrapped in what is now the doll's shawl. Stories can be such fun.

ℰ

An Exercise in Style and Connoisseurship

My wife's criterion a simple one: she has to feel deep affection for whatever she collects. The doll's size reminds her of Goldilocks and the Three Bears – not too large and not too small. It cried out for her attention with its curly hair, three-dimensional nose and eyebrows, and long fingers, (no toes necessary). The eyes are stitched, not buttons. The mouth is understated; a single red thread suggests lips. My wife sees beauty, but I find the doll alluring in her simplicity. No earrings or jarring ornamentation detract from her presence.

Compromises. Lacks original or old clothes (we could find them, I imagine, but they are hardy crucial to the doll's appeal).

At the same time there is more to collecting than the telling of stories, as important as they are, and I next turn to another important answer to the question, why collect? – the emotions a collector experiences.

Chapter 8

č

The Emotional

WWI, British poster, circa 1917. "More Aeroplanes are needed/ Women Come and Help." 76.0 x 50.0 cm. Ministry of Munitions. Condition is A. On linen and framed. No signature or information on who the artist may have been. Rare.

"Good morning Mr. Smith. Ready for our session?"

"More than ready, Dr. Perlman. Some important issues to talk about today."

"Where do you want to begin?"

"I think today would be a good day to talk about my collecting, what it does for me, and the unease I feel at times."

"Sounds interesting and important. Tell me more."

"As you know collecting American antiques is important to me. Sometimes I feel it is too important. Oh, not in the sense of it being an obsession and my tossing everything else to the wind, but sometimes I feel as if I get a disproportionate share of my needs met by collecting. Is my normal life so barren that I must collect to feel alive?"

"An interesting thought. Where has collecting taken you and have you reached any conclusions about it?"

"It has taken me to wonderful worlds as well as ones I would rather not have visited, and I am . . . er (Smith thought: *at least I don't have to lie on a couch and free associate*), I am well aware of my feelings and that if I let myself enjoy them, they enrich my life. But all those emotions sure perplex me sometimes. I usually trust my instincts when it comes to judging people. And as a collector I am quite familiar with some emotions – thrill, disappointment, delight, desire, longing, excitement, passion, and love to name just a few. What collector has never felt like dancing as Tevye does in *Fiddler on the Roof* after falling love with an antique, or a great day visiting shops?"

"And?" Perlman asked. "It sounds like you think there is something wrong about what you described."

"It just doesn't seem normal sometimes. All of Shakespeare, the Greek tragedies, Broadway, the meaning of life, can they coalesce in a collector's emotional cauldron?"

"Normal? Some might argue you are lucky to have an arena in which to pour your feelings and soul. A tragedy sometimes, a comedy at others, the warp and weft of life."

"You make it sound okay." Mr. Smith was not convinced. "But to be so completely occupied with the hunt, to have no more reward than finding a 'thing' I've been searching for? It makes me feel uneasy. Is it normal to feel so excited and exhilarated looking for things? Aren't greed and the pursuit of material possessions . . . I don't know . . . unnatural, sins? "

"Here we are again – you agonizing about what is and is not normal. It sounds as if it is difficult for you to let go, to enjoy. As for greed, are you saying every museum curator the world over suffers from it, rather than, say, healthy curiosity? They get paid to pursue those material things. You'd never call them moral failure simply because they do their jobs, would you?"

"Well collecting doesn't seem very grown up. It's just a treasure hunt, going from one clue to the next until finally you find where 'X' marks the spot – the auction, dealer or collector who has what it is you seek. You weave through obstacles, go down detours and hit dead ends. Hunting requires hope, which is delightful, but . . . ."

"So you want to have hope but only if the matter is serious and you don't think collecting has sufficient gravity? Still, lots of people collect things. Nothing abnormal in that."

"But what about the competitiveness that collecting causes? I find myself needing to get to a dealer's booth before others playing sneaky games at auctions. That's hardly normal, is it?"

"You're tying yourself in knots. You once mentioned a book you had read about a collector – Jane Katcher I believe. You said that what was important to her was that an antique produced feelings that resonated within her, a 'stirring' as she called it. How lucky it seems for someone to experience such an intense feeling. Would you want to repudiate it?"

"Maybe I am focusing too much on my unease. I know that when I am surrounded by really good antiques at a show or at home, I feel great satisfaction. The intellectual satisfaction antiques provide is not as valuable as the smile they produce. For example, my wife is interested in women in aviation. I love her British World War One poster: 'Women Come and Help' it blares with biplanes on the tarmac and flying overhead. It truly makes me feel like a caretaker for the period and reminds me of both the optimism and failure of the "war to end all wars.' Non-collector friends find our passion for it is a mystery. And no matter in what way or how often I explain our feelings about the poster to them, they don't seem to understand how it can stirs something more than mild curiosity in the two of us."

An Exercise in Style and Connoisseurship

There is a great sense of motion within the rectangular outlines of the piece. It shows almost folk art proportions, given the size of the bi-plane flying over the woman. The bi-plane's wing piercing the border suggests freedom and motion, as the cursive "Apply At Once" evokes spontaneity. Sandy is captivated by the late-Victorian dress the woman wears. The poster is lithographed on paper and linen backed, as one would expect.

According to EBay (What is a lithograph – a clear definition):

The printing process that creates a lithograph is different from other traditional methods. Most printing presses require the printmaker to etch an image or text into metal plates or physically carve out the image on blocks of wood or other soft material. To create a lithograph, however, no etching is required. The artist uses a set of greasy crayons or pencils to draw a mirrored image of the original artwork onto a smooth stone tablet. This is by far the most time-consuming part of the lithograph process.

After the image has been recreated to the satisfaction of the original artist or other authority, it is ready to be turned into a lithograph. The lithographic process hinges on the principle that oil and water cannot mix. An oil-based variety of ink is applied directly to the plate and immediately bonds with the equally greasy crayon lines. Water is then wiped onto the remaining unpainted areas to discourage the ink from smearing. A sheet of paper, preferably one with a high cotton content, is then placed over the entire plate.

The inked stone or metal plate and the paper are placed in a press and light pressure is used to transfer some of the ink. If the original image were a monochrome pen and ink drawing, this would be the only press run necessary. A color lithograph of an elaborate . . . painting, however, might require several different runs with up to four different color inks – black, red, yellow and blue. The same paper would be placed precisely over the re-inked plates, eventually creating a satisfactory lithograph copy. This same process is used to create color pages in newspapers.

Since the process for creating a lithograph can be just as time-consuming and detailed as an original painting, printing runs are often kept low to preserve value.

The colors of the poster are true – remarkable given its age. The broad range of colors renders it more of a work of art than an ad. The scene is more complex than one might expect, showing several airplanes in the air and another on the ground with four people attending to it. Posters like these are rarely signed so we have no information about the artist. It is in near perfect condition and quite rare (the only other one I have seen was up for auction in 2018).

In the US, most of us think women entered the workforce in WWII, yet this British poster makes it obvious women provided critical support much earlier.

This poster was a must-own/keeper, for my wife. We decided to purchase it immediately on first seeing it. There appeared to be virtually no chance of ever finding another in such fine condition.

Compromises. Absolutely none.

"So you conclude?"

"I think that I lose sight of the balance between seeking and cherishing when I collect. The process can be disappointing, that letdown when I miss out or find a desirable piece beyond our means and it's worse when we feel we let a piece get away from us. 'It was too expensive. I will find another.' At auctions they call it 'under bidder's remorse.' And there is the unknowable answer for the question that keeps repeating: 'Why didn't I buy the damn thing?' There is no place to hide when the disappointment is the product of our own decisions. Phooey, if only it were not so."

"Okay, let's try to find some middle ground. What offsets the difficult feelings of disappointment?"

"Well, a least antique collectors tend to be optimists. Another piece will come along. It will be even better. We tend to have a sunny view of the future. Hopeful and confident, we persevere. At worst, we will get a narrative for a good conversation, training for our eye, a regret for something that stirred something deep inside us. And once in a while, we hit the jackpot! A proud addition to our collection."

"So collecting embraces the full array of human emotion, the highs and lows if you will. Let's continue with the positive for the moment."

"Collecting provides enjoyment, amusement, a break from the everyday, something challenging but not life and death, or on occasion a decision that seems to drag out dire consequences but turns out to be illusory. Regardless, it can be pleasurable, gratifying, and soothing, occasionally spontaneous. I have learned in therapy that when I am having fun, I less aware of the passage of time: It stops mattering. I think that is why collecting is so good for me. It is healing. And most antique collectors with whom I have talked will tell you that despite the aggravations, collecting antiques is fun. They enjoy doing it. I enjoy doing it."

"You could be a spokesperson for well-known auction houses or dealers, Mr. Smith. Yet apparently those positive feelings go away at some point. What takes their place?"

"Now and then I find my coveting of things and the strength of my desire is scary. I didn't know I could feel so strongly about mere objects. Desire is a powerful feeling – a strong wish of wanting, craving, coveting. 'I want that table and I will not rest until it is mine,' I tell myself. Or I think, 'I will find that Windsor bench I have been seeking, or an affordable redware apple pie plate, or . . .' The desire can be so overwhelming it sometimes feels like it is leading to obsession. When I become so fixated on the thought of owning an antique, I am unable to push it out of consciousness. To be candid, that just doesn't seem normal or healthy. Doc, if you remember teenage love, you know precisely the all-consuming power of desire. That desire for antiques compels and impels. Sometimes I feel lustful the longing is that intense. But mine isn't an intense longing for someone, but for something.

There's an author who wrote a book called *The One-Cent Magenta*. He describes stamp collecting as an obsession. His statement set me wondering. Can I build a truly great collection without being obsessed? Do I need an overwhelming, unrelenting desire to be a truly successful collector? I worry that the positive feelings of having a purpose will get mixed with the intoxication of desire and will morph into something else, something darker."

"Are you truly that obsessed? Does the hobby have a dark implication to you? It sounds like you are worried that you'll end up in Dante's second circle of hell."

"No, you're right. I'm tilting at windmills. I have never, ever completely lost my sense of proportion. Now that I am sensitized to it, I'll look out for those for whom the desire for antiques is all-consuming. They would be interesting folks to chat with. Yet I'm sure I am not 'that' obsessed or lustful."

"Hmmm. But it sounds like you like the passion for antiques as a feeling in the moment, many moments actually. If it doesn't last and last, it isn't a true obsession. Let's go back to the positives now. Give me another example."

"Well, collecting certainly is a worthy pastime; it has a value to me. Talk about negative feelings – filing taxes, politics, the state of the nation, the cost of these therapy sessions . . . just kidding, doc. Collecting tears me away from all of that. It dims my aches and pains, the sense of growing older, losing good friends. I don't even mind giving up once cherished pieces in order to improve my collection, even if that means selling a piece or two for less than I paid for them. All that is part of being a collector. Most of us don't collect to necessarily make money, you know. Unlike when I was working, even research and studying are not drudgery. If collecting antiques weren't fun, I'd stop." And Mr. Smith quit talking and listened to what he had said.

"What are you thinking about right now?"

"I was thinking that collecting has been good for me. But then I think again of strong feelings I get I find uncomfortable. For instance, at times I get frustrated and angry. Oh, it disappears quickly most of the time. It's easy to be angry with myself for doing something stupid. For how I treated someone in the moment. For simply wanting to cuss out the gods of collectors who dealt me such a lousy hand. But those are mostly transitory emotions. Well we're told that pride goeth before destruction, a haughty spirit before a fall; that's Proverbs you know. I have found I feel prideful sometimes. Oh I am hardly the sole collector to fall into that trap. I've worked diligently to build a collection that suits my tastes and get great pleasure from how some people react to my efforts. Collecting is time consuming, sometimes expensive, and often difficult. It is natural to want my collection to be appreciated and respected. I know that many collectors or their heirs take pride in an auction catalog in part or whole devoted to their collection crossing the block. But still, 'pride.' You know, that a sin,"

"You seem to look too hard for negative connotations. We're back to the seven deadly sins and circles of hell again. I think of biblical pride as corrupt selfishness – putting your desires even whims before the welfare of others. Most of the time you seem pretty humble. Isn't the pride you are talking about nothing more than deep satisfaction and gratification with something that is important to you, that gives you meaning?"

Mr. Smith paused and was silent for some time. "I hadn't thought of it that way. You make it sound so normal. There are times I feel triumphant, exhilarated, even gleeful. I am elated and euphoric. Then life is good and worthwhile. I feel like shouting 'To life!' We collectors are familiar with the feeling of exuberant triumph. After all of the looking and searching, the amassing of purchasing funds, the frustrations and disappointments, once in a while it all works out. I find a beautiful antique, one that gives me aesthetic pleasure, and even one that talks to me. I feel happiness and joy in response to touching, and looking at antiques or works of art Perhaps that's what Jane Katcher meant when she talks about being 'awoken and stirred?' She feels joyful when she looks at pieces in her collection. The feeling sustains her in her collecting."

"Let's stick with these positive feelings. Tell me more."

"I've experienced much joy in my years as a collector. The Roberts' wooden works tall case clock was too good to be true (pictured in Chapter 12), and it is so very beautiful. I had similar feelings when I attended a top-quality antique show for the first time many years ago and was actually awed at being in the presence of so many beautiful objects. It felt right and 'good' to be there. I get a special feeling when I see my wife find a piece she really, really wants."

"I hear you saying that your search for, owning, and researching antiques fulfills you. Now you've achieved something you had long searched for. While you're concerned about being a bit abnormal or crazy, you actually sound contented. Some thinkers argue that fulfillment in life is more important a feeling than happiness. If collecting gives you meaning and meets many of your needs, isn't that good? When you collect you feel alive."

"Have I felt fulfilled as an antique collector? As they say in Minnesota where one of my daughters-in-law is from, 'you betcha.' And not to get gushy, collecting gives me an intense feeling: I am deeply emotionally attached to the world of Americana. I think I'm feeling my way around to describing what most people call love. I didn't seek love as my collecting evolved and unfolded. Love was the outcome of a sense of synchrony with everything antique collecting entails. It's not the intense feelings of romantic connection but more like the way one loves a good friend or family member, 'companionate love' that involves commitment such as to my wife of many years. Some of the romantic passion is gone, but the commitment is deep and long lasting. That's how I feel about collecting antiques. To steal from Shakespeare: 'If collecting antiques be the food of love, play on.'"

"We are almost out of time today. Are you still so concerned about your collecting, uneasiness and lack of normality?"

"No, I feel better. It's just so hard to understand the emotions involved in collecting, let alone explain them to others. But I think I understand them better after going through this process and that will make it easier for me and to share what collecting means to me with my wife, kids and friends. Thanks, doc."

"See you next week."

And Mr. Smith left the confines of the therapist's office for the world of collecting he now felt much less ambivalent about. *To life, to life, l'chaim.* There were other antiques to seek out. He'd let others worry about deadly sins and Dante's circles of hell. It was time to get on with life.

Chapter 9

ℰ

A Hobby and What It Offers

Circa 1790-1815 Vermont triple back Windsor chair in old red surface. Found in Vermont, no repairs, original condition, 25"l, 16"d, 47"h.

It is possible in our excitement that we exaggerate both the nature and value of the things we most cherish. Antique collecting is no exception. I have known more than a few collectors who have assigned the chase and the capture of desired objects significance not far from life and death (in the case of Western noose collectors, that may not be far from the truth, of course). Still, collecting fills out our days, letting us set aside the tedium of repeated decisions on whether Fruit Loops are an appropriate breakfast for our six year old or whether to put real or synthetic oil in the crankcase of the pickup.

In collecting Americana I have found pleasure, excitement, fulfill-ment, meaning, and an opportunity to pursue and share expertise. While I am not an adherent of Dale Carnegie, when he said, "let the winds of enthusiasm sweep through you; live with gusto," he had to have been talking about something very much like my collecting experiences. Not to wax poetic or invade the religious realm, hobbies are good for our souls. They counterbalance everyday Fruit Loop decisions and offer us a path to sane choices. I need that sanity in my life, since I am too readily a Type A personality. While I say I am more laid back since I retired, Sandy just smiles, sighs and shakes her head. I'll say, "I have changed; see I can be more relaxed." She responds in her own way, "If you think you have reached a state of calm, the rest of the world is comatose."

As we continue to investigate why it is that we collect, the actual decision-making process increasingly begins to look like a Rubik's cube. Turn it this way and one set of reasons appears. Turn it another and alternate and sometimes contradictory explanations crop up.

Following hard on the trail of the preceding chapter, I can think of no better example of collector certainty or uncertainty than the influence of feelings. We are quite accustomed to having revered dealers and collectors in Americana giving high praise to "instinct," which sounds a good deal like an emotion. An unsigned piece is attributed the hand of some famed craftsman because it "just feels right." That instinct is little more than the product of long study and profound experience: Reason was its foundation, and now the expert is so bathed in "real" things that he unconsciously assembles all the clues, bold and subtle, and confidently makes his attribution. OK. In contrast, an inexperienced collector who has not studied the field intensively can be easily misled by his or her feelings: The penholder is attractive and appealing, so it must be genuine. There is a simple emotional formula for the experienced collector: liking = authenticity (to be followed up by a very close look at the antique and sometimes extensive research as to its attribution). Both parties followed their feelings but the outcomes – mainly because of the way in which the feelings were formed – were very different. Ah, the joys of a hobby.

In what follows I discuss how identity, everyday rituals, competition, relationships, and the intellectual affect and enhance collecting.

Identity

It is alleged that everywhere in the British Empire (from the 16th century onward), each afternoon the Brits had tea. The custom was a powerful reminder of who and what they were: until 1947, when India defected, pretty much masters of the East. The ritual of sipping tea, just as did their fellow citizens and colonials around the globe, unified Jolly Olde England, even for those sweltering in the far reaches of the empire. It hardly stretches the truth, if one is to believe contemporary histories, that the consumption of tea became the closest thing to a religious ritual the notoriously reserved English ever came. Amid shot and shell, in the blazing tropics and frigid poles, the kettle came out and the wallahs sipped their Darjeeling tea. They were British – this was their identity and their expression of it.

One's personal identity is powerful and meaningful. Think of identity as the assembled self each of us knows is inside, at once making us individuals and giving us a sense of belonging to a community. Others may define who we are, but more importantly each of us defines ourselves. When others assign us a group identity they place us in societal categories – Jewish, educated, middle class, father, husband, aging (to name a few that apply to me). We are uncomfortable when someone tries to give us personal identity we have not thought of, or is not respectable or valued in our own opinion. Your wife or girlfriend says you are really "sweet." Being sweet may conflict with the Bogart tough guy image that you have of yourself. Or that you yearn for. Or the fact she sees you as sweet may come as a complete surprise. Inside, you reject the characterization as insufficient to your self-perception.

When we define our identity what we end up with may not be accurate, but these self-beliefs steer many of our behaviors and feelings. Over time you may have come to define yourself as an antique collector of refined tastes. What implications do that carry? Quite important ones as it turns out.

If being an "antiquer" is a recent part of your identity, you may feel as if you are trying on a new coat. Are you comfortable with it, does it fit? If the answer eventually proves to be positive, antique collecting becomes part of whom you are. You try to act like an assessor, casting a critical eye on the things that surround you, assigning them value. You may even spurn certain things – say costumer jewelry – as unworthy of ownership (yet there are collectors who covet it). The more serious you are as an antique collector, the more indelible that label is as part of your identity.

Yes, I am an antique collector. However, I cannot tell you exactly the moment I adopted that facet of my identity. I have been purchasing antiques since I was in my early 30s. I think the commitment became heart-deep when I began finding myself tracking the dates dealers I had purchased pieces from were venturing into the Midwest from their New England markets. I was determined to be first to see what they had for sale. Not long after that I began subscribing to periodicals about antiques. Finally, I began spending more for antiques without letting it nag me (well, at least not as much). I reveled in the antiques I owned and spent time thinking what I might find next for our collection. My identity had firmed up. It fitted me. I was comfortable with and in it. I knew that was part of who I was.

Notice that having an identity embraces behaviors, thoughts, and feelings. I was doing things that an antique collector does. Therefore I thought of myself as a collector. Therefore I grasped and responded to the emotions antique collectors described when they wrote about their hobby or when I talked with them.

All of that is well and good. What is critical to realize is that changing one's identity – one's personality – can be a messy and sometimes unconscious process. We all have wished now and then we were different: better able to get down to work, better able to enjoy time off and relax, better able to be on time and be more responsible, happier, more serious. That is the reason shelves of self-help books in a bookstore go on and on; everyone is delighted – for a price – to let us remake ourselves. And despite their titles these transformations take more than 30 minutes, an hour, or a month. Once any identity is firmly in place – including that you are an antique collector – it lingers. It can be modified over time but it is amazingly difficult to reverse it. You keep collecting because it is who you are. Even if you stop collecting, you may regretfully or delightedly identify yourself as a "former collector" (which real collectors may equate with being, say, a former streetwalker). And if you identify yourself as a collector, you will engage in everyday collector habits I think of as "rituals."

Rituals

Most people engage in simple and almost unconscious behaviors – squeezing the toothpaste in the middle of the tube, loading the dishwasher from bottom to top, usually in a way with which your spouse always disagrees. Such habits help ground us and keep our world seeming rational and even providing something to look forward to (French fries without catsup are *meh!*). These activities are our rituals. They provide harmony, are familiar and give us pleasure. We miss them greatly and feel out-of-sorts if we can't indulge them. Rituals connect us with ourselves. They are congruent with our identity – tea in the afternoon for the British.

These rituals have importance beyond reminding us of our social or cultural identity. Everyday rituals can become sacred. We would not think of doing without them. We know such "rites" are important to us, when as Samuel Johnson said, " . . . they are too strong to be broken."

Others may not understand our rites and habitual actions, but they are ingrained. Think of the importance of Starbucks' coffee to millions of people every day. Watching the barista prepare and serve it, the first sip, savoring the aroma, all help start the day right. We are better able to face what may follow. For me, the ritual is tea. The first mug of tea in the morning, reading the morning paper, looking at the schedule of what lies ahead (full disclosure, being retired it may be a full day or a fairly empty one). I must have my tea.

So what are the actions collectors imbue with meaning? Speaking for myself, I check the websites of several antique publications almost daily. I learn what new articles, often with wonderful photos, are posted. I look at dealers' offerings. Technology sometimes lets me view all of the booths in a good antique show while sitting at home. Doing so I feel like I have participated, and I get a chance to learn not only what wares dealers have for sale but to hone my appreciation for antiques. If there is an object I covet, I can pray it has not sold and contact the dealer. I am involved with social media sites too, reading and responding to posts and photos. I would feel lost if I did not do those things. I also try to write a bit each day or two for a column in *Maine Antique Digest*. Given the winters in Wisconsin when the weather outside truly can be frightful, writing is a welcome distraction as well as an established ritual.

I have never seen any writing on the everyday rituals of antique collectors and learning about them would be fascinating. The social scientist part of me wants to survey collectors and gather data. Perhaps another time.

Of course, none of these practices is fated or immutable. Our identity changes as the years pass, life challenges us, or opportunities appear. We can and probably should introduce new rituals now and then, complementing or replacing the old. Worn and tattered rituals may make us weary over time, no longer providing the meaning and sense of completion they once did. But for the moment, whether a few years or decades, the collecting of antiques is part of my daily life as well as my personality.

Competitiveness

It's a dog-eat-dog world I've been told. Some folks have to come out on top in everything. Others couldn't give a hoot. As for me, I lost 10,000 straight games of *Chutes and Ladders* and checkers to my kids when they were younger. None of that induced suicidal impulse or thoughts of revenge.

Still, I like playing card games, trivia and the like. I find low stakes, what-the-heck competition to be fun. There is certainly reward in competition. We love it when David beats Goliath in sports, unless Goliath is quarterback on our favorite team. We get mentally and emotionally involved, even as spectators. But sheer winning isn't everything: talk to an everyday marathoner who finishes long after most other racers, or the golfer whose handicap has gone from a 19 to a 15 after years of hard work. Notice how gratified they feel even though they have not won anything by accepted criteria.

Collectors' needs and personalities seriously affect how they compete. Some face plenty of confrontation in their everyday life – the commute, preventing a co-worker from stealing credit, even gaining the recognition they feel they deserve and their sibs seem to get effortlessly – and collecting is an escape from conflict. Others go into any sort of competition, say to buy a piece of glass, with a savagery and heightened feeling that baffle their colleagues and observers. Personally, I do not want to sacrifice good sportsmanship and class. Naturally, the rules allow us to guiltlessly indulge in a bit of gamesmanship in pursuing our collecting goal (not bidding until the auctioneer says "third and last call" at an auction) but no one is hurt by it, not to mention it is fun.

Think of competition as a means of putting yourself in the best position possible for finding and purchasing pieces for your collection. It seems only common sense not to tell a fellow collector of like pieces about a dealer who has an antique you are looking to buy. It also seems the exercise of sound judgment to do a quick walk-through at an antique show to discover whether it has something you are searching for. Implicitly you are working against the interests of others who might capture the prize, but these competitive behaviors are sensible, common and socially approved.

We may even compete with ourselves when collecting. Honing our eye and sharpening our mind to choose and bid wisely is not only a matter of self-discipline but of survival. Knowing the market allows us to get a fair deal. Missing out on a winner is a reminder we need to sharpen our game, not an excuse to exact retribution on the collector who proved better prepared or smarter than we were. Sometimes competing is simply hard work and involves the expenditure of time and real mental and physical effort.

My wife collects fiction about girls and women who fly. No flight attendants for her; only pilots will do. The first series touching on the subject began in 1911, shortly after the Wright Brothers' inaugural flight. Collecting them is real work. Finding first editions with book covers in good or better condition involves prowling a number of web sites on a regular basis, firming up relationships with book dealers willing to look for possible purchases, going through endless lists, and luck. In building her collection Sandy competes with a cadre of mysterious addicts to the genre. She does not know how many such collections exist in the world. Not many is my guess. Truthfully, most of the competition lies in her ability to endure in her quest.

A dark side to competing lurks in the antique world's shadows. I have thankfully not experienced it yet. "Collecting" as a concept has a nasty edge for some: They absolutely need their antique collection to be the best. They take pleasure in the envy of others. Winning becomes everything and they miss few opportunities to lord it over those churls who are just second best. I once read about a national contest for book collectors, the *National Collegiate Book Collecting Contest*. Panels evaluated not merely the collections submitted, but the descriptive essays and bibliographies entrants presented. Sounds to me more like a neglected form of professional wrestling; everything depends on getting an advantage by any possible means. Am I being unkind? (Participants may enjoy the process and the competition it entails.)

Competitiveness offers its own pleasures. I like the research on women in aviation I do for my wife. Other collectors may enjoy the subtleties of auctions and spend more time watching human behavior than bidding. Still others wait years for some toy to come to the market and have the delight of beating fellow fanatics for the piece of their dreams. Frankly, I am surprised no one has invented a board game (probably a video/computer game at this point in time, but I will wear my years with pride.). Roll the dice, make decisions, earn dollars and points, move ahead or be penalized. The end goal is purchasing the antique you seek before other players can do so. The truth lies in plain sight: Competitiveness and how you practice it is judged by its outcome and how it makes you feel.

So we often compete with others. One way or another, collecting necessitates relationships; the degree and nature of our competitiveness determines, in part, how good those connections are.

Relationships

Most of us cherish having relationships despite their complexity, the pain they can cause, and the difficulty in sustaining them. As the playwright Tennessee Williams once wrote, "Life is partly what we make it, and partly what it is made by the friends we choose."

Through our connections with others we give a peculiar new dimension to our world. We laugh, cry with, remember, and validate our lives with good friends. I remember my mother telling me once, after my dad died, how lonely she felt. There was one less person, out of only a few left, who knew what it was like to live in Chicago in the 1930s, during the war, and afterwards. She had no one to share memories with who would understand.

Collecting antiques is interpersonal. I have found I enjoy my passion more when I share it with others – my successes and failures. Laughing with folks makes the day seem good, life worth living. Ken Kesey wrote in *One Flew Over the Cuckoos' Nest:* "Man, when you lose your laugh you lose your footing." All of the forewords in books depicting famous collections, written by dealers or friends who helped the collector amass what they are now displaying, talk about the joy of getting to know the principals and the privilege or observing or participating as the collections grew.

Relationships allow us to learn – talking with fellow collectors while waiting in line for shows, at auction previews and through correspondence. These dialogues (and now and then monologues: They are collectors, you know) have helped me better understand my tastes and refine what I know or think I know. Others have provided information about details in furniture or redware that I might easily have overlooked.

What have I discovered through these chats? Insights into a piece's aesthetic come to mind. When I was still collecting painted boxes, I had walked a show and not seen a single one I liked. A collector I knew told me about a dealer's booth with a prime example I had missed. Furthermore, she told me why she was recommending it; it was a good example of Maine black and red paint with nice scale and originality. Had I been curmudgeon and never talked with this collector, I (and one of my sons who now enjoys it) would have missed out on the box.

Interpersonal relationships build camaraderie. They let me feel I am part of something larger than myself (a sense of belonging is one of our most important and basic needs). I like being part of the distinguished group of people who prize Americana.

The Intellectual

Finally, collecting as a hobby involves intellect, reason, thinking . . . whatever. At the simplest level, this is mostly bookkeeping work: saving auction catalogues and receipts, meticulously cataloguing appraisal lists, making note of available and desirable pieces and their dimensions, and keeping track of auction houses' upcoming sales. Beyond this – and I am not trying to minimize the importance of these common tasks – collecting provides us many ways to use our mental capabilities. I think of a triple back Windsor I purchased. It was wonderful, but I had never seen a seat quite like the one it had. I looked for clues in Nancy Goyne Evans, *The American Windsor Chair*, and Charles Santore, *The Windsor Style in America* and drew a blank. I studied auction catalogs and articles in magazines and still no illumination. The chair remains a mystery, which is part of its charm. Build a relationship: if you can shed light on the seat in this chair, please let me know. I will keep studying.

C

An Exercise in Style and Connoisseurship

Here is another Windsor chair (see the Exercise in Chapter 3 with the Tracy chairs). The bases of the Tracy Windsor and this one are similar, with excellent turnings and splay to the legs. The original red paint on this chair, worn down in all the right places, provides the only ornamentation. As it rises in height it tries to keep the proper proportion but its style seems to slowly diminish. It does not squat on the floor but leave an impression of lightness.

This is a true Vermont country chair. From the seat up the chair seems a "little stiff:" the spindles a just a bit heavy, the arms slightly odd in shape, the arm supports of a familiar pattern but not as finely tapered as in other examples. The base looks a lot more refined than elements from the seat up.

Ah, the seat. I struggle to understand how a chair maker who could craft a base and the three backs in such nice proportion could make a seat like this one. While not crude, it comes close. Exceedingly plain in form, the seat nonetheless has two incised parallel groves in it. Obviously this was purposely done to dress it up a bit. The maker would surely have known how Windsor chair saddle seats should look, since he knew the form of the spindles he turned so well and how to splay the legs. Did someone want a seat like this and order it? I would not think so; even country Windsors often have nice saddle seats.

Compromises. The seat. Everything else about this rural Vermont chair rings true. Some may consider it a bit "funky." Because it made such a good impression on me, I did not hesitate to purchase it. I only hope some day to learn about and understand why the seat is as it is.

More grandly, and perhaps importantly, many antique collectors feel compelled to research what they own and the period in which the antiques were made. If you ask such collectors why that is, they will tell you, "Because it matters." The belief in comprehensive research goes back a long way in American decorative arts. Stillinger wrote about Irving W. Lyon who first published *The Colonial Furniture of New England* in 1891. The book is still in print and is described on the flyleaf as " . . . one of the great enduring studies of early American furniture." Lyon's research is both impressive and fascinating. His use of inventories with dates, often for estate purposes after someone had died, is exemplary. The photographs add to the text. I learned, for example, that Windsor chairs were in use as early as 1736 in Philadelphia, earlier than I had imagined. Who knew that what we now call a "gateleg" table was originally known as a "thousand-legged table"? Or that what we call "lopers" to hold the slant front of a desk were called "supports for the flap?" What we label a "corner cupboard," often built in, was named a "buffet." A buffet was not a counter on which dishes of food were served. Cupboards were named as early as the 14th century and started as boards on which items were placed, evolving into both open and enclosed pieces of furniture.

Lyon's depth of scholarship deserves our respect. Many collectors follow in his footsteps, though perhaps not with the sort of painstaking detail he provided. Researcher/collectors believe they are stewards for the antiques they own and that they are responsible for preserving them, while constructing records for those who follow. They love and respect history. Their interest allows them to place what they have in a historical context, adding meaning.

Such researchers, whether museum librarians or collectors, often are the detectives of our history. They look for clues in the antiques or works of art themselves, in newspapers, magazines, in letters from long ago, in changing maps and the evolution of conveyance (that is, how things are preserved and passed down over the years). They research to discover who might have crafted, formed or painted the object, why and when its style or function was popular, and its history down to the present moment. Such endeavors can be strikingly revealing as well as very gratifying.

Chapter 22 devotes itself to research on a simple painting of a schooner I own. Research librarians at well-known maritime museums and former experts now retired or working as art dealers contributed to the scholarship, as did the historical society in Madison, CT (where the ship was probably built). The end result is a cherished narrative of who its captains were, what cargoes it carried, and where it ended its days. The result of this study has made the piece doubly attractive to me and filled me with appreciation for the era. In the process I learned a great deal about the world of the working schooner that is now gone forever. The painting now has its own historical and geographical context. Using intellectual tools has helped bring the E. A. Elliott alive once more.

In the same vein, I own redware made in Norwalk, CT so of course I had to look Norwalk up on a map and learn something about it. In 1830, about when much of the redware I collect was made, its population was 3,792 – a good-sized Connecticut town back then. Owning a Hudson Valley painting, I studied the Hudson Valley, its place in this nation's history and the school it came from. Liking Connecticut Valley furniture I located where the Connecticut Valley was and is. To better understand a painted candlestand I read two or three well-worn (by now) books on painted furniture, and I still scrutinize painted New England furniture whenever I encounter it. Leonardo da Vinci captured what I feel when researching antiques; "The noblest pleasure is the joy of understanding."

And in Conclusion

Collecting antiques is our heartfelt activity; so maybe the answer to "why collect?" is unnecessary for us to be happy. We are already pleased with the choice. I still remember all those sci-fi films in which the aliens only want to be understood (and of course when they are not using their superior technology to destroy the world). I am in the same position: I have a commitment non-collectors do not fully understand. I need to explain myself first of all. More important, I need to transmit a message about the hobby of antique collecting (no, not "we come in peace, earthling," but that mine is a valuable and legitimate – and complicated – passion).

The best answer to "why collect?" and at the same time the most incisive is an existential one – collecting gives us meaning in our lives. Existentialists write that meaning does not exist out there in the world but that we decide what has weight and significance. For those of you who have accompanied me on this journey you, like I, have decided that being an antique collector provides some of the meaning we need in our lives. If you are a new collector I hope it gives you the meaning that I prize. And if not giving it meaning, collecting can nurture our being. Pablo Picasso got it right when he said: "The purpose of art is washing the dust of daily life off our souls." The effort, venture, struggle, or enterprise – however you want to describe collecting touches us and becomes part of us. And we would have it no other way.

If you have traveled with me this far, you have done so either because you yourself collect, you are trying to understand someone you know who does, or because you are fascinated by what would call the mania behind the hobby. In the next chapter I will explore some psychological phenomena that maintain collecting behaviors (as a psychologist this topic is a natural jumping off spot for me) that I think you will find interesting.

Chapter 10

℮

Psychological Explanations

Mid 19th Century homespun blanket. 71" x 87". Indigo and natural wool & linen windowpane check. Center seam, perfect condition. The design "explodes" at one end.

Once I began collecting, I wondered if my discipline – psychology – could help me explain what sustains the collecting spirit over time. A resounded "yes" peals across the land. Psychological writings and research contain implications and even clarifications (as rare as they may be from psychologists, at least generally speaking) for the antiquing passion. I present three concepts here and hope each illuminates why we antique collectors, and any collector for that matter, are such compulsive gatherers of things, treasures, whatever.

Let us begin with **instrumental (operant) conditioning**, part of the theory of learning. To understand this notion, we have to venture to Harvard University and the research of one of the legendary psychologists on its faculty, B. F. Skinner (1904-1990). Skinner studied the types of circumstances or consequences that make us likely to increase, maintain or decrease a particular behavior. These consequences he called "reinforcements;" think broadly of rewards and punishments, both those of which we are aware and those we are not.

Skinner developed his thesis by working with pigeons and rats. And while these animals do not collect antiques, what he found applies to humans in general and certainly us antique collectors in particular . . . with one exception I will describe in a bit. The rats and pigeons were hungry so food pellets were a reward ("reinforcement"). Skinner learned that these animals work long and hard without a positive outcome if the reward is variable (it occurs every once in a while or over "x" number of behaviors on average). In this system, the subjects never quite know when the next reward will show up so their behavior is persistent and consistent.

Let us look at an example of how humans fit this behavioral paradigm. It takes, on average, 10,000 casts to see or hook a muskellunge (a big fresh water game fish; Wisconsinites call them "muskies"). The rod, reel and plug are heavy. The weather is often cold and rainy. It's a heck of a lot of work in lousy weather to throw the lure time after time, hour after hour with no result. And then comes the 9,999th cast (on average) and some mighty water creature explodes at the end of the line. The sportsman's passion for fishing for muskies is instantly revived: a fish!

Golf for the average golfer is another example. Perhaps four or five shots out of an 18 hole round are sweet ones. But that handful of good shots is enough to keep a golfer taking lessons and driving back out to the course and paying the greens fees and buying new balls to replace those that went *ker-plunk!* in the water. Someday, he tells himself, the sand traps and water hazards will not be on a first name basis with me. Someday the ball will roll across the green as if guided by a divine hand and give me the right to brag ("Shot par today, boys! Drinks on me!").

Proving that psychological studies are not all exotic babble, remember that slot machines are programmed on a variable ratio (after an always differing number of pulls on the handle, the machine pays off). That next pull could be the big winner. As a result people sit for hours and push the button or jerk the handle.

Anyone who has ever been friends with an avid fisherman, golfer, or gambler knows the power of intermittent reinforcement. And if you do not fish, golf, or gamble, how often do you check your cell phone? The genius of Apple – emails, tweets, texts – is that once in a while one may be important or interesting. So you keep hoping and check your device, ping after ping. Mobile phones offer us the perfect variable reinforcement schedule.

It is time to apply Skinner's experiments to the antique collecting.

Happily, this passion fits his variable reinforcement scheme perfectly. If I found something I wanted every time I went to an antique show, collecting wouldn't be much fun or any fun at all. Inevitable success would make the chase boring, leading me to stop the pursuit. I am reminded of a Twilight Zone episode ("A Nice Place to Visit") I saw on television in black and white (how primitive we were back then!) in 1960 (and yes I am old enough to remember 1960). Bad guy Francis Valentine dies in a shootout with police and finds himself in a place that seems like heaven. All of the women are gorgeous. He plays pool and when he breaks the rack all 15 racked balls sitting in a perfect triangle go into pockets. You get the idea. It turns out he is not in heaven at all but in hell.

The reward for collecting antiques is a perfect model of a variable schedule. What makes the hunt so much fun – although it can become frustrating at times – is that now and them when you visit a dealer, look on the Internet, or go to shows or auctions you may see something you want, or a piece that is truly beautiful. You never quite know when that will be. Every few weeks, months or years you may find or see an antique that knocks your socks off, but such epiphanies are hardly predictable. Of course, discovering such a treasure is only part of the process. You also have to be able to purchase it. Experience tells us that not every time we find an antique we want do we take it home. Sometimes it is too expensive, or sometimes purchases it before we are able to, or we are outbid at auction.

From a reinforcement schedule perspective, our collecting behavior is going to be rewarded and thus strengthened occasionally and randomly. That is why we will continue to look for antiques even when the reward doesn't appear. No wonder we keep going back to a dealer's shop or a show where years ago a great piece miraculously appeared. "Maybe this time . . ." we mumble, though it is likely we will be disappointed. The principle of variable rewards may explain why wealthy collectors become so choosy: If no antique is beyond their budget, they have to find reasons not to buy everything they want in three months and be done with it. Perhaps you personally want antiques from a certain craftsman or city (formal Philadelphia, for example) or a certain artist who rarely comes on the market. If it were easy to find these antiques, your collecting days wouldn't last.

I mentioned that we differ from Skinner's pigeons and rats in one important way: We have greater cognitive abilities. It may not sound as much of a compliment, but collectors are quite a bit smarter than pigeons and lab rats, contrary to what some shady dealers believe. We may think about (fantasize) how good it will be to attend the next show or auction. These thoughts in and of themselves can be reinforcing and sustain our collecting behaviors. Additionally, sights and sounds associated with an antique show or auction can be an incentive, even if we purchase nothing – just as the aura of an auto show is a sensory delight to someone who collects classic cars.

I remember the New Hampshire Dealers' Show in 2016. Over the years I have seen much painted furniture and endless versions of painted boxes. Nonetheless one of the dealers in 2016 had a Vermont painted box in pristine condition that took my breath away. Variable reinforcement was at work, and I remember the moment I saw it as if it were yesterday and my regret when I realized I could not have it. I am still looking to find its mate, unappreciated.

Let us turn to a second psychological concept, **transitional objects**. Here, briefly, is a psychological description. A transitional object is one that provides an internal sense of security. The object soothes the child, and theoretically substitutes for mother. Excellent examples of transitional objects are a child's blanket, doll, toy, or a favorite stuffed animal. How many parents have turned the car around and headed back to the motel, beach, or friend's house to get one of those back? The transitional object anchors the child like nothing else. Eventually children outgrow such simple things. They learn to provide their own internal security by controlling their behaviors, and develop a stronger sense of self. Many a parent has wondered whether her child will begin school with that stuffed bear, or bring it with to his wedding someday, only to find it in the back of the toy box and junior perusing the adventures of Babar. The bear is suddenly baby stuff.

Even adults can find objects soothing. ("I always loved seeing this bowl and pitcher when I went to see grandma Ally"). I once heard that adulthood is not all that it is cracked up to be. About 35 percent of adults in our society still sleep with a stuffed animal. Intensive care unit nurses give these totems to adult heart patients after surgery. And I know many adults have their own sources of security that are objects – a favorite chair, coffee mug, flannel shirt, and the like.

Some antiques are clearly adult transitional objects for collectors because of their associations, particularly the ones we cherish most. They bring back happy memories of warm fires and newly baked bread and create in us a feeling of well-being. While not a substitute for mom, granny or Father Lou, touching, looking at, and living with them is somehow satisfying. These need not be the best antiques in our collection, but for whatever reason they carry with them an aura of serenity and safety. I think of a homespun blanket or two in our collection, a silver teapot, and a small redware creamer. One of my wife's black dolls serves the same purpose for her. My hypothesis is that these adult transitional objects resonate with us unconsciously. We do not decide that this antique or that antique will soothe. At the macro level I know I find my home, with American antiques everywhere, one large transitional object. I love the feelings it evokes and its ambiance. It provides safety and sanity in a tumultuous world.

ౘ

An Exercise in Style and Connoisseurship

A homespun blanket mid-19th century. Vivid colors, perfect condition.

Made of linen and wool (some are made with cotton). Such blankets were woven for warmth and to last a long time. They could take a year or two to make. The pattern here is a common one except for the one end shown in the photograph where the pattern becomes fancier (explodes). The knowledgeable dealer from whom I purchased it did not know the pattern's name. Usually folded on its center seam, the two halves' patterns match perfectly when completely laid out.

Blankets are wonderful because they offer so many ways to display. Fold one in half or thirds at the foot of a bed, fold it differently and put on the back of a wing-backed chair, hang it on a bed tester, stack several folded lying on top of each other in a small cupboard with the door open. We snuggle under ours too, especially on cold winter days. Sitting and reading with a blanket like this beauty folded over my legs I feel like I am in the 19th century. Its color and pattern add life to a room. Homespun has always been affordable. Still, I have trouble finding ones in good condition. And as far as collectors are concerned, quilts are in right now.

Coverlets, like homespuns are affordable and great bargains. A novice collector can find ones that are signed, their region of origin known. Coverlets are as useful and homey as homespun blankets. The fact my wife and I love homespuns and not coverlets is a nice example of personal taste determining what you collect.

I have never seen a homespun blanket that was signed. I have never seen a book that seriously and exclusively assesses homespun crafts. I have no idea whether this piece is rare or common, Eastern or Midwestern. What I do know is that it caught our hearts on first sight.

Compromises. This is nothing more than an attractive, simple, honest piece with a great vibe, an object that makes the owner feel good while looking good. We made no compromises in purchasing it.

Lastly, let's explore **over-determined behavior**, a psychological explanation for lots of tics, including collecting. Behavior that is over-determined has multiple causes, any one of which can be sufficient to provoke the behavior. I like to think of the concept a different way: A single behavior can reflect many motivations and that is why behaviors that are over-determined are so difficult to change or give up. Think about Jane Katcher, who I referred to in Chapter 6. ("Well Known Collectors"). Does she collect solely because antiques arouse in her an appreciation for their beauty? The answer is "no." She talks about collected objects restoring feelings she first experienced as a teenager, being emotionally involved in the quest for finding pieces to add to her collection, and being intellectually challenged through learning about antiques. She collects antiques because she wants to share them with others. What she is doing is hardly one-dimensional. Collecting refines her aesthetic sense, expands her mind and ties her into a larger community, Her avocation meets a multiplicity of needs.

While a single need may be enough to motivate and reward collectors, when many of them come together simultaneously the drive to continue to collect will be stronger. One may even imagine complex motivations contributing to a compulsion, addiction, or passion.

Speaking for myself I know I collect for a number of reasons, some of them more readily identified (or admitted) than others. Yes, I have a passion, but a compulsion? "Aw, come on: I can go cold turkey any time . . . maybe." Truthfully, I think it will be nigh impossible for me to discontinue collecting. I love the intellectual part of collecting, researching pieces and learning/knowing about them. To top it off, at this stage of my life I am able to write about them and I very much like to write. I also like what antiques stir up in me – positive feelings, an oasis from the world's craziness. I cannot always put into words how or why the many antiques I own resonate positively with me, how they conform to and contribute to my persona, but they certainly do.

And that, *compadres*, is our journey through psychology. Those complex cerebella on which we pride ourselves as human beings have been mapped and explored . . . and continue to be. Behind all we do, particularly collecting, we see the outlines of glittering hope. This may be the day, the hour, when the object I most want, most like, most admire will pop up. Now and then something approaching the ideal appears, maybe to be lost to another paddle raised at auction or maybe to the misfortunes of Croesus. Yet the occasional intermittent reward keeps us collecting. Some antiques provide us with a feeling of security and safety, although we may have no ready answer as to why. Finally, collecting can satisfy a plethora of needs – capturing or recapturing the past, fulfilling our needs, encouraging research and learning, satisfying our aesthetic impulse, affirming our identity, allowing competition, and so many more things – over-determined behavior.

Now that we have a better idea of why collectors collect, let us turn to "A Study of Collectors," the next leg on our journey. More specifically we will talk about the different types of collectors one is likely to meet, couples collecting, and the stages of collecting.

Chapter 11

ℰ

A Typology of Collectors

Wirt, Mildred, A. (1930). Ruth Darrow in the Air Derby or *Recovering the Silver Trophy. NY: Barse & Co. Rare. Extremely clean attractive copy with bright, beautiful color copy dust jacket. Near Fine, 1ˢᵗ Ed.*

If we think of antique collectors as a species, subspecies abound. One group of collecting enthusiasts attends antique shows or studies pieces for sale on-line. What items sold for how much at shows and auctions absorb another. Some appear at exhibits by accident or are dragged there by friends or family. Others are diehards: They line up for antique shows hours in advance of the opening. Some can be spotted shuffling through shops where they visit dealers in their lairs and finger the goods. The less bold may lurk in dark corners of auction houses. Dealers report that sometimes collectors actually spend money rather than just behaving as what they are – curious, skeptical, involved, knowledgeable and frustratingly unpredictable.

The "we" who comprise the collecting species fascinate me. What are we like? Or to put the point more succinctly, how would dealers describe us? What are our sorts, our ilks, our taxonomy, our kinds, our categories, and our genres?

Let me present for your inspection a typology of "us." The lexicon includes type, Latin translation, and synonym. Since scientists may still discover and a new subspecies now and then, this lexicon by definition is necessarily incomplete.

My Grandma Had One (*Historia in familia*), n. Synonym – It's about me.

Not all accumulators of stuff are "collectors," of course, though they would prefer to be thought of in such dignified and elevated terms. *Historia in familia* are best thought of as Snoops. Shows, antique malls, and catalogues are nothing more than occasions to spot a familiar ancient apple corer (described as in mint condition) or a weather vane (somewhat rusty, but still bearing a gasp-inducing price tag) and to relate it to themselves and their past. Usually it offers an opportunity to crow something like, "Gramps had one just like it on his barn. I shot it full of holes with my .22." To the Snoop all things are overpriced or silly (meaning no relative had one when she was a kid). The word "attic" is used often. Such folks do not buy. These peripatetic wanderers gasp with self-righteousness over prices and condition, remembering the good old days that oftentimes were not good at all. The reward? Superiority.

Tire Kicker (*Goodyearus testicum*), n. Synonym – Pain in the butt.

Woe unto the innocent who is plagued by this pest, who will twirl a nice piece of redware carelessly – "just checking the balance" – or wildly poke at your 18th century demijohn – "sure this hasn't been mended?" While the Kicker's elbows fly, dealers are tested on how long they can hold their collective breaths. *Testicum* drifts from booth to booth, leaving behind panic in his wake. Buy? You have to be jesting! These collectors are anxious to touch everything in a dealer's booth except for their wallet or purse. They are one of the more dangerous subspecies of collectors, at least to the antiques they inspect.

True Window Shoppers (*Per accidens existential*), n. Synonym – What in the hell am I doing here?

For whatever reason – luck, fate, a failed sense of direction – these folks have ended up at an antique shop or show. Their presence seems a total accident and you can tell it from their befuddled expression. Perhaps a friend dragged them along. Perhaps they took a wrong turn on the freeway. The truth is unknowable. They are not interested in learning. They simply exist. A beautiful antique has as much attraction to them as the batteries in their smoke detector at home. They are not really, to be serious, part of "We, The Collectors" except that they passively cluster where collectors have congregated. Dealers can spot them a mile away. They have a lost, bored, 12-year-old look on their faces; "how long am I going to have to be here?" Neither benevolent nor malevolent, they simply are . . . and waste dealers' time if they ever step into a booth with a question. Sometimes they are the spouses of true collectors coerced into keeping them company. These (latter) window shoppers have the patience of a saint and often are heard muttering, "Yea, though I walk through the valley of the shadow of death . . ." Dealers can only wish that were exactly where they are headed.

Here and Gone (*Spiritus*), n. Synonym – The ghost.

These supposed customers (collectors) are essentially ghosts. We often find them near the front of a line at a show. They rapidly walk through the entire array of booths in minutes and if nothing speaks to them they leave shortly after they have arrived. What is it they are looking for? No one knows. One second they are here, the next they are gone. Perplexing to say the least. Ghosts are little studied and less understood, as they are impossible to keep in focus for more than a moment. Perhaps setting up cameras to capture their existence would help. If you wanted to categorize all the subspecies of collectors, as bird watchers do, and check them off your list, *Spiritus* would be a great find.

Always Another Question (*Expellam te insanis*), n. Synonym – My task is to drive the dealer crazy.

Seldom if ever do these sorts buy anything. They think they might someday, but "someday" never comes. *Expelli* return time and again to look at antiques and ask questions, but they never reach for their checkbooks. These collectors may not suffer the anguish of *nofunius* (see below) but they are equally obsessive and ambivalent. One would call them one of the most creative types of collectors. Their mental gymnastics and reasons for not buying a given piece defy rational explanation. They would find fault with a signed Townshend desk or a simple, perfect piece of stoneware. (The Goddard and Townsend families were known for crafting furniture sold in their Newport shop. They made exquisite

18th century furniture with a block and shell motif, and a ball and claw foot with spaces between the two. Other makers had similar motifs so a label bearing their name is useful [and increases the price markedly]). It would be interesting to learn the best question *expellam te insanis* has ever asked a dealer about a piece – best not in terms of educated or incisive, but best in terms of marking this species of collector as one who really accumulates doubts rather than Americana.

Close But The Deal Is Not Closed (*Dolor in asinum*), n. Synonym – I wish you would go away.

These sorts are a dealer pain in the ass (pardon my language but no other term better captures their essence and I have already used the more polite version). They put items on layaway, ask for first refusal on a piece at shows, or tell dealers, "I'll take it" but they never do. The definite commitment to buy is predicated on first talking to a spouse or an antique seer, an investment banker, a confessor. The item placed on layaway is never paid for: *Dolor* usually vanishes, even when having first refusal on an item. (A first refusal means that a collector has told a dealer he wants the right to purchase the item but not at that moment. A piece may have someone with second right of refusal and even third.) One wonders about the psychology of such folks. Wouldn't it be simpler to spend the money? Perhaps, but alas, for reasons often known only to themselves, they cannot and do not buy. More malevolent than many folks at antique shows, they deliberately take up dealers' time, leading them to believe a piece may sell or have been sold. If vendors have murderous fantasies about collectors, these folks are often at the top of the list. I am unaware of a dealer moving from fantasy to actually throttling such a collector, but hope springs eternal. If a dealer was ever to do so I am sure that fellow dealers would put up bail money and chip in for the best attorney available. Alas, *dolor in asinum* associates with compatriots no less difficult.

Collecting Is Torment (*Nofunius*), n, Synonym – I do buy antiques, but appreciate my agony.

Finally, someone who actually buys antiques. But *Nofunius* finds no joy in collecting, only drama and personal pain. The plusses and minuses of each piece, every purchase, every place it will be sited must be deliberated, obsessed over, and then mulled once again. "If the piece is a *10*, can I find an *11?* (The theater of the absurd keeps this character company.) What about that normal wear on the painted blanket chest? What about the craquelure on that painting?" *Nofunius* lives to say "what about?" Positive emotions are completely absent, replaced by an overwhelming self-pity, torment, anguish, and suffering (*solotis, dobribus, curcatus*, and *dolor* for you Latin fans). What underlies this trauma? The usual suspects – harsh toilet training, genetics, fear of friendship, and attention seeking – spring to mind. But don't overlook something as simple as money. Most collectors have a budget for the year; even with loans and payments only so much can be spent. *Nonfunius* wonders, what if yet another, undiscovered, piece surpasses this one? What if I should have waited? What if . . . Of course a better example could come along, a similar example at a lesser price, one with slightly better form, or surface, or provenance. The robins' egg blue might be a tad too faded. The 35¾ inch width might be perfect, or is it? There is no end to this obsession, only more agonies, more queries.

These dickens drive dealers crazy even if their checks are good. They are miserable to be around and worse to listen to. Even dealers hope someone else comes along to be the caretaker of a special piece. Self-medication might solve the problem, or so vendors think, until the next one appears.

I Have No Money (*Ego non habetis argentum*), n. Synonym – Pleading poverty is next to godliness.

A group of collectors exists who insistently plead poverty, no matter the price of the item. They may have a good eye. They may be educated about style and connoisseurship. But they simply will not fess up to their financial status and ability to purchase antiques at a certain level. At times, they may admit to having the financial means and buy something, but they drive dealers crazy in their whining about price. (You will note, as an aside, that many folks drive dealers crazy. This situation may account for the mental state of many dealers. Perhaps this is a topic worth taking up at a later date.) Their protestations are not necessarily an attempt to get a better price. It seems instead to be part of their personality. Maybe all the dealer should say is, "oh, in that case let me hold it for someone else;" you'd be surprised how fast the mendicant finds reverse gear.

Mortal Combat (*Mortalis certamen*), n. Synonym: I really, really wish you would go away.

This sect of collectors engages in mortal combat disguised as negotiating on a piece's price. Buying antiques for them is about their winning and dealers' losing. They need the best price for every piece, every year, at every show. Here are the collectors who drive dealers to drink, though their parsimony only leaves them with cheap hooch. Other collectors avoid the dealer's booth if *mortalis* stands within. My opinion: Life is too short and the hobby of collecting too precious to have it sullied by warfare.

But You're a Female Antique Dealer (*Mulieribus sunt horriblis*), n. Synonym – It's the 21st century; get with it.

Comprised of almost entirely male buyers, this sub-group of antique pests feels more comfortable buying from those with a prominent Y-chromosome. Call them misogynist, call them traditional, call them out of touch, to them women simply cannot know as much about antiques as a man would. How embarrassing for a woman antique dealer to be asked if she is minding the booth until Mr. He Must Know More returns. Sigh . . .!

In my experience gender plays little if any role in the antique or collector world. Yes, early in American antique collecting dealers tended to be men, but not always. Customers too were often men, but not always. If younger generations become collectors of American antiques (and there exists great concern that this will not happen) *mulieribus* will be become extinct. At least one hopes so.

The Novice (*Novitius*), n. Synonym – The field needs more of you.

Most antique dealers love to educate collectors, teaching them style, aesthetics, and history. They love what they sell and want others to love their goods also. (On the other side of the line, experienced collectors continue to train their eye and learn.) Novice antiquarians want to learn; everything is fresh and new, and they are a dealer's delight. Whether these early experiences and education will translate into their loving Americana and becoming a committed collector is a mystery for the ages. But all collectors started as novices. We all at one time ended every utterance to a dealer with a question mark: Even a statement like "I'll take it?" showed we were unsure, hesitant, and didn't know if we had fallen in love with the piece or not. Dealers need novices to expand their collector base. The complaint today is that there are fewer and fewer new collectors, *novitorum* if you will.

Novices crawl; walk slowly actually, before they stroll briskly. No advantage awaits them from a quick walk-through at an antique show. They amble; looking at pieces, looking for dealers who will spend time with them, excuse them for their not knowing. Educate them. Novices do not mean to be *Goodyearus Testicum*, although they may act that way on occasion.

Experienced collectors love *novitorum* for several reasons. They remind us that we know something. They remind us of ourselves years ago. They are the future of the antique world. More crassly, they will be buying our antiques when we die or cash out. Long live *noritorum*.

As an academic I learned that I really did not know psychology (theory, research, and application) until I explained it in plain English to my students. It is difficult work indeed to try to get those new to a discipline or to collecting antiques interested in them. I would love to have a *novitius* or two to mentor. I believe I would learn a lot about myself and what I truly know. And it is always fun to see someone grow in knowledge.

Behold The Role Model For All (*Gravi collector*), n. Synonym – I write checks; count on it!

Serious collectors also love to be educated. They know they will be living with these fascinating, special objects in their homes. Knowing about them makes them even more noteworthy. By educating experienced collectors dealers have the opportunity to assist them in expanding their collection . . . and in spending more money. I have jokingly told people that for years my eye caused me to love objects that greatly overreached my budget. I had learned what was truly good – a desk, Windsor chair, or blanket chest. But my income did not keep pace with my developed taste. As I grew older my disposable income increased. In some genre, on occasion, I can sometimes afford that which fully I love and appreciate. Serious collectors embrace the identity of "caretaker" for what they own. They love antiques of all genres, shapes, and sizes. They are the guys and gals who make the antique world go round.

My wife is a *gravi collector* of fiction about girls and women who fly.

Sandy always carries with her "the list" (just in case – title, condition, etc.) so she can upgrade her trove if the opportunity presents itself. Of special interest are anthologies of short stories where well-known authors (at least to her) may have penned and published something relatively unknown. She does not hesitate if one pleases her. Brava!

℮

An Exercise in Style and Connoisseurship

The pen and ink and color illustrations in books that comprise Sandy's collection of girls/women who fly are wonderful. As an aside so are the plots. Susie and her friend drop everything to visit gramps in South America. This before the time of glass panels, GPS navigation, and other avionics to safely get you there.

The cover of *Ruth Darrow in the Air Derby* (1930, one of a series) depicts Ruth (young lady indeed) ready to go flying. Aviation has advanced. Her "bird" is a single wing airplane with enclosed cockpit, not an open cockpit bi-plane. As for the plane, it is described on the back cover as a racing Monocoupe. It is accurately drawn including its radial engine. (On a radial engine the cylinders radiate outward from a central crankcase.) The prop looks a bit short but that could be the angle at which it is viewed. The plane lacks the "pants" (covers over the wheels and cowling cover) one often sees. In the late 1920s, Monocoupe manufactured a sporty and speedy, relatively affordable, high-wing light plane, often raced. Following the era of the larger, more costly, open-cockpit biplanes, Monocoupe offered the first enclosed cabin, smaller, two-seat, popular plane in the United States. The Monocoupe would be a competitive air racer indeed.

Imagine being a young lady in 1930 and viewing this book cover. Oh my: leather helmet with goggles. A gorgeous leather coat. A bright yellow plane just waiting for you, and a modern smaller enclosed cockpit plane at that. What adventure; let the fantasies begin. "Thrilling adventures in the air" the back cover reads. After all, isn't that what fiction for young people is all about? "A rollicking flying series for girls, tense and startling . . ."

As for the book, it is a first edition in near fine condition with an original dust cover in excellent to near fine condition.

Compromises. We have never seen this book in better condition. One may not exist. My wife keeps looking.

℮

The Aging Collector (*Senex publicanus*) n. Synonym – A new caretaker is needed.

All collectors, as is our species' fate, grow old. Yes, some of us divest our collections when in the prime of life. Perhaps we found another hobby such as stock-car racing (highly doubtful, I admit). Divorce may have forced us to share or sell precious antiques. At times, however, these apostates are tired. At other times end of life planning or death cause antiques to enter the marketplace. It is not as if there are no options for the aging collector or executor: consign some to a group shop; let a dealer broker some; auction them off. Better yet, for all involved, you can give them to heirs who have admired and may have coveted them. Sadly, sometimes heirs want nothing to do with that old stuff and once again, educating them may be the solution.

Now and always *Senex publicanus* is and has been critically important to the antique world. I imagine Queen Elizabeth still hopes she will finally get the one British Empire stamp she lacks in her collection. The faith in the process and the love of antiques does not die easily, and it is what keeps the collecting hobby going.

So there you have it. Since this is not the *Oxford English Dictionary* of antique collectors, I would love to hear from readers about other subspecies of collectors I have unintentionally omitted. Who else needs to be included in the antique collector taxonomy? In the meantime, *bonam fortunam* (good luck) in your collecting. May you avoid the *Goodyearus testicum* and *Mortalis certamen* of the antique world.

Chapter 12

ૡ

When Couples Collect – A Most Interesting Dance

Circa 1810 northern New England birch tall case clock. 18"w, 9¼"d, 89"h (top of center finial). In excellent condition, decorated floral face, refinished case, quarter columns with brass stops. Inlay below quarter columns and above feet on front and sides. Lipped door, Hepplewhite cutout base. Bonnet has 3 square finial supports with open fretwork. Frame surrounding face (inside bonnet door), brass finials, hands and bell are replacements. In working order, 24-hour wooden works. Identified as a Roberts' clock.

Anyone who collects knows that collecting is not (always) a solitary pursuit. Yes, it may be a man who has a collection of antique toys, and his wife a collection of 18th and 19th folk art silhouettes. And sometimes couples collect together, walking the aisles of shows, waiting in line, negotiating all that is involved in getting their treasures, all the while compromising on and discussing each other's tastes, wishes, and sometimes power.

It is time I take a look at the issues that arise when partners collect. Maybe then some collectors will feel less idiosyncratic, less silly, and more as if they are not alone in their interactions, frustrations and successes. Perhaps the rest of us will even gain a useful insight or two. And their friends or grown children might finally begin to understand the patience and tolerance shown between loved ones.

Most of what I have read about collecting antiques focuses on what the solo collector is to do. Train your eye. Talk to dealers. Attend educational forums and symposia. Decide what it is you want to collect. Buy the best you can afford. Talk with other collectors. We have all heard and maybe even heeded this advice. But when you have a partner, the possibilities for complexity, negotiation (not with dealers but with each other), and what you (plural) want to purchase and live with exponentially increase. The calculus grows more complicated. Speaking from experience, I can assure you landmines are plentiful. A misstep can do more than blow up the collecting experience. Partnerships hang in the balance.

Dealers see collecting couples all the time. Sometimes they split up at a show, following separate paths. They will meet up later to talk about what pieces they saw and want to look at again. Other couples hold hands or stroll side by side – at least at the beginning – sometimes with a well-defined goal (finding a mirror) or looking for a treasure that captures the heart of one or both of them. At times only one of the partners is looking, perhaps taking or texting photos to discuss now or later. More than you might like, you see what is evidently half of a pair slumped at a table sipping or noshing, dragged along once again.

Dealers observe the soft-spoken conversations, the murmurs, the "we'll think about it." Wise ones know better than to get involved too deeply or to press too hard. They know that couples cannot always agree. Sometimes tastes diverge and all a dealer can do is wait for the storm to pass (Roberts, 2010). I once was at a show where the male wanted the horse weathervane and his partner wanted the rooster. I never did learn which one sold, though I personally thought the rooster was the better of the two. Chances are neither left the dealer's booth, since the preferences sounded suspiciously like a draw. This is one, of course, but there is a roomful of reasons couples do not reach for their checkbooks.

Who am I to give advice? I have a horse in this race (and several horse weathervanes), having collected antiques for a long time and having been contentedly – and now and then tensely – married to a collector for all of that time. We have survived couple collecting, and learned our lessons. Sandy already had an antique or two when we married. Her old kitchen table is still in use; I would like to upgrade but it has too many emotional attachments for her to let it go. That piece taught me my first lesson regarding the need for compromise and understanding. While I am on the subject of our kitchen, I'd like earlier period chairs around the table, but that also is a non-starter for my wife. And (I will stop kvetching in a moment) there is the cherry cupboard we bought decades ago, covered with refrigerator white paint that we removed when we refinished it. The cupboard has great meaning to Sandy but I'd like to . . . When collecting as a couple you learn the wisdom of sometimes biting your tongue, being gracious, and muttering to yourself softly, all in the interest of now and then being absolutely delighted when you agree on something you both love.

I remember seeing a caption to a photo from a show that read "after some negotiations with the dealer and a conversation with his wife Bob was happy to purchase (you may fill in the blank)." I always thought the caption could have easily read: After some conversation with the dealer and extensive negotiations with his wife Bob was happy to purchase (you may again fill in the blank).

One of the feelings that must be worked through when couples collect is disappointment. One party sees a piece that is wonderful but the other just shrugs. He wants to expand a single delightful piece into a small collection (in my case, perhaps prints or paintings of 4th of July celebrations); she is indifferent to the idea. Sandy wants to upgrade and give a cherished piece to one of our sons, trade it, put it up for auction, or store it for a while. I feel it is too much part of our lives to do something so "callous." These disagreements do not last forever. Still, there are inevitably instances when you passed on purchasing an antique because you could not find common ground, yet one of you still wish after all those years you had purchased. The consolation is that all collectors can probably name every piece they should have bought but did not, not just couples.

There is another form of disappointment that can drive one half of a collecting couple crazy. One partner hunts for some particular piece for years, does research, and makes repeated wistful remarks about how nice it would be to own such a wonder. When the object of her desire enters the market, the decision not to buy it seems mean, arbitrary and inexplicable. "Buy it, buy it," chants he. "No, it is just what I thought I always wanted but I can pass," is the reply. Learn to duck quickly and gracefully.

Sometimes to prevent disappointment couples horse trade (figuratively of course). I remember one show where I saw a tavern table I really liked. Sandy was unsure. She saw a piece of jewelry she really liked. You can see where this is heading. She wore the jewelry home. I brought the tavern table with me in the trunk of the car.

But disappointments, when do they occur, can also lead to opportunity. When couples collect, it is often true that as one door closes another opens. A candlestand was passed on but a great small tea table proved a better and more pleasing buy. My collection of 4th of July celebration prints and paintings did not materialize, but the decision not to accumulate them freed up dollars and space for a still-growing collection of redware plates with slip names and initials. If you are truly fortunate, your partner will become interested in pieces that you like; just remember that is an ideal, not a requirement.

There are times when I am involved in pursuing some object or other that I feel great gratitude to my wife. She puts the brakes on my ardor, forces to me reassess. I really liked a candlestand once, inlay in the top. High country. She liked the top but pointed out the stand seemed to squat. I said that is common when there are Queen Anne legs on a base of that type, and desirable. Sandy was not moved; having taken ballet for over 30 years she knew that a ballerina when landing should look as if she is lifting off the floor. She wanted a stand with lift, and thus life. I reluctantly but, I now believe, wisely decided she was correct.

Some collectors handle conflicting tastes by having a man cave (she-shed?) for elements of their collection. For the guys this may mean nailing up license plates in the garage or sticking tools in in the basement. For women, old utensils – apple corers and such – maybe have to be hidden in an out-of-the-way cupboard. Their mutually loved collection of burl wooden items can still be proudly displayed for both and all to enjoy.

Of course differences of opinion and feeling can seem almost insurmountable. If he loves high country furniture (made in the late 1700s or early 1800s, having style and grace but lacking the more expensive woods, scale, and ornamentation of many metropolitan pieces) and she loves Victorian, the couple faces an unbridgeable chasm. Having one room with one period's style and another room with the other creates an aesthetic clash like that of wearing plaids with stripes. Still, a certain amount of tolerance is not only called for in cases like this but crucial; the two may have to be content with small pieces in their styles, spread out so they do not compete with one another. And such clashes are more rare than you might think.

Not infrequently, one partner collects antiques and the other does not, sort of an aesthetic mixed marriage. The collector must be patient, realistic (my partner thinks "this is all old stuff; why would I expect differently?") and hopeful. Face the fact, not everyone can be convinced that being a curator of the past is fun, relevant, or even desirable.

Whenever couples are involved in collecting, the one crucial element is full, honest and open communication. That will take you a fair distance in understanding why Sandy likes Black Americana (I, on the other hand, can live with it but have little feeling for the genre), and I like weathervanes (which she probably thinks is little more than a fancy). Now and then a like or distaste is so deep, however, that all the chatter in the world cannot sway the doubting party. I like hooked rugs and my wife tells me they remind her of what her grandmother would have made or had in her house long ago. The memory for her is negative. She might reluctantly let me hang one in display but I would like to stay cheerfully married, so I demur. At least for now. The merit of keeping one's mouth shut is never to be underestimated, particularly when you are involved in collecting.

Perspective is paramount. A collector must appreciate that some, maybe most, of serious collecting involves the stories and memories one gathers along the way. The history behind a treasure can be more precious than the object itself. We purchased a chest of drawers from a gas station decades ago, sort of. We had first seen the piece at a dealer's shop in Mattawan, Michigan and decided not to purchase it. About 20 miles down the road we changed our minds. Our conversion took place long before the advent of cell phones; we had to use the coin-operated machine at the local Shell station to call the dealer and ask him to hold the chest for us. The results were still marvelous: We enjoyed that chest for years and its curator is now one of our sons. Before giving the chest away, Sandy and I had agreed that we wanted to upgrade and found another chest of drawers even more to our taste. For some objects, of course, such a harmonious and fortuitous outcome is little more than wishful thinking. Take our kitchen chairs, already tagged above as less desirable for me than my wife, as just one example.

117

Couples should share the best elements of collecting with each other, especially the stories. Memories regarding where we found a piece, of schmoozing with dealers, of the thrill of the chase, even losing out at an auction can solidify a relationship and elevate the experience of building a collection.

While it may be difficult to believe when you are new to antiquing, if you stick with it eventually the shelf, room, or home fills up. That state of affairs provides another avenue of agreement or dissent. If your children like certain pieces, you face a tough decision. Can you agree what are you willing to give to them because it would make them happy? How much loss would you feel if you did that? Sandy has a rule: Nowadays, nothing comes into our home unless something goes out (except for antique jewelry. It is her rule after all.) For us, the trick is making choices we both agree on. Looking ahead, I provided her with a list of what I could live without if we moved tomorrow. Even though she has not given me a similar inventory, I just know hers would be different from mine. We will need to talk this through over time.

In brief, compromise is what couple collecting is all about. Discussions on the subject range far and wide. How happy, if bought, would a certain piece make your partner? Can you agree to add to your collection? How petty are you being by protesting an acquisition? Further, feelings must always be acknowledged, even if not shared. And both members of the team certainly can and should take turns in pursuing collectibles. At some show, the two of us will look for a black doll for you. At another we will look for something both of us would like to find (really nice 18th century Windsor chairs). When my turn comes, redware plates will be on the agenda. While compromise is always involved and desirable, putting some pieces away for a while, moving items around, and throwing tantrums all help.

You will by this time have noted I have not yet talked about money. Money is a commodity usually in limited supply. And of course pelf has other uses besides buying antiques. Finances are often difficult for collecting couples to discuss. But a couple that collects must pose and deliberate important questions. "What can we afford this year?" "Are we willing to take out a loan if we find a great piece?" "When do we take a break from collecting and use our money for other purposes?" "How do we decide that?" Of course if both partners are working, one may choose to use discretionary income on antiques as long as doing so does not adversely affect the other. The problem is that how one defines "adversely" may be difficult to agree on. And in my experience, only in retrospect do I know that I should have gotten a loan for that blanket chest, or that one-of-a-kind bi-plane weathervane (who knew in 30 years we would never see another). Money is notoriously easy to fight over and not just for those who buy antiques. It carries many burdens: power and control; an avenue to enjoyment that both partners may not agree on; identity, self-worth, anxiety or lack of it; escaping one's past; securing one's future. I merely repeat my cautions regarding the crucial roles communication and honesty play in this hobby, not to mention partnerships generally.

When couples collect, each of them must be supportive of the other, often in nursing wounds. Sandy, despite her efforts, has only found three Black dolls she loves. I let her bemoan her ill luck. In the process, I have learned a good deal about why she yearns for these dolls, and at least she knows I sympathize with, even if I don't share her frustration. No, being empathetic doesn't solve the problem but it joins us in a peculiar fashion.

Couples who collect also need celebrate their successes. We purchased a wooden works tall case (most people say "grandfather") clock decades ago (pictured below) that we had only seen in a Polaroid photo before asking the dealer to bring it to the Midwest for us to consider. We walked right by it in the dealer's home because it was too beautiful. That could not be the clock we liked we told each other: The one we were looking for could not be that beautiful given its price. When the dealer stopped laughing and asked why we had not looked at the clock, we realized how lucky we were. This was a real find. It was a memorable moment of shared delight.

ℰ

An Exercise in Style and Connoisseurship

This exercise uses more research than is touched on in previous chapters, since much information on this particular timepiece is available. A recurrent theme: My experience is that the more antique collectors know about an item in their collection, the greater their enjoyment and pride. I corresponded many years ago with Ward H. Francillon (now deceased), a noted expert on wooden works clocks who served on the Research Committee of the National Association of Watch and Clock Collectors. More recently I talked with a noted authority on American clocks. Mr. Francillon said that Gideon Roberts or his sons produced the movement in our clock in Fall Mountain, Bristol, Connecticut. We also learned that its painted dial was typical of Gideon Roberts Sr. and suggests the clock was built between 1808-1813.

Roberts was born in Bristol, Connecticut on March 5, 1749. No one knows who trained him in clock making. Bristol was at one time one of the largest clock making centers of the world. Gideon made clocks powered by wooden gears. His design for the works was trendsetting because of its smaller scale, and other clock makers soon emulated it. He married Falla Hopkins of Farmington after the Revolutionary War, settled near Fall Mountain and set up a clock shop near their home. He peddled his clocks as far south as Pennsylvania, where he was introduced to the Society of Friends, and he soon joined the Quaker faith. He is described as also taking his clocks to New York to peddle and even became involved in the Southern market (Morris Jr., *American Wooden Movement Tall Clocks 1712-1835*, 2011). He and Falla had at least five children, all of whom eventually worked in clock making. Gideon experienced great success in manufacturing clocks and it is estimated he made over 600 in his lifetime.

Roberts may have been unique in using water-powered machinery in his business and probably used foot powered lathes and saws. His clock factory failed in 1813 after both Gideon Sr. (typhoid fever) and Gideon Jr. died. Initials like those found on the seatboard of our clock (*HR*) were frequently stamped (incised) and quite often are not those of the principal maker. These may be the initials of a workman and used to keep track of one individual's assembly efforts for accounting purposes. The *HR* could also be the initials of one of Gideon's sons, Hopkins Roberts.

A peddler (Gideon Sr. himself perhaps) probably sold the clock and it may have begun its life as a "wag-on-the wall," *i.e.,* the works, dial and pendulum without a case. According to the expert with whom I spoke our clock's case is especially nice for a country piece and in all likelihood was made in the Concord, New Hampshire, area, possibly for Timothy Chandler (a prolific, well known clock maker in Concord). It has a mahoganized finish. A number of clocks similar to this one are signed by Chandler or the Hutchins Brothers and are cased in a manner almost identical to this one's. Its form is in the "Roxbury" style. Those cases were made almost always of mahogany but here an available wood, birch, was used. It is possible, also, that Gideon's daughter, Candace, painted the wooden dial. The paint she used to color golden apples in the dial may have contained actual gold. Its extensive history has lent our clock deep meaning. (For those of you who want to learn more about wooden works clocks I recommend Morris Jr.'s book.)

With that background, we need to address style and connoisseurship criteria. The proportion of the case's height and width pleases the eye. French feet, a lively fretwork, and inlay on the front and sides of the case dress the clock up. The golden apples and the flowers on the dial draw a viewer's attention. Well-executed ornamentation on both the dial and case make the clock a superb example of the craft.

Wooden works clocks were widely produced and evince a wide variety of details, but some elements set this particular piece apart. The lovely dial is unusual. The mahoganized birch case also is unusual for a wooden works clock and lends the clock some of its appeal. The case is considered very special. The vast majority of wooden geared clocks are cased in pine, not in hardwood like this. The clock carries its years well. Condition is excellent, the refinished case and its few replacements are acceptable. Of course, the dial and case have softened in appearance over the years.

Wooden works clocks are not rare, generally speaking. This one, given its condition and the quality of the craftsmanship, meets all the aesthetic criteria. It is worth less today than when we purchased it in the early 1980s. Still, we acquired it then without hesitation and would do so again.

Compromises. Except for perhaps more originality, none.

I have based my remarks regarding couple collecting on years of involvement, but I am smart enough to know that every couple has had to find its own way of coping with individual tastes and preferences. One thing remains paramount: Couple collecting is a mutual, sensitive and cooperative endeavor. Somehow the fun vanishes if it becomes competitive, or the balance skews toward one person always getting his way. To everything I have recommended, add a large dollop of good will. Both of you will need it.

Chapter 13

༄

Stages of a Collector's Life – A Curious Journey

Queen Anne Massachusetts walnut drop leaf table, circa 1740-1760. 41"l,14"w, 27½"h, each leaf 13¼", leaves extended 41" x 40½". Walnut with white pine and cherry secondary woods. Cut out skirt, tombstone center scallop, and shaped apron. Top reattached; several glue blocks missing, and plugged, pad feet. Initial "R" script on support (shaped) apron.

Collectors differ in what they collect, in how they interact with dealers, in their approach to money, and in how much they spend (and how rationally). They also differ in where they fall on the continuum I think of as an antique collector's journey. Some never move beyond an early stage of collecting whereas others progress, grow and mature. There are those who start to collect antiques yet it never gets into their blood. And not all collectors reach the final goal; individuals pause at different way stations – some stopping, some not – before reaching a full-blown collecting commitment. But for the rest collecting antiques becomes a life's journey. Like those fabulous characters in Chaucer's *Canterbury Tales*, those who gather the detritus of history can't resist sharing the lessons they have learned.

Antique buffs are tainted by every personality trait from naiveté to brutal cynicism, and their experiences have molded and shaped them and sometimes shape us. I think it fair and enlightening to scrutinize the progression of most collectors. Perhaps you will find yourself or someone you know who collects somewhere in this sketch. I did. As a social scientist, I have a penchant for data: robust sample sizes, reliability, and validity. But in describing the life stages of an antique collector, none of those is readily available and we have to fall back on experience, analysis, and observation.

Stage 1 is one of *Innocence.* ("I knew not what I was getting into, but wish I had.") When I married, Sandy owned two antique pieces of furniture: a refinished Victorian washstand, circa 1900, and a country style (likely from Ohio) drop-leaf kitchen table in pine. It may have dated to somewhere around 1850 and had also been refinished, with a shiny surface. We have kept both because of their associations for her. Her wedding present from me was a nice bowl and pitcher. (Does anyone buy or sell those anymore? I rarely see them now. In my day, they were a beginner's introduction to collecting.) I might have settled for that modest collection, but our next-door neighbors in East Lansing, Michigan, owned some country antiques. Charlie's mother had been a dealer in Maryland and he was most likely destined to become a modest collector. His assemblage somehow caught my attention, though I thought nothing of it at the time. Little did I imagine where this would lead me.

The ominous words "if only" are found often in an antique collector's thoughts and utterances. Innocence of the magnetic attraction of antiques is replaced by an inexplicable need to see, learn and have more. If only (see?) you had known where those first little toddling steps were leading you, well then you could . . . but allow me to be cynical for of course you were already trapped. At some point you discover you are a collector, that you have a preference for certain styles and that you have developed expertise (maybe even insight).

Stage 2 is *Looking for something to do.* ("Oh, had I only filled my time in other ways.") And so came the gorgeous spring day when Charlie and Betty, the neighbors, asked we wanted to go antiquing. Sure, I replied, though I had no notion what this entailed. Still it was a chance to wander the countryside and so off we went. We had fun dashing about over the next few months and even found a favorite shop or two (looking back, the collected goods motivated our return, not the dealers themselves). It was fun, inexpensive (do you hear that, inexpensive!), and my wife and I still had a bare-bones apartment that needed furnishing. Looking for bargains in old pieces became a bit of a habit. A $12 (asking price) Boston rocker, mid-19th century, stripped to bare wood comes to mind. We paid $9 and Charlie did major restorative surgery on it. One of our sons enjoys it still 40 years later, now a nice looking ocher in color. And so many pieces we saw looked enticing then. Over the years, things have changed a lot. Now that our house is full, I must force myself to ask what I would give up to fit the dealer's or show's prize into our abode.

Stage 3 is when *It begins to get in your blood.* ("Intoxication with collecting is a subtle, initially benign, process.") The hobby with its fervor was a logical outcome for me, but I realize not for all collectors reach this point. What causes people to stop being mere buyers and become antique collectors? I don't think what first tyros immediately fall in love with are objects that are *10*s. Instead the total environment, physical and psychological, captivates them surrounding antiques. Be aware this is only a theory. I still struggle to fully explain how and when I became an ardent antique collector. My early days of collecting in Michigan were a landscape of antique shops, most often hiding along picturesque two-lane roads off the beaten track. Sometimes they were true shops, sometimes a room in a dealer's home. I still remember the smells after so many decades as if it were yesterday – an amalgam of dust, rot, sequestered air, old wood, furniture wax, oil, and varnish. And the sense of touch lingers, the sensation of running my fingers over pieces as I looked and learned. Sunlight crept through dusty windows and motes danced in the air. Antique shops were (and are) a world unto themselves. I guess I am a romantic.

Part of the charm of collecting was good conversations. Voices were low. The shops had a church-like hushed, sacred feel to them. We were not looking necessarily for anything specific – that determined, dogged, single-mindedness develops later. Even then the truth of Israel Sack's comment (I did not know who he was yet) that pieces talk to you if only you listen, was felt, even if not consciously.

After some experience I usually knew a good antique when I saw one, but I lacked the range of exposure and learning to put my appreciation into words. I knew the time would come. With fewer shops nowadays perhaps less seduction occurs or it takes more time, making it more difficult to fall in love with antiquing. Older collectors such as myself lament the gradual extinction of readily accessed byway antique shops. Still, I have always found shops to have a slower and more benign pace than antique shows. Of course with the Internet, viewing a dealer's wares can be done from home with bunny slippers on. Yet I miss the ambiance that seduced me long ago.

Once collecting gets in our blood, we are vulnerable. Fulfillment seems to lurk around the corner, and we feel near certain that some spirit of old things is going to spring out of the shop's gloom to tempt us. You'd be surprised how few people are immune to the charms of the past, and devotees readily use words such as *love*, *temptation*, and *magic* in talking about their involvement in the hobby. These terms describe the affective world. Collecting is not a totally intellectual, cognitive enterprise.

The next stage, **Stage 4** I think of as *Cataclysm*. ("The twists and turns of our lives can be unexpected and unpredictable."). I use the term deliberately; for me it does not connote violence, merely upheaval. I do not know if all collectors who become serious about the hobby experience a life-changing event, but the ones with whom I have talked did. Sandy and I underwent two such epiphanies. The first was aided and abetted by our neighbors, who recommended a trip to Colonial Williamsburg. The year was 1974. Their message was innocence personified: Go there for a vacation and you will love it. We did. I had never seen such antiques or the settings in which they resided. We took tours, went to the Abby Aldrich Rockefeller museum, dined at the taverns, and walked for miles. We stayed at one of Colonial Williamsburg historic houses, the Orlando Jones Home on Gloucester Street, the main avenue through the colonial town.

Late in 2017 we went back again, having visited many times by now. We stayed next door this time: Orlando Jones' office. Jones is less well known than his granddaughter Martha and his father, the first rector of Bruton Parish Church. Martha was the widow Custis, who ultimately married a promising young man named George Washington. On this visit, we recalled the fresh, pristine and powerful memories of being in Orlando Jones' presence again as we had been 43 years before and it added a dimension until then missing from our collecting journey, a realization of the way time flowed through what we collected and what we did.

But it was the first visit that provided the impetus for a question I have pondered but only recently somewhat satisfactorily answered. Collectors are taught to train their eye, to become discerning, to learn, to know. And we are told to buy the best we can afford. But what if the best a collector can afford falls short of the guidance provided by the eye and taste? The best I can offer is that each collector should make decisions based on the style and connoisseurship criteria, and he ought to know and must accomm-odate the compromises imposed by availability, finances and all those niggling imponderables he has to live with.

Colonial Williamsburg changed us both intellectually and emotion-ally. It cast our commitment to collecting Americana in concrete. It made us converts to history, culture and quality. We were never the same.

In the next stage, **Stage 5,** you are Hooked. ("Unbeknownst, I began to get serious about it all.") My passion for collecting now seemed fated. Of course I was going to subscribe to the *Ohio Antique Review* (no longer published), *The Magazine Antiques,* and *Maine Antique Digest.* Loving books, of course I was going to begin to read extensively. *Good, Better, Best (Fine Points of Furniture: Early American)* by Albert Sack (the son of Israel) became my bible. The book shows the same form of furniture in three photos, one that is good, one better, and one that is the *piece de resistance*. My wife and I began to go to more antique shows.

As or if devotees of the old and significant reach Stage 5, they begin to choose their style. "We collect high country." "I collect old ironware." "Pewter is my passion." "Our house is furnished in a mish-mash, but we gravitate towards antique toys." Collectors begin to learn which auction houses, dealers and shows specialize in what they like. They form strong opinions about collecting –"I like mid-level shows;" "I like prestigious shows with the best stuff, even if I cannot find anything I can afford, because they help me train my eye;" "I like to go to auction previews to learn the difference between how pieces appear and are described on-line or in a catalogue and how they really look."

Several hypotheses now. As I have noted, our friends and mentors Bernice and Jim collected and sold high country. I think to this day, almost 40 years after we met, I am trying to emulate their collection, taste, and pleasure in antiques. I wonder if all serious collectors have someone, somewhere (a dealer, a fellow collector, a museum docent) who becomes their model, consciously or unconsciously.

Another part of becoming serious concerns money, and a second hypothesis arises: The dealer or a fellow collector you trust makes it feel safe to plunge into your first really big purchase. For Sandy and me the "big gamble" was buying the Roberts' wooden works tall case clock I talked about in the previous chapter. It cost a lot of money back then. We have never forgotten that feeling in the pits of our stomach, that silent cry of "what are we doing? This is crazy." We have never regretted purchasing the clock despite that feeling, mostly because our mentors encouraged us to take risks as the price of owning good pieces.

Once a collector breaks through the barrier and spends a lot on a single piece, it becomes easier to do it again. All that happens is that the numbers on the check are bigger the next time. A small, walnut, Queen Anne drop-leaf table followed our clock. The commitments are substantial, by the way, and it is in this stage that a relationship with a local financial institution and a line of credit may be necessary. Once you are a convert, it is entirely feasible that you may forego a vacation or new kitchen appliances for another antique.

An Exercise in Style and Connoisseurship

The rectangular table with curved ends (rounded tombstone center scallop) becomes round when both leaves are raised. Massachusetts's tabletops are generally applied with glue blocks, while Connecticut tops are pinned on. This table was made in Massachusetts. Though it does not significantly compromise the piece, several glue blocks are missing. You can see where they were affixed if you look at the table's underside.

The shaped apron, cut out on the sides, and curved cabriole legs (although a bit stiff) add angles and curves that appeal to the eye. Proportion is excellent. The smaller size adds to its desirability and to its fine scale. The table was probably intended to be pushed against a wall and pulled out for meals or games. The only ornamentation, its side cutouts, are much more visible when the table is fully extended. The center cutout is shaped like a tombstone, thus the label. The cutouts make the table better. Construction is well executed. One leg is attached to a support and swings out to hold the leaves up.

The eye sees a smooth object and the table's patina adds depth. The walnut has a rich, dark color that has softened with age. The craftsman used walnut for the primary wood and cherry and pine as secondaries. The Queen Ann pad foot is well formed. Craftsmen did not sign such tables. I wonder if the "R" script on the support apron was not written when the top was removed for repair.

Overall this is a sweet, small, aesthetically pleasing drop leaf table. We have owned it for a long time. It stands in our living room with a lamp on its center and is my reading companion. Because of its color, scale, and craftsmanship, we find it beautiful. It was the first walnut piece of furniture in our collection.

Compromises. A more fluid leg would add a bit more to the form and movement to the table. The top is plugged (patched) in several places. At one point in time it was removed and repaired. As noted, its original glue blocks are missing. We could only afford the table because of its repairs. We have learned since that such repairs are acceptable. We have never considered replacing the table with an undisturbed one.

131

℮

Sometime during this stage, a collector starts buying from and working with a smaller universe of dealers. Most of us end up thinking of these few dealers as special - a great eye, fair prices, and captivating antiques. These dealers you end up with should be the ones who truly want to help you build a collection. Whether buying a houseful of furniture, or antiques for one wall, or enough good items to fill one shelf, a good dealer can help you find what you truly love.

At this point a collector usually begins to ask other collectors which dealers they like, which ones carry merchandise that is right, whom they have heard positive stories about. Another recurrent theme by now: The maturing collector knows getting a really good deal is not what collecting is necessarily about. The piece must be correct. It needs to be as represented, what is supposed to be. Many collectors will willingly to pay more for that "true" addition to their collection.

Another hypothesis – collectors would buy from the devil if he has a piece to add to a collection, but only a devil they appreciate. A few dealers I really like, others I like, some I don't care about, and a few I refuse to deal with. I need to feel good about the person to whom I am handing a check. But for a collector at this stage, the quality antique – assuming now the dealer/devil can be trusted if not embraced – comes first. If Satan and Sons Antiques have the right piece for sale, I will seriously consider it if vetted (as necessary) by a third party. Temporarily abandoning our faithful friends and dealing with someone louche seems to happen to all collectors now and then.

And a final symptom: In this stage collectors are looking for particular pieces. But pursuing such narrow goals sometimes creates a mystery. On the one hand, I am a birddog when I am on the trail of something to add to our collection (another weathervane, redware, painting). Just as when you are going to reroof your house, the whole world becomes house roofs – "look at that one, I like those textures, that color, that style." The Japanese have a saying: "To a man with a hammer everything looks like a nail." What happens is that the treasure you are pursuing becomes a consuming fixation. How can other pieces really talk to you when you are on such a focused quest? What do you shut out of consideration when on the hunt?

There is a cure, of course: a fast walk through at a well-attended antique show reminds you that there is much out there deserving of attention, a few items deserving deliberation, and a very rare item that actually elicits attention, thought and maybe even temptation. It is my slow stroll through an antique show later in the day after the crowds are gone, or on the second or third day, that I find most pleasurable and instructive. What is more important, finding the piece or enjoying the hobby? Maybe we should ask fewer questions and enjoy the outcomes more.

Of course a collector in this late stage follows auctions and websites on-line. Email allows him to converse with dealers and let them know what he is interested in. At this point, the casual antiquer has become a serious collector. The pursuit and the acquisition of a desired object affect the blood stream, sometimes cutting off the ability to think clearly.

In **Stage 6**, *You have it bad.* ("If one must be afflicted, 'tis a glorious disease to endure.") Yes, the passion can become more intense. The love of antiques is not necessarily corrupting. I find conversations with collectors who are in line for three hours before the New Hampshire Dealers' Show opens fun. I find the long road trips required to go to an auction enjoyable. Perhaps I am discouraged or depressed when exactly what I want at a show has a SOLD sign on it. It can be painful when a piece I really want to add to my collection goes to someone else at auction. Yet feeling intensely about anything contributes to living life fully, so why not feel about antiques? The disappointment of show after show, auction after auction with nothing I am interested in (and can afford) is at times maddening. I vacillate between despair and the hope that in the next show aisle, in the next auction catalogue, in an email waiting for me is IT! (Intermittent reinforcement at work.)

It is in this stage of collecting that you wonder if you should attend 12-Step meetings, if they exist, for antique collectors. You cannot imagine not collecting. Yet there is less and less you need or want. Having it bad gives meaning to life, suffering too. You value being a caretaker for your antiques. You worry about who will take your place. You know you bought some pieces you should not have. You know you bought some when the market was very high. You simply do not care. The pursuit and the pleasure make up for a great deal. This is antique collecting at its fullest, its best and its worst.

Then, as is true of almost everything in life, you reach **Stage 7** – *Culmination.* ("All good things come to an end.") Death and divorce are both pretty conclusive (although you can remarry). Even antique collecting may cease contributing to your life. You may find other avenues of satisfaction (grandchildren, travel, cooking, crossword puzzles). The significance and charm of a collection may finally come from sharing parts of it with children or others, or selling pieces to people who truly appreciate them. It is said as we age we must become Buddhist and learn that things are just things. We will let others be their caretakers. The fire that burned so brightly flickers a bit, the pleasure dims, the passion cools. Favorite dealers die or retire. The thought of one more show or auction no longer exhilarating. The joy of the chase becomes over familiar.

But from my experience, the joys and temptations of the collecting spirit never go away completely. You may no longer buy pieces but you will still spend a Saturday trying to dope out values on Antiques Roadshow, or find your feet taking you to an exhibit at the local museum, or realize you are leafing through the rack at the library in hopes of finding another good book on antiques.

Mine is the story of one collector and his observations. As I journey toward Canterbury I agree with my fellow travelers that love is a delight, nobility a sham or torment a disease. In my case I am blessed and cursed with a love of antiques rather than some fictional maiden in an ivory tower. In this journey, I hope my tale holds up competition we seem to have developed. The overriding consolation is that the collector's life is richer for the journey. Someone, somewhere is just taking that first step. I wish him the joys of a collector's journey and life.

Chapter 14

෧

Collectors and Their Money

Queen Anne, probably eastern Connecticut rare country candlestand, circa 1750-70 with octagonal top, crisply turned shaft, sharply raked knees with "spurs." Maple and tiger maple in old surface. 25 h, 13½" to 14"d of top.

Money in its many forms has existed for millennia. But psychologically money is never really just what it is – shells or gold or scrip. Money lets you sleep at night ('I can replace the washing machine if it breaks, care for my family, put food on the table'). It tells the world how successful you are *via* your home, automobile, jewelry, antiques or a costly trip. Money lets you make the world a better place if charity spurs you. Money is a road to pleasure, power, prestige, peril (ever try investing, gambling?).

To state the obvious: Anyone who collects needs money. Even as a boy I needed funds to purchase comic books (oh, I wish I had kept them), baseball cards and stamps. And except for the very wealthy, those who collect often wish they had more disposable funds. Every collector with whom I have talked over the years knows of at least one, and often several, antiques she would have lent her soul to the devil in order to own, if only she could have afforded them. One of the famous early collectors of American silver is quoted as saying ". . . as I look back upon my career as a collector, I rather fancy the most important thing I learned was the expenditure of money" (Sallinger, *The Antiquers*, 1980, p. 138).

The thesis of this chapter echoes Richard H. Thaler, a behavioral economist (often thought of as the father of this fiscal school). Thaler won a Noble Prize (2017) for challenging established economic thought and theory. His idea: For the most part, people are not always rational when buying things and making financial decisions. In other words when we spend money we are influenced by emotion, suffer self-control difficulties, and are victims of distraction. As collectors, therefore, many forces influence how we spend our shekels, though we are barely aware of them.

As a retired psychologist, people's spending behaviors interest me. Of course as a collector I am fully confident I am managing my funds in ways that will allow the purchase of future antiques I covet. Claudia Hammond's 2016 book, *Mind Over Money*, got me thinking about the scholarship on money, social psychological research in general, and how both apply to collectors. Add to the list of scholarship Jonathan Clements' *How to Think About Money* (2016). But before we explore some of the irrationalities of our spending, unconscious influences on us, and ways we approach money, we need to talk about *pricing* and *value*, words many people equate but that are distinctly different.

What makes the collecting world go round is that I am willing to pay X amount for Object A while another collector will not. The reason I am ready to do so is that my judgments are not the same as another's. If we all agreed on the goodness of things and actions, life would put us asleep. But when two or more of us concur, for whatever reason, that an object has some sort of monetary, aesthetic, family, historical or other value, competition sets in. We vie for or envy possession. The painting Julia and Robert purchased in Chapter One was rare but in their case such rarity did not lead to an astronomical price because there was little demand. Only two bidders were left seeking the painting. In a way Robert and Julia were lucky, especially Julia. She really liked a painting few others avidly sought. Only two bidders felt they truly wanted the painting as its price ascended.

A disclaimer us in order at this point: The findings of any body of research may not apply to every particular person. What motivates me may not move you. Some findings apply to the world in general and others are specific to certain situations. Still, behavioral economics and the research on the spending of money can give us insights into how others and we behave. Perhaps what you read here will save you a few dollars or help explain your monetary behaviors in the antique world. It may also make you more cautious or less willing to keep on collecting. In what follows I offer a series of vignettes, each illuminating a different monetary percept, followed by commentary. While I try to keep things simple, don't forget that what you do in any given situation may be driven by more than one force.

Sam loved to attend antique shows. He always paid by credit card when possible to earn points for his airline travel. But when the end of month card statement came, Sam was often surprised at how much he had spent on antiques, sometimes too much for his budget. 'It will all work out,' he tells himself, sometimes grudgingly.

Make your money real. This statement needs a bit of clarification as I assume you are not building your collection with Monopoly money or counterfeit Benjamins. Like most of us, you probably shop using credit cards and checks. With one swipe of a small rectangle of plastic or one signature on a small piece of paper you can spend a heap of cash, though it doesn't look like it. Cards and checks often don't feel like "real" money, and therein lies the problem. Imagine a charming piece of classy Americana has caught your fancy and fueled your lust and it is priced at $2,000. Now imagine dashing to an ATM and getting $2,000 in $100 bills. Visualize counting out that stack of hundreds and handing it to a dealer. To make the stack thicker and the transaction take a bit longer, change the $100s to $50s or even $20s. Count them out in your mind's eye. As you see yourself doing this, would you still want to purchase this piece at that price? Most of us find it is more painful parting with cash than signing the money away. Those green and black pieces of US specie seem more real than other forms of payment.

A second way to make your money real is to transmute a dollar price into the hours you have to work to amass that amount of money (be a realist and subtract the taxes, insurance and such are that taken out of your gross pay). For years I consulted at a mental health clinic in a rural county about an hour from home. Every week, for a long time, I spent two hours on the road, and eight hours working. When I look at an antique I think of how many hours of commuting and consulting I spent to purchase it. This exercise brings home the effort and fatigue it took to gather my antiquing funds. As a result I am more alert to fiscal reality when I make a purchase.

Bob received a call from a dealer from whom he often purchases antiques. The dealer had found a candlestand he thought Bob would be interested in. Bob knew it was something he wanted. To his surprise when he visited the dealer's shop the dealer had not one but three stands for his viewing. One was Federal and what Bob had pictured in his home; one was better yet and more expensive, a Queen Anne country stand with some tiger maple; and the third was clearly out of Bob's reach, a wonderful high country Queen Anne stand with original finish and great feet and base. After looking, Bob purchased the Queen Anne maple one. It was better than the Federal example although it cost more than he had planned to spend.

ℰ

An Exercise in Style and Connoisseurship

I can understand why Bob liked and purchased this candlestand. Tiger maple is a wood greatly desired for its appearance. (This is a good time to talk about "figured" woods. Tiger maple is one example and pieces with this wood typically cost more than a "plain" maple desk or chest of drawers. Birdseye maple and birch – due to unfavorable growth conditions; the "eyes" are tiny knots – also are popular. Craftsmen use figured mahogany, often veneers, of such figured woods on fronts of chest of drawers, desks, and the like. These woods lack a straight grain, producing undulating lines known as "flames." Flames add curves, texture, and ornamentation, softening and enhancing the piece of furniture and making such pieces highly desirable.)

Perfectly in proportion, the stand has a substantial cleat (a piece of shaped wood underneath the top where it is attached to the base). Some collectors and dealers like these pieces as much for their cleats as for the stands. This cleat is chamfered and the top has a thumbnail molding all around its lower edge. The screws holding the top to the base appear old. It is tempting to leave it upside down for a day or two on occasion to enjoy the details that reflect such expert craftsmanship.

These stands were constructed to support a candlestick. This one now sits next to a sofa. Having a history of ownership or a craftsman's signature is unusual for small country pieces such as this one and it has neither.

139

The six-sided top, base, and gentle shaft appeal to the eye. The base, legs, and shaft exhibit nice proportion. Nothing jars. It takes up little space of course. The decorative elements, tiger maple wood used in its construction, and its "knees," add greatly to its appeal. It is smooth to the touch. The stand has aged well, having both softened and darkened. The tiger maple grain is visible to the eye but not strident. The stand's scale is small and somewhat delicate.

Overall this is an antique a person can live with. It rates highly as a country stand and is rare because of both the wood and its knees. We find it wonderfully simply and purchased it almost immediately after seeing it.

Compromises. Sandy would probably want a stand that looks a bit lighter on its feet but one does not find that in Queen Ann pieces like this. Otherwise we made no other aesthetic compromises.

Beware of, or be aware of, the power of three. The research predicts that when a consumer is faced with three alternatives choices – one with all the bells and whistles; one perfectly acceptable; and one in the middle – more expensive and nicer than the basic model, he will purchase the middle one. Sometimes he will spend a good deal more than he had planned. This rule of thumb holds true for appliances, computers, and most assuredly antiques.

How can you keep a collector down on the farm after he has seen Paree? The answer is, you cannot. The best candle stand was out of the question for Bob because of its price, but he found himself willing to stretch for the middle one, which was better than he had anticipated buying and was far superior to the base model: no obvious faults, no nosebleed price, no missing features. Do dealers know about the power of three? I would imagine they do although I have never asked. Now you do.

Sarah simply would not bid for something at a live auction. She would leave a bid or have someone bid for her, always setting the price she was willing to pay and not surpassing it. Her reason for this behavior was straightforward: She had bid at auctions once or twice in the past but could not control herself when items she liked came across the block, so she ended up spending far too much.

Auctions can be tricky. This statement is true in several ways. Everyone who has bid at auction knows that they sometimes fly past what they planned to bid and spend. Julia in Chapter One did so in purchasing the Hudson Valley sandpaper painting. Auctions are emotional, particularly for highly competitive collectors. That is one reason why a lot of items sell far above the high estimate.

But psychological research has uncovered another pitfall to beware: Purchasers are likely to pay more for an item at auction than they intended if it follows a more expensive one in the queue. The previous collectible may be of a completely different category (American furniture versus the offered far Eastern jewelry for instance). It does not matter. This research finding was verified in the real world – at classic car auctions. At these venues almost all buyers do their homework and know what a vehicle should sell for, yet they still often paid more than real market value when the preceding auto on the block was more expensive. You may be drawing the conclusion the game is rigged. The fact is more simple and less tawdry; as Thaler notes, almost all collectors are irrational with how they spend money at times.

Susan had a food budget, another budget for monthly expenses such as insurance and utility bills, a third for clothes and other necessities, a fourth for everyday expenses such as her daily coffee, a fifth for saving for unexpected expenses and retirement, a sixth for antiques, another for medical expenses, yet another for travel. Her problem was that when she went antique hunting she found herself borrowing from her travel or retirement funds to support her purchases.

We all have mental money accounts. The research says that most people have eight or nine accounts for funds in their heads, just like Susan. Many collectors have enough self-restraint to not raid Peter to pay Paul, unlike out fictional collector. They set immutable mental boundaries between one accountant and another. Others – and I don't exclude myself

– sometimes raid another category to rustle up the money I need to buy an antique. As might be expected, I tell myself that I will pay myself back. Unexpectedly, I do. Still others collectors buy antiques cavalierly, giving no attention to how this may affect other needs. Generally, I think that passionate antique collectors act like Susan and borrow from other categories of expenditure to purchase antiques. We stretch so we can buy something we love. In moderate amounts, this is understandable. Just bear in mind you might need a financial chiropractor eventually.

Chris was prudent with his money, or thought he was. He visited three different grocery stores to get the best prices, only purchased clothes when he really needed them – and then on sale – and had a ledger at home to keep track of his monthly expenses. But he thought nothing of adding extra features to the used car he purchased, some of which – driving lights? – raised its price by hundreds of dollars.

Relative thinking is interesting. We make judgments on what we are spending as a proportion of the total cost of the purchase. Our attention to what we actually spend is really pretty hazy. While you may bend down and pick up a dime or quarter you find lying on the sidewalk, you may not be so careful when it comes to large purchases. After all, what are a few extra bucks when you bid on an expensive antique? So when you spend time on-line to find cheap flights to travel to an antique show, and you gas up the car at the discount station to save a few pennies per gallon, doesn't that justify spending perhaps a few hundred more than you planned on a beautiful piece? In doing so you are behaving in a predicted irrational fashion. Thaler didn't get the Nobel Prize by saving Green Stamps: again we are inconsistent in our monetary behaviors.

Donna always enjoyed the very reasonable parking rates at the antique show she went to in Philadelphia and the free shuttle bus the promoters provided that carried her between it and another show she enjoyed. When parking became expensive and a fee was instituted for the shuttle bus, although the cost was nominal, she quit attending.

Loss aversion is powerful. Most of us dislike losing, even a little. Loss is a powerful motivator as a matter of fact. The research on this behavior is what social scientists call "robust," meaning most of them agree with the conclusion, no matter how self-evident it seem to the rest of us. People put great effort into not losing, even more than they put into winning. That is one reason that we may bid more than planned for an item at an auction instead of walking away from it, even if we later think the price was "too high." We overpaid but at least we didn't lose it! The loss might seem even more bitter considering the time and money we spent to travel to the show and on the motel and meals. We came out a winner!

In Chapter 14 I talk about a redware plate that says "apple pie" on it. I wanted one. But the price to me really was too high. I did not purchase it. I chose to lose, a lesson we sometimes need to learn.

Loss aversion shows up in other common situations. Once we are rewarded to do something, we get used to the compensation, and react negatively when it is taken away. So if a show has a zillion complimentary tickets (the New Hampshire Dealer's Show in Manchester, for example) and you are used to entering for free, you may well be upset if the show changes its policy (I hope it won't). Your reaction might be to refuse to attend. The fact is we do not like losing good things we have become accustomed to. The obverse also is true: an incentive has to be large enough to truly motivating or we will not care if it exists. Allowing children to enter an antique show for free, even though adults pay a nominal fee means nothing at all. The quality of talks or tours at shows had best be outstanding or they will not attracting patrons. A reward has to be perceived as a substantive benefit before it seems real.

Ralph was getting on in years and had begun the process of gradually divesting himself of his collection. But he was frustrated; was everyone out to get him? The group shop and two auctions houses he had contacted all undervalued the pieces he wanted to sell. Was he the only one who knew what antiques were worth these days?

The "endowment effect" may not be your friend. Collectors know they should be realistic when valuing their collections, especially when it comes to selling pieces or trading up. Still, being realistic is psychologically stressful. The endowment effect is well known to auctioneers, dealers, real estate agents, and automobile dealers: Everyone tends to value what they own more highly than the market may. This effect holds true even if you have owned the antique (or auto or lawnmower) for a short period. If we cannot keep what we have we want to be rewarded handsomely for giving it up. Real estate agents go crazy, for example, as they struggle to convince sellers to price their house at what the market will bear. In the same vein, auctioneers try to persuade consignors to set reasonable reserves on their treasures. Dealers face the same problem. My advice: When you shed something(s) from your collection, settle for a fair price and don't hold out. Dollars in hand sometimes trump principles and feelings.

Amy has attended antique shows for years. At the present time she is looking for a piece of stoneware. She has now seen several that would fit well into her collection, and she buys a nice stoneware jug with a cobalt blue bird decoration, circa 1800, from a dealer who has exceptional wares and prices them accordingly. She could have paid less for another jug equal or better in quality and rarity but did not.

We are all contortionists when it comes to money: The mental gymnastics we perform with price is one example. Amy, you have to learn that a high price does not mean the antique is of higher quality. One of a collector's responsibilities is deciding what constitutes a reasonable amount to spend on an item. Any collector reading this book can probably name two or three dealers who always seem to list very high prices. Some of their items sell at those prices. Some seem to linger for years. Perhaps the marketplace is making a decision on which antiques are worth the high cost, and which are not. Surely individual collectors are.

What happens is that we, the purchasers, engage in what is called confirmation bias: the antique looks right, we have struggled to find one for some time, and the dealer's booth contains many other glorious objects. Based on that, we convince ourselves not only that the antique is genuine but also that it is worth the price. We look for information to support our bias. "The prices support my opinion that this is an exceptional, high-class show. The prices are in keeping with the show's quality." The high price that is being asked helps confirm that the antique must be special. It is said the Roman dictators had a flunky who walked at their side and whose only job was to whisper to them at intervals, "remember, man, that thou art mortal." I have often thought of hiring someone to accompany me to antique shows whose sole job would be to toss cold water on my face and give me a talking to when I am falling victim to money over mind.

And what about dealers? Certainly some (and maybe not a few) of them figure a high price adds to the lure of a piece. Heavens, only a madman would charge that much for a toby mug or whatever were it not the very, very best of its kind. And it sometimes works, collectors being collectors and dealers being. . . .

David is at a show he attends annually. He greets a dealer he knows well, gives her a firm handshake. The dealer shows David a piece or two in her booth that she thinks he might be interested in. As they talk she lightly touches David on the arm once or twice. David eventually purchases an item. The dealer has made a sale.

We are influenced by information we do not consciously process. What David is experiencing is a form of personal intimacy. The dealer's light touch on the arm seems an act of friendship or camaraderie. It certainly may be that. On the other hand (will we ever trust anyone again?) the behavioral research into such matters concludes that we are more likely to purchase an item if we are lightly touched. Even more, we are likely to rate the seller as more "impressive." The touch implies David is a nice person and tells him the dealer is focusing on him. No matter how genuine, little gestures may still cost us money, lots of money.

Cynthia is well known to dealers. She has built an impressive silver collection and is knowledgeable about its craftsmen and history. Her collection of Southern silver is really quite good. Dealers regularly compliment her on her eye and judgment. Such feedback from them is validating to her. A dealer has just talked with her about her collection in glowing terms and brings out some Carolina silver. She purchases several items.

145

Be cautious and alert to the dangers of praise. How many people say positive things to any of us even on an occasional basis? It feels good when someone recognizes what we know, admires our taste, or values something we have done. The dealer may know more about buyer psychology from experience than you can find in a book. Praise, like a light touch on the arm builds rapport, and makes us feel like experts. You already can guess the punch line. A kind word from an auctioneer leaning forward at the lectern with a smile: "The handsome gentleman in the back, this is a wonderful piece, one more bid." Keep your hands in your pockets. Beware the dealer who praises your eye or commitment as a collector. You are more likely to buy that antique and to pay more for it.

Ethan collects antique toys. He regularly attends one or two of the auction houses that specialize in them. They know his taste and value him as a customer. Each auction house keeps in touch with him about what will be coming up in the future, and they keep their eyes out for pieces he has talked about buying. The impression they give, probably true, is that they are working hard to help him add to and improve his roomful of old trains and accessories.

Social obligation is a powerful force. The pressure to repay others is called the "reciprocity principle." In social situations we try pay back what we get from others: We invite people to our parties who have invited us to theirs. When the need to reciprocate goes unmet we feel uncomfortable (anxious even as the pressure builds) for being an ingrate or hurt for being overlooked. Ethan may buy a toy train just to say "thank you for the attention and for working so hard to assist me.' You see this impulse in action in movies when the gentleman, after someone has been kind to him in some small way, doffs his hat and says, "much obliged." What he is saying is there is a social debt that needs to be squared (I am obligated to you). Even as a psychologist who has taught about the reciprocity principle and knows it well intellectually, I still feel its pressure.

How does this relate to buying antiques? If a dealer or auction house goes out of his or its way to be helpful, only good business practice, you may feel pressure to repay them by purchasing something. You have to resist buying something you do not love just to relieve that uncomfortable feeling of obligation. At the same time, reciprocity is a two-way street. If I praise a dealer over time, say nice things about her, tell her how nice her booth looks, comment on her eye and how good it is – will the dealer work harder for me and will I get a better deal?

I was shopping for an automobile and the saleswoman (it was something rare back then to have a female car 'salesman') asked if she could help. I said she could help me by leaving me alone and letting me look, and just be available when I had questions. She honored my request and that was one (among several reasons) I purchased a vehicle from her.

I like people to let me feel autonomous. There is no touch on the arm, no praise and yet we still can be hooked into buying. We want to sense we are trusted to be on our own but do not like to feel ignored. *Maine Antique Digest* publishes letters to the editor every once in a while in which collectors complain that when they were in a dealer's booth, he sat and ignored them (e.g., did paperwork or chatted with a fellow dealer). Maybe they are being overlooked, but the dealer may have learned that a fair percentage of customers simply like to be left alone. Many dealers let customers look and ponder because that is how a lot of people go about collecting. As the potential customer moves physically closer to an item to look at price, surface, or description, dealers make themselves available. The dealer who lets you make up your own mind with no hard sell may be exploiting the psychology of customer autonomy.

Martha is driven as a collector. She has visited people who share her passion and one or two have collections that outshine hers. She is on a mission to 'show them.' If anyone is going to have a great antique collection it is going to be her. Additionally she wants dealers' respect and pays handsomely for her antiques.

It is easy to lose our grounding. The yellow brick road Dorothy followed to Oz would well serve many collectors (since it promised reaching a cherished goal and actually did show her there's no place like home). "Social comparison" is the tendency to evaluate ourselves against others and is the source of competitive behavior. Professional athletes judge their worth, oftentimes, not by what they earn, but by what they earn compared to what other athletes are paid. The same thought process seems to apply to a Wall Street brokers' bonuses; it may be a few years' salary for you or me but if it doesn't exceed the amount Joe received, Troy may feel he is underappreciated.

There will always be someone with a better antique collection than ours. Perhaps she had more resources or may have inherited the lucky gene. We need to stay grounded. Throwing money at antiques to increase our sense of self-worth or to "show them" is not the way of Tao. You will be out harmony with the antique universe. Yet as you will read in Chapter 18 such harmony can be hard won and difficult to maintain.

Martha also represents someone called a "love buyer:" Some people use their money to purchase respect, admiration, and liking. Their thinking goes: "The dealer will like me because I am writing out this large check." Some people leave extra-large tips at restaurants or indulge their grown children so they will spend time with them. The truth is there is only a small group of people who love and care for us (family and close friends). Spending money to buy caring doesn't work.

Martha is also a poster child for terminal materialism. Listen to Will Rogers: "Too many people spend money they earned to buy things they don't want to impress people that they don't like." Well said. Her conspicuous consumption's goal is to communicate to others how rich and important she is. She thinks their knowledge of her status is the payoff for the high prices she pays for antiques. Besides purchasing love we can also be fooled into thinking that envy also can be bought retail. Terminal materialism uses a person's financial resources to improve social status and generate jealousy. It is fascinating to me that many of the page-long obituaries laud collectors who never lost sight of acting the common person, who would talk with and assist the new collector, who kept friendships over the decades. I cannot remember seeing such a eulogy where the person was described as rich or a snob, blessed with an excess of great antiques.

My wife and I attend an antique show in Wisconsin twice a year. It is small and the offerings are mixed. We have found some nice objects there over the years, and it is always fun to look. The show in no way compares to prestigious shows in the quality of its offerings, nor does it pretend to.

Collectors are wise to remember and pay attention to their roots, what collecting was like when they first started out. Surely it was simpler and it may even have been more fun. In other words, going for the latest, the biggest and the best sometimes works against the collecting gene. The research shows that the top 1percent may find little pleasure in simpler activities. If you only eat in exclusive restaurants, a street vendor may not appeal to you, even if the food is spectacular. As you work your way up in antiquing – more dollars to spend, fancier shows, and more prestigious auctions – don't forget the simple outdoor market or a down-to-earth small antique show. Broadening your experiences will keep you grounded, and keep you from becoming an antiques' snot.

Sam collected painted boxes and firkins and was building a 'tower' of each. He needed a box of a certain size and found one. It fit the tower perfectly. When Sam brought it home he wanted to beat his head against the wall. When he looked at it closely he wondered if the paint had been touched up, and it did not measure up to the better ones he already owned. Within a few months he replaced it.

We have to *learn to recognize our losers.* Some pieces should have never been purchased to begin with. Typically when people invest they take credit for their winners and blame others for the rest. "Those wonderful antiques I own are due to my diligence, preparation, and skill in collecting." Perhaps so. Or we say to ourselves: "The dogs I own were due to weakness in judgment brought about by my mood, slick selling by a dealer, or being led astray by someone convincing me the piece was really good when it was not." The trick is to avoid rationalizing bad decisions and look at them with eyes wide open. The answers will help you avoid such mistakes in the future that waste your money. Sam recognized his loser and improved his collection.

Elizabeth was searching for an antique dining room table. She had consulted with her decorator, who recommended one of a certain size. She went to a couple of antique shows and shared with dealers the dimensions of the room and the size table she was seeking. She purchased a country table of the 'correct' dimensions and passed on an earlier, much better one, nearly identical in size, when the dealer focused on aesthetics and surface.

Elizabeth is a wonderful example of the designer or decorator approach, and how we process information. *We give information validity when it confirms what we already believe.* And the corollary is also true. *We discount information that flies in the face of what we know, or think we believe.* If you are seeking a particular piece, get others' opinions as to whether they have seen any of them for sale, how frequently they come on the market, and their quality. In other words, indulge in reality testing. The table Elizabeth purchased may fit the dining room perfectly but a better quality one, even a bit smaller or larger, would have added to her collection and looked better. Perhaps she felt obligated to the decorator who had assisted her. Talk with Oriental rug dealers some time about decorators. For it can be a revelation.

Larry is at a dealer's shop looking at a chair. The dealer impresses on Larry how rare and important it is. Larry purchases it, in part because 'rare' to him means he may not see one again for years and years. 'Important' means it will be a major cornerstone of his collection.

We are influenced by how issues are framed. It is a wonder we ever make good decisions with our collecting dollars. If a dealer tells you an item is rare, does that mean he has seen one in the last twenty years or sees one annually? And rare is not the same as good. A rare piece can easily lack the aesthetic qualities you are looking for. If a dealer hasn't seen a piece like this in some time does that mean he hasn't been looking? Is such an item unappealing to most collectors? Just because the antique is truly special, does it not need to be closely inspected?

If a dealer tells you an item he is selling is really good ask him: "What would make it a *10?*" Sack's book, *Good, Better, Best* is so useful because readers can see the difference between average and wonderful pieces of furniture. That is the reason I have always wished there were several similar tomes covering high country furniture, homespun blankets, and clocks. They would allow collectors to better train their eye.

Language is powerful. "Important" implies that we should pay attention: something significant is in play. Just as the sold sign or red dot causes many collectors to linger, the word important may have the same effect. It can make us pause, even to value the antique more highly. Seasoned collectors most likely have learned to not accept the adjectives or arbitration at face value. "Why is the piece important?" they ask. "How many pieces do you handle in a year that you feel are important?" "Aren't all antiques somehow important to someone at some time?"

To motivate buyers the product has to be made desirable. Thus the "important," the "rare," the "unique," the "significant," the whatever. These words are the salt on the boiled egg, the VSOP on the brandy bottle, the Baum and Mercier on the wristwatch. The usages have a secondary effect, implying the dealer or auction house is tasteful, established, re-spectable and somehow deserving of buying and selling antiques of great significance. The so-called halo-effect lends other items in a dealer's inventory a new grace, deservedly or not.

Let's assume the dealer or auction house wants to suggest a host of positives qualities for a piece. Its attribution is well known. We know what craftsmen made the desk in Philadelphia, to whom he sold it, and who had it in their possession as it descended in and out of the original owner's family. Provenance of this sort is crucial for some collectors. Hence, the piece is significant and worthy of pursuit.

Sometimes, the term *important* is a synonym for rare. If a craftsman made a limited number of clocks, sets of chairs of certain types, tables and the like then finding one has to be an important discovery. Of course this logic begs the question whether the piece meets high standards of style and connoisseurship. It may be important, but is it any good? No matter its rarity and provenance, any antique can be average in design, proportions, ornamentation, condition and a host of other ways. What determines whether or not a piece is important is to be taken seriously is not the seller but the buyer.

Of course the critical question is always whether a potential buyer, Larry in this case, loves the piece that has been put on the market. Does he find it beautiful? That's what counts in the long run.

We use so many shortcuts in our reasoning that it becomes automatic. Carefully rephrasing what we are told, accurately describing reality, takes practice and work. Kirk (1979) has a marvelous story of a dealer who advertised a piece as having descended through a famous family. The claim was factually true, but only since the late 19th century. It was what is called a "centennial piece:" a duplicate constructed 100 years after the 18th century piece readers probably thought the ad was selling. Ignore the hoopla and hype, to deconstruct terms such as *extraordinary* or *important* and see the antique for what it truly is.

Billie Jo attends an antique show and sees a Delft bowl (think Dutch, blue and white) she really likes. When she talks with the dealer she tells him the price on it seems high. Can he do better? Yes, he says, he is willing to dicker and comes down in price a goodly amount. Billie Jo purchases the bowl only to see one or two equally attractive ones in the show for sale by other dealers that are less expensive.

Billie Jo experienced what is called anchoring. Show someone an antique carrying a high price and her expectations about the value of the item shift upwards. The lower price that the dealer finally offers increases the attractiveness of the antique, even if it ends up being more costly than comparable items. The psychology at work is that people give inordinate weight to the first piece of information received and make later judgments relative to that first piece of data. Billie Jo sees the large discount and feels she is getting a good deal. Anchoring can be avoided by knowing the market and range of prices for an item, depending on its quality. The downside of anchoring for a dealer is that he may gain a reputation for high prices, despite the discounting.

Dan visits a dealer's shop and finds a Windsor chair priced at

$1,499. It has a nice splay to the legs, no major repairs, and a good paint surface. He buys it.

No description of behavior economics is complete without the famous "number 9," i.e., a price one dollar below a nice round number. Try to find a house for sale for $200,000 or $250,000. The research shows that a dealer is more likely to sell that Windsor chair at $1,499 (assuming it is an equitable price for the piece) than at $2300 or, interestingly, at $1,100! There are many theories as to why this is so. The one I like is that somehow we feel we are getting a bargain at $1,499, a price just below $1,500. Fascinatingly, I could not find a definitive explanation for this phenomenon.

About now, despair is setting in and you are probably wondering why learn the basics of style and connoisseurship? Why struggle so hard to make truly rational decisions about purchasing, only to have them undermined by deeply buried and unconscious motivations? Learning about these mental traps increases out awareness; that hoary cliché about knowledge being power assuredly applies in antique collecting just as it does in other pursuits. For collectors must beware just like anyone else. After all, isn't that how our education and knowledge are meant to be used, some would insist, best put to use?

As the song in the musical Cabaret aptly runs, "Money makes the world go round." Cash keeps things turning and churning. I hope this has helped you learn something useful about yourself as a collector, and about other collectors, dealers, and auctioneers you have encountered on your journey in the world of antiques. It may even have explained why you have now and then acted in a way that you can't quite fathom. It is difficult to condense so much good advice, but in the final analysis the collector has to learn how to thoughtfully allocate and use resources. Failing to do so casts dark shadows on what can be a delightful and fulfilling hobby.

Chapter 15

𝒞

Reasons Collectors Do Not Buy

*Pan American 1930s China Clipper Hong Kong. A++ condition
with great color and pop, one of the rarest of the Pan Ams. Linen
backed. 30" x 44½". This poster was rolled (never folded) and has
no imperfections. It was in a historical society collection that was
deaccesioned to an auction house.*

Collecting involves spending money, often a decision evoking
something other than rationality. One falls in love with a piece, with the
assessment of it using style and connoisseurship criteria supporting this
ardor. Or as Chapter 14 depicts, a number of forces, many out of our
awareness, lead us to reach for our checkbook. In other words, a panorama
of dynamics is in play when we purchase for our collection. Interestingly,
the same holds true for when do not buy. The reasons collectors refuse to
purchase items for their collection, although sometimes obscure, deserve
probing. I am not referring to rejecting objects that fail tests of provenance,
aesthetics, style or taste. It is easy to understand why we may pass those
by. Nor am I describing a collector who is making sense of whether he
wants to continue the hobby and has withdrawn from shows and auctions
to decide. What I explore in this chapter are our motives when we fail
to buy objects that seem to all of the qualities we value, at least initially.
Some of these reasons are financial; we lack sufficient funds to purchase

the piece in question. Some are not financial at all. Welcome to *Dollars and Sense* (or perhaps some collectors might argue, lack of sense).

Two common reasons we do not purchase fine additions to our collections are that we are discouraged or broke. How much energy and time can I invest in looking for the perfect silver English egg poacher from the 1820s before finding one? (I would be surprised, but not terribly so if such a rarity exists, though I imagined this piece.) Even if a dealer or two said they would keep an eye out for one, how long would I stay in touch with them, reminding them I am still interested? Unless this unicorn were to complete a set or was I one could not die happily without owning, it would be easier to just move on. So there are times when not buying reflects the waning of a particular passion. The chase has lost its joy. The pursuer has lost his spirit.

In yet another instance, Sandy and I hunted for an antique cupboard for our kitchen for some many months. Space constrained its size and we fell in love with one or two, which after careful measurements were disappointingly large. We gave up. By all criteria each of the cupboards that we coveted was gorgeous. Unhappily, we grew tired of the search. Both fatigue and our vision of the ideal cupboard (more on the ideal later) contributed to stopping the hunt. The silver English egg poacher, and the cupboard are both examples of a collector having the financial wherewithal to move forward and buy, but lacking the energy.

For a collector, "being broke" has its own definition: It means having run out of the sum set aside to collect, not living under a blanket on a street corner. The most common reason collectors do not purchase nice pieces is because they have no dollars to spend. They are tapped out, penniless, bankrupt, busted, impoverished, cleaned out, insolvent, strapped for cash, down and out, without any pieces of gelt to their antique name. You ask, "How could such a state of affairs come about?" "Easy" is my answer.

My bank account is usually full when I attend Antiques' Week in August (in Manchester, NH and surrounding places) with several shows, some overlapping. Several auctions take place in subsequent weeks as well. Suppose I see my imaginary egg poacher at the first show. Should I purchase it? If I do so, I may lack money for the rest of the week, and for the upcoming auctions. If I see a great piece on Tuesday or Wednesday the same dilemma presents itself. I can wait for the last show, but by then I may have passed on a number of highly desirable antiques and there may be nothing I want at the last show. My advice: If you see a piece you truly love, buy it.

It is a waste of time to try figuring out how to avoid going broke. The best advice I can give goes something like this: (1) If you are a serious collector, you really need to have a budget. (2) No matter how much you like something, don't borrow from junior's college fund to obtain it. (3) If you find items you love of course there will be periods of time when you are broke, as you must replenish your antique funds. (4) Recognize that patience (so important I devote a separate chapter to it), is a major weapon in the collector's arsenal – you can't always have what you think you want, but sometimes you'll get it later . . . or something you like as well. (5) Collectors would never have any good stories to tell if they weren't like fisherman who can recount that record-breaking Muskie that got away. I doubt a collector ever existed – except for the truly, fabulously wealthy – who could afford everything she wanted. Saying "no" to an antique, in this case because you are broke is not only virtuous but also sensible.

To switch gears, let's talk about objects we have sought for a long time, loved at a distance, and yearned to see, touch and possess. I have endured all these feelings and then not purchased the antique in question. I was surprised the first few times I experienced the "not buying syndrome." What the heck is going on? Being broke is not the answer. "Love is the answer." (John Lennon crooned the song in the album, *Mind Games*. Who knew he was talking about purchasing antiques?) I will explain.

In many areas of my life looking is more meaningful than buying. To leave the realm of collecting for a moment, looking is an idle and pleasurable pastime. For example, the Friday *Mansion* section of the *Wall Street Journal* is great fun and the next time I have a loose $14 million or so, I will start thinking about that ski lodge. It is fun to fantasize about what I would purchase if I ever had all the moolah I needed. Fantasy looking takes place at auto shows, while reading travel brochures, when my wife visits jewelry stores, and even in dealers' booths at shows. But maybe it is worth examining this daydreaming in a real-life situation, when the object was affordable.

We almost became classic car owners, emphasis on "almost." My wife piloted a 1964½ Ford Mustang that she loved. She will tell you that

I made her sell it. This was 1971 or so. My response is that if we all kept everything that someday might be missed or become a "classic," we would need warehouses in which to store the items. "Exactly," she replies. That didn't mean the fire had gone out, though. Years later we became interested in owning a classic fastback Mustang. We searched for about 18 months. We had a chance or two but always passed and then finally gave up.

The rationale for not buying that car fail to capture the decision's essence. Sure, we live in Wisconsin and the Stang would have to be stored for several months each year. And our garage and driveway are not large or wide enough to accommodate our two non-classics as well as the Mustang spring through fall. The thrill of listening to its V-8 or having people enviously wave at us as we drove by seemed sort of small-minded. In truth, we were unwilling to give the car the attention it would have needed. What classic car owners find fun we would have felt a hassle. Put simply, the car did not deserve us. Now voyeur-ship trumps ownership.

Returning to American antiques, the same scenario replays itself. I once desired a jeweler's watch sign to hang on the wall, one that looked like a pocket watch. I read about them and knew their pricing, saw a few, and zeroed in on what I coveted. I found one, exactly what I wanted. Then I realized I could be happy without it. There was no ambivalence or regret in not purchasing the sign. Was this a rational decision, an emotional decision or both? I believe it was an emotional one. I was infatuated with such a sign, but once we met I did not fall in love.

Perhaps we have to be confronted with our own needs and tastes to know how badly we appreciate, lust after, and need to add an item to our collection. I haven't seen this topic written about, so I am somewhat on my own here. I believe the "passion threshold" was not reached in this instance and that without sufficient passion the sign would not fulfill me. When Neil Sedaka sang that *Breakin' Up is Hard To Do*, he was singing about being in love. I did not love the sign enough. Breaking up was easy.

This discussion brings me to the present moment and a story yet to be finished. I have been seeking a Windsor bench, constrained by a 76-inch length, although they are rare enough that few of any size have come to market in the last decade. The question is: If one became available would I purchase it? A fine question indeed. I am growing weary of waiting; I have no sense whether I will be elated, relieved or disappointed if one shows up in my price range. As with the jeweler's sign I will not know until the choice presents itself. The bench may take my breath away and I will be in love. Alternately, in that instant I will know my affair of the heart is over, the infatuation gone, the quest ended.

As I have mentioned, my wife and I collect aviation (posters, fiction about girls/women who fly, small steel toy airplanes). We live in Oshkosh, Wisconsin, which welcomes the Experimental Aircraft Association's annual convention (drawing 12,000 aircraft each summer). Add to that the fact that Sandy is nearing thirty years of volunteer work for EAA's Vintage Division. In addition we have a son who is a commercial pilot. Our interest was foredoomed. Sandy loves the Pan American Clipper airplane and had no problem saying, "I want it" when a poster of one became available years ago. To complement it, we started looking for a TWA poster showing a Lockheed Constellation punching through the clouds. (The Connie is perhaps the most beautiful commercial aircraft ever produced. We have seen her in person several times and she always makes us smile. She was first built in 1943.) We found a marvelous example and had the opportunity to purchase the poster in good condition, yet we decided not to. The emotional response carried the day. The fact our wall space was largely filled worked was a rationalization. I ultimately concluded that we did not love it as much as we first thought. The image couldn't do justice to seeing Connie in person. Once again, infatuation never matured into love. I believe our love in the Pan Am Clipper was well placed.

An Exercise in Style and Connoisseurship

The Pan Am poster is rectangular but the image offers many forms, curves, and angles. Everything depicted in the image is in proportion. Its texture is smooth but does not appear so as the eye views it.

The poster is lithograph printed on paper and is linen backed. (Additional information on the printing process is provided in Chapter 8.)

The colors are intense and vivid. Its overall impact is a riot of colors in an exotic setting. The artist (Lawler) did a superb job; his techniques well honed. The poster is one of a set printed in the 1930s to advertise Pan Am and the faraway places it flew: Hawaii, South American countries, the South Pacific, and the China Clipper to Hong Kong. Posters promoting Ecuador and Peru are the most commonly found; Brazil is found rarely, and the others are almost never seen. No records exist of the printing runs; survivors only abide in private or institutional collections.

Such posters were not labeled. The dealers we purchased it from may know the historical society that consigned it to auction, but we never asked. The condition is perfect with no wear. The poster is completely original. An overall evaluation would be that this is one of the few *10*s my wife and I own. It is rare and to us beautiful. We found it worthy of purchase and have never seen another for sale.

Compromises. None.

⸒

Let us leave love for the moment and turn to missed opportunities and the concept of the ideal as another explanation for not buying. As I have written, almost all antique collectors with whom I have talked can tell me exactly when they passed on something they still wish they had purchased, often years or decades later. And sometimes they never did buy such an object, even when pondering comparable examples. A personal story may clarify. When first collecting, we had the opportunity to buy a gorgeous robin's egg blue blanket chest, but could not afford it (a true case of lacking the necessary funds). We still rue the day these decades later. Now we can afford one but we have never seriously looked. Would the color be the same as on the one we loved so many years ago? For us, it is more fulfilling to carry that original blanket chest in our memories than live with one that might not quite be up to it. We loved it then and do so now. I know this may make little sense, but it is the best explanation I have. I am confident that there are more than a few serious collectors out there who could tell a similar story. It all boils down to the fact that at its core, collecting is a human exercise.

I talked to a friend who is steeped in the classics and taught classical literature, asking him to shed some light on why we behave this way. He pointed me to the literature on the ideal. The explanation goes something like this. The collector envisions the antique he has been seeking for so long as a sort of Holy Grail. The real object cannot possibly measure up. We have made the desired antique perfect – the blue blanket chest from long ago, the kitchen cupboard, perhaps a Windsor bench. Eugene Delacroix, a French romantic artist of the 18th and 19th century, said, "the artist who aims for perfection in everything achieves it in nothing."

161

Perhaps the same is true for antique collectors. We will have to temper the ideal picture we have built up of any long-sought piece if we are to own one. How to persuade ourselves to moderate our desires and fall away from the perfect remains a mystery. I wonder if and how others have managed the trick. Still, if I abandon the ideal, I wonder if I can truly love the piece in question. Will it be an eternal compromise? Thomas Wolfe captured the soul of the challenge in his novel, *You Can't Go Home Again*. When it comes to certain antiques we may have to preserve their feeling and memory but never possess them, their essence or effect on us a remembrance.

Robert Fulghum may have summed up one of this chapter's theses best in *All I Really Needed to Know I Learned in Kindergarten*, where he wrote: "I believe that imagination is stronger than knowledge. That myth is more potent than history. That dreams are more powerful than facts." I wonder if the blue blanket chest, and comparable examples for other collectors, carries with them mythical associations?

Another reason for not buying is that a collector is dipping his toe in new waters. Genre long time collected may have to be put on the back burner to accrue funds for a new area of collecting. Not long ago I went looking for a painting of a schooner. I knew nothing of maritime art and was aware that I needed to develop the requisite knowledge before I purchased one. For a period of time I held onto my money, not buying other antiques for my collection, waiting to see what would happen. My changing tastes (this would be my first maritime painting) accounted for that decision. My waiting was rewarded. You can read about this painting and see photographs of it in Chapter 22.

Another reason collectors do not buy is because they fail to trust their own judgment. They seek objects that have not been shopped around. They assume, often erroneously, that if the object is still pictured on a website after some period of time, available after an auction, or at a dealer's booth at more than one show that other collectors have found it wanting. This conclusion is true some of the time but not always. The desire for an antique that only the dealer and perhaps a handful of others have ever seen before a collector whisks it away for his collection gives the object a cachet. Just as rare should never be confused with good; fresh to the market does not mean an antique meets style and connoisseurship criteria. I know of several dealers who have had antiques for quite some time, only to receive multiple offers almost simultaneously (life seems to work that way). Our dealer friends, Bernice and Jim often would have a beautiful antique that for one reason or another did not sell. Sandy and I would always bring over a bottle of champagne to celebrate when we learned of its sale. Oh how I wish I could have afforded some of those "dogs" that languished on the market.

As I think about looking and not owning, it seems obvious that over time Sandy and I have changed and matured in our tastes and desires. Some antiques that seemed endlessly attractive a year or two or longer ago now seem less attractive. As a psychologist I know that time is not a casual variable. It is what happens over time that determines disease, changing tastes, changes in who we are, and so forth. Yet my experience is that such shifts often are unconscious, even unwilled. Despite the lack of a debate with others or myself, change (I like to think of it is growth) is always taking place. It simply seems to occur.

What I do know is that certainty is a false god. It is often surprising which antiques in our collection we come to cherish and which are more easily given up. Items purchased because of infatuation may fall out of favor, or become cornerstones in our collection. Those we loved may endure, but not always. Those idealized from long ago may not brook any competition. Sometimes we may grow tired. Sometimes our finances make ownership of a desirable piece impossible. We may dismiss a great antique because others have passed it by. We grow over time and there always is a chance to refine or redirect our tastes. Above all, we cannot dismiss the word "no" from our collecting vocabularies. Whether the act is reasonable or unreasonable, nobly – even ideally – inspired, the product of gut instinct or lofty reason, stepping away is as intimate to the art of collecting as a nod at an auction.

Chapter 16

ॐ

I Will Not Pay One Penny More

Classic circa 1840 Norwalk, CT "ABC" plate. 10¼"d with excellent flourishes. Very good condition, only a couple of minor edge chips and one small spot of slip loss at the bottom of the "B". The exuberant curly-q's in the lower half of the dish are very nice and unusual.

Early 19th Century New England redware plate, 12½"d, ABC. Coggled rim decorated with trailed slip wave and scroll decoration, superb flourishes, exuberant. Excellent condition with a minor rim chip.

We buy antiques for all of the right (and sometimes wrong) reasons. We reject them the same way. In this chapter take I look at another conundrum: the frustrating and complicated challenge of fearing you will pay too much, even when you love a piece. Simply put, price affects consumption, although not necessarily in a straightforward way.

An example? Suppose a Sotheby's auction of American furniture is well underway. On the block is a wonderful 18th Century formal Philadelphian table, provenance impeccable, the piece itself in unrestored and almost perfect condition, showing a charming original surface. As the bidding intensifies only two bidders are left. "$800,000" says the auctioneer and one nods. "$900,000" the auctioneer quietly intones and the other's telephone representative raises his number card ever so slightly. At a million dollars you can hear a pin drop. At $1.1 million the auctioneer slams down his hammer and the piece sells, plus buyer's premium (of course). The bidder who bid only $1 million loved the piece, knew another was not likely to come on the market anytime soon, and believed that it would be a strong addition to his collection. Critically, he probably could afford to go higher but chose not to. It seems he decided that the piece was not worth the cost. Oh, and this happens all the time; even the Da Vinci that Christie's auction house sold in 2017 for $450 million enticed an underbidder who dropped out at a price in the hundreds of millions.

That prompts the question, when is an amount offered for an antique enough and when too much? We have to start with some simple understandings. First, the value of antiques is subjective: It is set by competitiveness, association, aesthetics, and to some extent rarity. Saying an object is "worth" X dollars makes no sense, unless all the variables – the market environment, the members of the audience, and dozens of other potentially contributing factors (even weather conditions) – are under our control – and that is of course impossible. After the serious recession of 2008-09 the price of most American antiques plummeted. Nothing had changed about them: They were just as old, beautiful, rare, and lovable. What had intervened was a new calculus: what collectors right then could and were willing to pay for these pieces. The very best of the best still fetched amazing prices, but uniqueness hardly justifies much if other contributing factors are absent. There may be only one Play-Doh hippo made by your granddaughter, and that makes it precious to you but assuredly does not render it marketable.

The market for American antiques has not vanished; it has just changed. The recession demonstrated that antique values were neither inevitable nor immutable. Something that used to cost $2000 now garners less, though it is the same object. A collector with $2000 is no longer willing to hand over that amount to purchase that same antique.

Every collector suffers from a different mania: I may be gaga over ceramics from Connecticut, you with smoothbore muskets from the Civil War. The guy next to you is in love with signed first editions. I am willing to bet, however, that each of us has encountered a moment when something deeply desirable came on the market, priced at the bleeding edge of what we thought was our financial limit. Oh the agony, the very hard decisions whether to buy or to step back. The challenge in figuring out how much to spend and when to duck faces all collectors. We can all benefit from sensibly examining why we behave as we do (or should) and how we can avoid paying too much by our personal standards.

What we are willing to pay for antiques depends on the market, how fair we perceive the price as being, the strength of our itch for it, what else we might pursue instead, what the piece might contribute to our collection, and what its ownership says about us. Let us descend into the real world and leave behind the rarified troposphere at Sotheby's. Not too long ago, a redware plate was for sale in good condition. It said "Apple Pie" on it. I had been looking to own one like it for some time. This type of Norwalk, Connecticut plate used to show up in the market fairly regularly, but more recently they had become genuine rarities. I liked everything about it, yet I found the asking price too high. Honestly I thought the dealer or consignor trying to get more than fair market value for it. While searching for Apple Pie, as I thought of the piece, I had purchased several other redware plates, including a fancy *ABC* example, this despite the fact that I already owned an ABC plate. Lack of funds was not the issue.

℃

An Exercise in Style and Connoisseurship

The first of the ABC redware plates pictured is a nice example of the genre. Its 10¼" diameter is a smaller size that makes it easier to display on a plate rack. Its condition is excellent, though it shows a bit of wear, only to be expected after all these years. The colors of this piece are bright. Its circular shape is traditional and the slip flourish ornamentation adds to its presentation. According to the Wilton Historical Society in Connecticut:

> Redware was the first pottery made in the American colonies. It was made from red clay found in most areas. Soft clay was pressed over a mold, which formed its shape. The notched rim was cut with a hand-held, wooden or metal coggle, a wheel designed for making decorative impressions. The inside of these wares were often decorated with a liquid white clay that was poured to form patterns, names, or sayings. To create a watertight surface, the interior was coated with a clear, lead glaze and fired. (Website)

Many of these redware pieces come from Norwalk, Connecticut, circa 1825 or 1830 or so. (To show the value of a bit of research, I learned when reading *The Antiquers* [Sallinger, 1980] that a friend of Edwin Atlee Barber's, Albert Hastings Pitkin also wanted to interest Americans in American ceramics. He found some redware with slip in 1884 when little information existed about such pieces except they were probably fifty years old. He called them Red Clay Pottery and was told that at one point in time they were quite common. He knew of no examples in the hands of collectors or dealers. It is possible that he was the first collector of such pieces. I also took away from Sallinger's book a lesson: I need a middle name if I am to be remembered as a collector.)

The second redware plate is larger: 12½" in diameter, almost platter size. It is very nicely formed and may also have been made in Norwalk. The craftsman let loose his creative instincts, covering the plate's surface with scrolls and patterns. Even the *ABC* is exuberant. Again, condition is excellent. The red clay on this plate is lighter in color than that on the first.

Owning both plates goes well with my display style: having similar objects grouped together. Even if this was the first ABC plate in my collection, I couldn't pass up a second specimen with so much aesthetic appeal. The larger plate is a vastly superior example and an A+ for slipware ABC plates. Some collectors and dealers consider the larger size more desirable because it diverges from the usual. And they value them more highly even if the slip decoration is the same on two examples.

Compromises: For the plainer of the two plates, I'd like one in better condition. For the exuberant one, I see no shortcomings.

Though the tariff was peaky, I could afford to purchase the plate and lusted after it. The difference between what I thought was fair and what the dealer was asking was not measured in tens of thousands of dollars – more like $2,000, but a third higher than I thought the plate deserved. "Take it out of the kids' estate and they wouldn't even notice" is what I could have muttered. Yet I could not bring myself to purchase the piece, and that started me tasking why. The more I thought about it, the more intrigued I became: what does overpaying mean?

Being a good academic, I talked with other antique collectors and a dealer or two. I spoke with a colleague in psychology at the university where I formerly taught. I sat on my porch and cogitated. While I came up with a few answers there are still some gaps, mostly because I was largely forced to look inside myself, always a painful, chancy and dispiriting exercise.

Value theory looks at why, how much and when we set the worth of something. From an economic perspective, if an item is too expensive, we are reluctant to pay for it. To us, it lacks "value" equal to its price. Either the object itself or our rational and emotional assessment of its worth is insufficient to make us reach for our credit cards. Axiology (whew!) is the philosophical study of value; for our purposes the part of axiology that looks at beauty is relevant. The apple pie redware plate on offer was not beautiful or harmonious enough to me to entice my buying it.

Offsetting my worry about being excessively focused on my ego is the fact that the plate had been on the market for more than a year, with no takers. Had other collectors felt there might be something wrong with it because it had generated no interest? This is the sort of skepticism that drives antique dealers crazy, of course, and as noted before there are landmines hidden in such glib leaps to conclusions. Still, on examination, nothing about the redware plate seemed wrong with it. I think it was just too pricey for people with enough knowledge to spend real money on such a piece.

Another reason for not buying the plate was that I need to avoid feeling that I am being taken advantage of. In this case, interestingly, paying more than the plate is worth would constitute "self-exploitation." It is not the dealer who would be taking advantage of me. I would be insulting or defrauding myself. Or so it seems. Outside of the realm of collecting, we go to great lengths to avoid being exploited on the price of goods and services. The same seems to be true here.

Many different thoughts and feelings can lead us to conclude the price of something is too high. Returning to the plate I didn't purchase, let's start with what I think of as my good angel, sitting on my shoulder and whispering in my ear – surely an imaginative delusion but useful. One reason I refused to overspend on the redware plate had to do with my self-image: I think of myself as someone who pays reasonable prices for quality antiques. Buying the overpriced plate would contradict – or at least undermine – that persona. There is a rational aspect as well: I think of myself as a collector knowledgeable about the market. Not buying this attractive redware plate for too much confirms the value of thinking before acting. The emotional and rational motives reinforce one another, and living up to what I believe seems more worthwhile than owning the plate at that price. Unlike the tension between infatuation and love described in the preceding chapter, you can love something (but perhaps not love it enough), be able to afford it, and still bristle at an outrageous price and decide to let it go.

I could have capitulated. The emotional bad angel on my other shoulder might persuasively whisper that I should surrender to lust. Why bother with worrying about a few dollars? Though I wanted the plate, I did not feel compelled to throw caution and money to the wind. Looked at in the broadest possible perspective there is probably some antique somewhere that would lead me to overspend in order to have it. This was not it. Was I somehow mistaken about how much I want the plate? The baddie on my shoulder mutters that I should enjoy it, own it, can afford it. She – assuming angels have gender, a question I refuse to pursue – could not win the argument.

Wise to these things, the auto industry has devised an abundance of ways to convince consumers to purchase luxury vehicles, and other sellers, antique dealers included, have enthusiastically adopted not a few of these manipulative techniques. Think of Lexus at Christmas time. Put a red bow on the top of the auto. The car becomes a gift, and Lexus' commercials always show a family ecstatic about their surprise $70 thousand Christmas present. Mercedes depicts the long history of its luxury automobiles. When you buy a Benz you supposedly fulfill a life's longing and now own a piece of history. All you need to do is convince me that to buy this redware plate is to . . . be persuaded it is a gift to myself? Think of it as an irreplaceable historical artifact? Be offered an option with it (better stereo, perhaps)?

Note that in auto commercials there is a strong emphasis on what groups of people feel and value. Not many people who see my collection know what they are looking at. I have few fellow cognoscenti – people with the same passions and knowledge – to share it with. If I could say: "Isn't it a beauty? Paid a bit more than what I thought it was worth but there it is," and the person with me could actually understand what he was looking at; I think I'd be more likely to purchase this redware plate. So the realm of interpersonal give-and-take may be a significant element in the calculus I am describing. A *Wall Street Journal* article ("Why Cameras Outshine Fridges;" 2018) supports this hypothesis. Those lacking the expertise will neither recognize nor praise my redware collection or my taste.

One dealer I have worked with over time with recommended that I wait to decide on buying this piece before leaping one way or the other. He counseled me that more of them would enter the marketplace if I waited and perhaps prove more reasonably priced. Valuing his wisdom I have so far heeded the advice.

Let me point out that the tension between reason ("do not buy") and emotion ("oh go ahead") is in fact simplistic. Two facets of reason and two of emotion exist simultaneously. The question is, which carries the greatest weight in making the decision? Reason takes into account the relatively paltry amount involved, my mortality and the like. Do we pass up golden opportunities for mere pelf? Emotion says I should throw caution to the wind, yet a sense of guilt at having splurged, anger at myself for acting foolishly, or regret from demonstrating that I am in fact neither as frugal as I thought nor as wise also await. Collectors cannot let the fear of making a wrong choice (buyer's remorse) paralyze them, but the guilt you experience when you realize an extravagant expenditure brought little satisfaction or happiness is painful. After all, most of the time the irrationalities touched on in "Collectors and Their Money" leave us with no one to blame but ourselves if we feel buyer's remorse.

There exists in psychology and psychotherapy the notion of "reframing a situation." Reframing means that the circumstances remain constant; what changes is an individual's perception regarding what is taking place and the conclusions he draws. To reframe is to change how one thinks and feels about something (if the thoughts change, the feelings will follow). So instead of thinking of myself as a chump for buying the plate, I could think of myself as someone realistically dealing with the marketplace, his own mortality and the need to feel satisfied with and build my antique collection. To re-frame would be to say: "Once in a while I pay a bit too much for an antique because I choose to do so."

A psychotherapist would call that rationalization. She would ask why I would feel resentful if I purchased the plate and then lay on me, accurately, the charge that I am choosing to feel resentful. There are alternatives. Certainly the best solution that gets rid of the mess would be a fair price but that is not available. Facing reality head on, not buying is the best possible alternative and the one I adopt

What I have just gone through is a detailed *cost-benefit analysis*. I weighed the pros and cons to decide whether my decision was sound. Part of this scrutiny took place at the emotional level and that is perfectly permissible, not to mention human. After adding up the pluses of seizing the plate and subtracting the negatives (its financial and emotional costs), I concluded that owning the plate would not outweigh the assessed negatives.

Part of any cost-benefit analysis a collector undertakes must include what other antiques he is seeking. A redware plate is not the only piece on my "I'd really like own" list. As a matter of course I took the money the plate would cost and added it to the fund available for purchasing something else I really wanted. The new funds to buy the braceback Windsor chair in original green paint was not only soothing but, I admit, self-affirming. I had done the right thing, so there!

More important to the final decision was my inability to rationally decide buying this piece of redware was sensible. No matter which angle I tried I could not persuade myself to buy the plate at the price being asked.

We make mistakes when we create credible motives for buying something to the exclusion of all other facts and feelings.

Yes, I understand that what I have said sound like the classic: On the one hand/on the other hand. It is, and that may be the real point of this whole discussion. Collectors (and poets and artists and others) are attracted to the good, the true and the beautiful. That's an ancient saw (and from Plato, to boot). What draws us embodies beauty: craftsmanship, rarity, aesthetics. We want to possess what we cannot create. We want to save what is evanescent and fragile. That's why collectors feel so strongly about their antiques. The very authenticity of things – an almost two hundred-year-old piece of redware in this instance – builds a bridge between our past and this moment in our lives.

The reluctance to spend freely may simply arise from our sense of good, of what is fair, of what is reasonable. I judged the price to be unreasonable and my emotions are congruent with that conclusion. My willingness to say "no" is not a rejection of the antique I have used in this example: It is a confirmation of my need to see things in balance, to act prudently and to still appreciate what I don't possess. Avoiding feeling like a sucker outweighs any argument in favor of the purchase. A collector has his limits after all.

And there you have it. This is the calculus of not overpaying. And these are some of the ways we deal with the conflict between desire for an antique and its worth.

Chapter 17

ℰ

An Antique Show

Circa 1740-1760 New England, probably Stratford, Connecticut or Long Island, bannister-back rush seat side chairs (pair). 37" chair height, 16" seat height. Trumpet legs and side posts, stocking foot and bulbous front stretcher. The surface is original with paint decoration, early 19th Century. Rush seats are old.

Shows featuring American antiques come in all shapes and sizes. Some are intimate and have 20 dealers, give or take. Some are large and jammed with more than 60 vendors. They may be only a few hours long, but a handful last three days. Shows can take place outdoors in parks, on historical grounds, or fairgrounds. Indoors, they take over hockey arenas, museums, hotels, armories, school gymnasiums, and the like. Now and then they provide lavish opening nights, edible food and tolerable (sometimes better than that) music. Previews may serve alcohol, but at high summer shows in the countryside cold water or lemonade is crucial.

Why shows like this, the fancier ones that is? At the core, the dealers or promoter who arrange and sponsor them hope the visitors will buy something in the midst of meeting, greeting, being seen, seeing others, and noshing. Altruism and PR go just so far, of course and "free" is not a widely used enticement. Such shows can be expensive, especially for those offering more than wandering-around privileges. More than a few charge a premium for entry during "early admittance," the idea being collectors will pay more to have first shot at what is exhibited. Others cost just a few bucks.

I have always been amazed at the number of antique shows to be found advertised in publications and online. Especially in New England, they appear to sprout like tulips in spring. I asked someone knowledgeable about the trade whether there simply weren't too many of them. "Folks," said he in his best Downeast drawl, "say too many. Always did. If they weren't makin' money, wouldn't be doin' it."

As collectors look forward to and queue up in line, (we shall talk about their behavior in the next chapter) the promoter and dealers will already have been fully occupied and often have been bustling for quite some time. The show's promoter reserved the venue and months ago sent out contracts to prospective dealers, some of whom appear in the same shows every year. Before inviting vendors, he had to decide what mix of antiques and types of dealers he wanted. None of it is easy; timing, venues, the slate of dealers all raise daunting challenges. Should she stretch a bit, include more art, invite someone who specializes in Mid-Century modern, a dealer with jewelry or Native American pieces? What forms of publicity should be budgeted? Is a special show insert to be arranged for one of the major antique publications (some shows do so year after year and a change in habit could be disastrous)? Will dealers be given cards for free admission they can send to their most loyal customers? Can we get local television to cover the event? More recently, the promoter has had to decide whether to advertise on social media.

The nitty-gritty details are endless. Porters need to be available both at set-up and tear down and to assist moving large pieces once purchased. If booths there be, constructed they must. The promoter needs to oversee lighting, seating, and to minister to headaches (sometimes physical, more often bipedal). It is not unknown for a dealer to cancel at the last minute, contract be damned, for illness, important family matters, bad karma, whatever. The promoter is the go-to person for all problems and details, on-call from before setup until the last seller has packed up and left the building counting his profits.

As part of being the "go to" person a show promoter becomes father confessor. In the high holy church of antiques there are always souls that need attending, murderous impulses to be salved, sins to be forgiven or hidden. Consider the collector who purchases an item, takes it home, has a friend swear it is a fake (whether he knows anything about the topic is no matter), and for that reason brings it back to the dealer to return. From thence arises the classic it's real/it's not discussion (shouting match?) and the promoter must step in as mediator (promoters have learned long ago that being a judge is a sure-fire way to lose both buyers and sellers). Or a collector buys a nice piece, looks it up on the Internet once home, decides he overpaid, even though what he purchased may be a century older than what he saw online. Being unhappy with the dealer, he wants his money back. Being a customer, he wants the promoter to be his enforcer. None of these scenarios even borders on the fictitious or alien. Why in the world would anyone want to put up with all this? Some folks simply are born to be a show promoter, love being one.

The second vital element is dealers, and they are as varied as their specializations. Some work at the trade full-time; for others it is a part-time gig. Some have deep pockets and built serious inventories, can tap a lengthy list of past buyers. A few are teetering on the edge of not making it and actively looking for a day job. Every single one of them would like to make a living selling antiques but to do so they must make a profit, which means finding good items and getting them for reasonable prices. Expertise, good taste, and persuasive skills are at the heart of their success, that and love for the pieces and the hobby. A few dealers have unappreciated powers to mold and shape the tastes of collectors. They elevate the desirability of collectibles and literally create a market. I think of one dealer, now deceased, who was instrumental in originating and maintaining two collecting genres: Nantucket baskets and Ralph Cahoon paintings of mermaids and sailors.

Dealers over the long term establish a reputation: They deal in specific sorts or periods or styles of antiques. In effect, they are toting their own images to these shows; selling is simultaneously a form of advertising. Within the show's parameters – venue, size, location and so forth – they display items that they think will fit the tastes of the collectors who show up, duplicate previous successes in selling there, and pick pieces likely to stir the interest of a few regulars certain to attend. If this is a prestigious show, dealers have been putting aside spectacular items for months, saving them. They have decisions of their own to make: Some unveil special items only when the opening bell chimes, antiques they probably could have sold weeks or months ago. Antique shows are theatre at heart but decisions can determine whether the play is a tragedy or comedy.

Perhaps most consequentially, no matter how much experience a dealer has or how often he and his fellows have sold at the show, deciding what merchandise to bring is often a crapshoot. If it isn't in the van or truck or fresh from the floor, it cannot be displayed. Will paintings be hot at this show? What about smalls and what sorts? Is this the show at which furniture will finally sell? Given the lousy market, will anything sell? Will regulars I am counting on attend and buy?

Dealers bear some responsibility for a show's scenery, too. They design their booths or display areas. Sometimes "booths" consist of nothing more than a clutch of tables on grass or a floor. At better shows, they may be separated from one another by pipe and drapes. Upscale types pay for side and back walls. To the veteran show maven, booths can be formulaic. No matter what show you attend Jim's booth is the same –furniture here, weathervanes there, a display case with small items. George is a master of the unanticipated, featuring different sorts of items every time he sets up. Do we buy because something is familiar (Jim's theory apparently) or strikingly original (à *la* George)? Only their bank accounts know. Some dealers are minimalists and make it easy to see what they have for sale, easy to set up the booth. Others seem to truck in a barn full and just scatter the pieces about. The scene has to be lighted dramatically too: Lighting is important; a special antique or two might be given center stage. A few pricey items bear tags limning history, dates, or provenance. Then there are the ones that blankly list a price (typically negotiable), just begging you to ask the dealer for detail.

Have you ever wondered what it is like for dealers to be on the floor at an antique show? What they experience? What they see when we – possible customers, potential friends, dismissive critics – wander past their booths? Come with me.

I shadowed a dealer during several shows. What I learned was enlightening, maddening, sometimes embarrassing (we think we buyers are so much nicer than we are). My experience led me to think collectors may want to be a bit more forgiving of dealers and that collectors themselves might want to pledge themselves to the code of conduct I propose in Chapter 27.

Let me introduce the *dramatis personae*: the dealer and Sandy and I.

Some time ago, at Northeast Auctions, the two of us were sitting in a sofa or on a table (I frankly no longer remember which) that was waiting to be sold, kibitzing with a stranger. Introductions were made and it turned out he lived in Wisconsin, as do we. Furthermore, he was a dealer who annually managed a show about two hours from where we lived, though we had not heard of it (clearly, more marketing was needed). Late that autumn we went there a-visiting and made the acquaintance of a dealer from out East. We talked, we returned, we connected, we purchased, and over the years he assisted us in building our collection and became a friend. So he is the third party, entering the scene from the wings. The stages for our anthropological study were Antiques Week in Manchester and a show in Nashville. The former used to open with a much-anticipated auction over the weekend, followed throughout the week by several shows, at least three of which were of high quality. Everything was there: buyers, sellers, shows and – most important – the freedom to play different roles as needed. I wanted to see the selling and collecting process from both sides, to look through the eyes of a dealer at a show, rather than as merely a consumer. I discovered a lot.

The first act for my sleuthing drama took place at an outdoor venue during Antiques Week. For the past few years, I had attended the shows as a solo player, scrutinizing what was available, keeping Sandy hooked in by texts, calls and photos. I had used the Internet, special show section ads, and dealers' websites to check what was on offer. Regardless of all the publicity, it is common to find great pieces for sale at a show that have not appeared in the media or previously been offered to the public. That is one of the reasons we attend shows.

"Great pieces," really? Let me share but one example. I attended a show once where a braceback Windsor armchair was for sale. Original green, darkened splendidly. The arms were original and were made from mahogany, a Rhode Island technique in the form's most sophisticated stage of development. The dealer was well-known and second generation; his father knew of this chair 65 years before I saw it. He and then his son kept in touch with the family that owned it and waited for six decades. And here it was, unheralded. It was fresh to the market, fairly priced and sold in the show's first hour. Had the buyer missed the show or waited for it to be listed somewhere, he would have been out of luck.

As an understudy I had kept a dealer company for the full day of the outdoor show, where he sold little. The next year we had visited Nashville and perched beside him in his booth during part of two days. And I now I had the opportunity: spend two full days over two years, being his shadow during Antiques Week. I must admit I enjoyed playing detective more than he did. Still, observing and listening was a revelation.

First of all, I learned that there are three ways that dealers make money. They sell to us collectors. They sell to other dealers. They can speculatively buy from other dealers, using the pieces to stock their booths or tucking them away for later. Buying well from others can make or break a dealer's day. They need time (and their wits about them) to walk the show over and over, to see if there is anything they can purchase that might yield a return. It is entirely possible for a dealer to be in the pink – or red – before the show's curtain goes up (So much for our importance as collectors).

Then the scrim finally ascends majestically (ahem, the curtain rises) and the rabid masses dash through the door. Their behaviors are not always civil. The anxious push and shove and mutter. The deliberate poke along and cast scornful glances at these obvious parvenus. There is a bit of throwing of business cards or shouts of "Hold that for me!" as the chattering hordes of collectors do their brisk walk-throughs. The traffic jam takes up the first hour or two of opening day and then slows down. Sales are not always immediate, but dealers like to flaunt some items with red tags or dots on them (sold!) early on. Buyers are still around in the closing hours, some finally decisive others looking for bargains. It is not unusual to have collectors call with interest in items days or weeks later.

Our own experience testifies to the truth of cautious decision-making (but not the only truth, mind you): We examined a pair of chairs in a dealer's booth at a show once. Months later at yet another show there was the same dealer and chairs. By then we decided we really liked them, and purchased them.

An Exercise in Style and Connoisseurship

This is a pair of chairs with a lot going on. Curves everywhere - the crest piece, side posts, legs, turnings, a bulbous front stretcher. They are well proportioned with bold, in-your-face ornamentation. The gold embellishment (paint) was probably added during the *American Fancy* period in the 1820s or 1830s. Collectors will disagree whether this sort of decoration adds to the appeal of the chairs. We felt it did. Their black paint is original and faded, the gold ornamentation more vivid.

Texture is rough, crusty. The chairs look old and are. They came with flame-stitch cushions that we liked, even though they are not original; they make the chairs more comfortable so we kept them. They seem well made, a common pair of Queen Anne country pieces. The two show some appropriate wear and age, a softening and fading of what once would have been crisper and brighter.

We found them brash and spirited. They were expensive but not overly so. Where are you going to find another pair with this originality and gold accent? Better yet, they fit in with our other furniture and accessories.

Compromises. Many. We could have waited for a pair of chairs with paint in better condition and more defined Queen Anne feet. After purchasing the chairs someone showed me a picture of one with a similar design at auction. It had a dramatic crest rail that was chamfered and had bolder and crisper turnings overall, with a leg that was a bit "lighter." The stile (side pieces) turnings were also more ambitious. Ignore the center splat and look at the space between the splat and the stiles. In the chair at auction the space was more interesting (that may mean pretty or attractive; I'm not quite sure). Our chairs are good; the chair up for auction was superlative. All were affordable. Some collectors would want a pair with no gold paint ornamentation. The chair at auction was not painted and displayed a nice patina.

Our chair buying experience in this case is an excellent example of how individual tastes affect buying, and at least signals the worth of the phrase "if I only had waited or known." In this instance, the superlative example at auction would not have fit into our collection. It was too good. It would have looked out of place with other pieces in our home. It was a superb antique and a bad deal at the same time. Since then, I have never seen a pair of similar chairs that sufficiently outstrips the ones we purchased. Before buying, I had no time to learn more about them, fit them into my style and connoisseurship classification, modify my judgment and preference (perhaps), and think at length about purchasing a pair – surely a perilous situation. But we love the chairs and have no regrets. Sometimes good luck is better than good research. Sometimes.

One of the first things I noticed was how attentive the dealer seemed. He knew who had entered the booth in what order, answering collectors' questions: "Please show me that." "Can you tell me more about this table?" "What are you asking for this?"

And then after an hour or two or three the show quiets and almost goes still. The aisles empty. That is a great time to see a show as a collector I might add, enjoying the attention of dealers. But as someone sitting in a both hour after hour, I found myself less alert, dissociating, my mind elsewhere, hearing the sounds of the loudspeaker, people's voices fading.

Being stuck in a booth is exhausting and boring (dealers are used to it). Einstein was correct: time is relative. The dealer's day can be long.

Some time later I began to appreciate what dealers sacrifice in order to pursue their profession. Unless a spouse works (with benefits) or the dealer has another full-time job (with benefits), health insurance must be purchased. The lifestyle may be desirable if you are young and footloose: be on the road a lot - picking, traveling to shows, checking on items up for auction, cycling between basic, mid-level or upscale inns. Anyone who has ever been a road warrior knows the challenges in eating well, exercising, and being rootless.

An antique dealer needs a powerful sense of self-worth and self-confidence. He is selling treasures he believes in, pieces he or she is proud to sell (I am painting with a wide brush but this was certainly true of many sellers I talked to). Some of what is for sale and on display comes from his personal collection, decorative arts or furniture he has lived with for years. And as the crowds thin out and if the sales have been sparse, dealers have to fall back on hope. "What I have is good; all it takes is the right collector." "Maybe later today." "Tomorrow is another day."

I also learned that collectors should be just a little, and perhaps a lot more, understanding. It is no surprise if a dealer is not always bright eyed and civil, energetic and ready to smile winsomely late in a show. He may need a little empathy from a collector and perhaps a lot of understanding. Collectors are wise to be less businesslike and more humane, giving the dealer a minute to make small talk and get back in the marketing mood. Doing this can be both respectful and advantageous. Nice people are often treated nicely in return.

Many shows have a second or even a third day. So out to dinner after day one, a stiff drink may help the dealer's mood. Hopefully she has some good customers/friends to dine with or good dealer friends at the show. Then off to bed, rising, restocking the booth if she has been lucky, and the reprise. Ahead may lie better sales, more enthusiastic and polite buyers, maybe even a treasure missed earlier. For sure, there will be more hours and (were it me) more boredom.

Of the five shows I observed and pretended to be a dealer at, I think my friend sold well at only two of them (I say *think* because I am not privy to the number of collectors who saw pieces at the show following up with him afterwards). He bought well at two shows, but not the same two, by the way. I think what energized him, above all else (when I was observing) is that there is something motivational and satisfying in selling. Your heart leaps when you can ties red sold tags on pieces. You learn something about your commitment writing item descriptions. All the while, money is being made to pay bills, to purchase more merchandise, to have some fun. The dealer feels useful and needed, the decision to go into the business validated. There are fresh relationships out there waiting to be formed. And now and then you get a great story to add to your stock – the gem that got away, the delight that sat undiscovered until you passed by, the collector who was so dumb, smart, mean….

We can't ignore the collectors at the show, for they are that essential element: the audience. They anxiously await the right dialogue. "What is in your collection?" "What are you looking for?" "Can I work with you?" Those words were music to Sandy's and my ears when we encountered the dealer fated to also be a friend. And even though we live in the heartland and he does most of his business and lives out East, he has visited our home. He wanted insight into our collection, its strengths and lacunae, and our wishes and taste (or lack thereof).

What makes antique dealing worthwhile (as part of selling)? The pure joy and smile on collectors' faces who have found a piece they want to add to their collection. That is a large part of what a dealer lives for. But don't ever forget: It is a show you are at, with all the implications that term bears.

Surely there are disappointing shows for both dealers and collectors. The weather can be too awful or too beautiful to draw much of a crowd. For some reason something that used to sell no longer moves. The stock market has recently fallen by a goodly amount and collectors, nervous about their financial means, keep their hands over their hip pockets. Another show or two, or an auction, may be taking place nearby, siphoning off some of the buyers and their dollars. Or the show, for whatever reason, may lack energy (see the next chapter).

In many ways being a dealer reminded me of King Sisyphus, except instead of the eternal struggle of pushing that rock up the hill only to have it roll down, there is always the next show to do.

Let the house lights brighten. I hope the audience exits, better informed.

Chapter 18

ê

A Collector's Energy and its Importance

Circa 1830 Vermont all original paint-decorated dome top trunk. Brown freehand decoration with green stripes on yellow ground. Decorated on back. 29¼"l, 14½"h, 14¾"d.

Auctioneers, dealers at a show, promoters, buyers – they all want energy, because it undergirds sales and robust prices. Antique collectors are attuned to an atmosphere that seems to crackle in an auction room or show hall. They can feel enthusiasm. The presence of passion mobilizes, motivates, galvanizes, invigorates and excites. Energy is indeed important to the antique world and its cast of players. Still, its presence is hardly a given. There are times when its absence is, by strict definition, palpable, and the effects are sometimes disastrous. Despite its central role, I could find little written about it.

I was waiting in line for the New Hampshire Dealers Show in Manchester, as I have done so many times. It was 6:45 a.m. There are about 40 people in line, many nursing hot coffee. People talk quietly. Most stand while others sit. The show will not open until 10:00. We are all still waking up. It is too soon to get the adrenaline flowing, but we hope everything will be energized by the time the doors open.

A few hours have passed. The waiting area in much noisier and everyone seems more edgy, more anxious, certainly more awake. The line has grown, snaking back from the show's door. The s-shaped line,

187

wandering back and forth, and there is a clutch of eager collectors waiting on the sidewalk. The show will open in 45 minutes. I renew old acquaintances and make new ones, just as others are doing. We talk about what we collect, what we are looking for, and the dealers we will visit early in the show. Our hopes, our past disappointments and successes, our history as collectors are stories to share and help pass the time. We need the show to begin. We have waited long enough. Anticipation builds.

I talk with a woman who specializes in chairs, both as a collector and dealer. She is from the Midwest. Ironically behind her is a sign that says "No Chairs," though it is not critique of her passion: The fire marshal has ruled those waiting in line now can only stand or sit on the floor, this despite the fact that in past years those in the queue could use hotel chairs to ease their wait. A devotee of irony, I swipe the sign after the show opens and give it to her.

The energy of the crowd soars. Five minutes to opening. I feel like a runner in the starting blocks for the 100-meter dash. Suddenly all of us are eager. We are focused. The hubbub is deafening. The herd will surge through the show doors in moments and then selling and buying will begin – frenzy. A local police officer assigned to the event looks at us as if we are aliens. Perhaps we are.

The same sense of excitement existed, albeit at a somewhat more civil level, at the viewing Julia and Robert attended (Chapter 1). It was unmistakable at the auction where they purchased their pastel sandpaper painting, for such events come alive when great items are sold. In the more formal setting of most auctions, the roar of the crowd is merely a restrained buzz in the ear. Watchers may applaud politely after heated bidding finally results in a sale. People will drift by to congratulate or console bidders. The auctioneer's job is to build and maintain energy and enthusiasm, and he uses his patter, demeanor and the ordering of items being sold to do so. If a show is a bullring, most auctions are slightly rowdy churches. Yet both depend on enthusiasm, energy if you will, for their success.

What is transpiring in these cases? Many things, as it turns out. I am sure our heart rates and blood pressure of we serious collectors are elevated as we wait for the Dealers' show to begin on the first day. We are filled with anticipation and excitement, causing increased adrenaline, faster breathing, and other bodily changes. Sometimes people feel that way when preparing to fight or flee. Instead, we are bracing ourselves to compete and acquire.

Part of my off-the-charts excitement is readily understandable. I have traveled a considerable distance at some expense to be standing here in line. I want to avoid being distracted or desensitized by being inundated with very nice antiques. While I am looking for redware, I know I will see other fine pieces I might want to inspect and think about seriously. I feel like I am walking a collector's tight wire. On the one hand I have to be open to all of the stimuli that are present – noise, jostling, passing remarks with people I know, dimensions, aesthetics, style, paintings, furniture, redware, silver – and on the other hand I have to be able to ignore that which needs to be ignored – shoving competitors, spilled coffee and the sort. I cannot lose my focus on the objects that are being sold and the people who are selling (and sometimes buying) them. It is not clear how we manage this trick; sometimes some collectors fail and end up owning something they really didn't and don't want. My house is about full so I must be selective. More importantly, my tastes and standards must be met and that demands concentration, not elation.

What I experience waiting for a first-rate show or auction reminds me of a National Public Radio piece from years ago. A reporter joined a group of English soccer fans. They were hooligans, soccer gangs, sometimes called "Firms," known for intimidating and attacking supporters of teams. The reporter described the tension in the air and waiting for the spark that will set off the mob. Fights seemed preordained. This is not unfamiliar territory: Think of mob behavior in the old oaters – "string him up, sheriff;" the opening moments of a sporting event; an opera or symphony lover waiting for her heart to be rent. Interestingly, the energy when waiting is contagious. We feed off the excitement and anticipation of others. The psychological label for this phenomenon is "emotional contagion."

The same electricity in the air as the New Hampshire Dealers Show begins. There are no fisticuffs but people push and shove in booths to view items or to touch them before other collectors do. They are expending their energy to gain "right of first refusal" (be the first one to put a hold on the piece). Their emotional involvement triggers similar feelings those who are nearby. We may even unconsciously mimic their stance, facial expressions and verbalizations.

I have noted before that the average age of collectors of American antiques is rising, creating a worrisome condition: Where can shows find young(er) people whose passion for antiques matches that of the dwindling cadre of veterans? Yes, I am not alone in hoping that I will find one antique I love, which guarantees some level of competitive excitement. At shows nowadays, most of the folks have been collecting for decades. Fortunately, their desire for the one great piece has not died. Like me, they can find energy in the possibility – no matter how far-fetched – that they will find one item at the show that they can love.

Soon sold tags or red dots pop up. "Did you see that wonderful table?" "How about the hooked rug over there?" You have to avoid calling out "I'll take it" or "Please put that on hold for me" when the energy in the room takes over your more logical faculties. I wonder how many antiques are purchased for no other reason than the crackle of excitement in the air. Antiques sell in the first moments that might have been passed by in the quiet of a dealer's shop or on the second day of the show when all is also quiet. In other words, doing our best as collectors can mean waiting instead of buying.

The realm of what I know about what I know (let's say *cognition* or *reasoning*) is another source for the energy I feel. Dealers save items for this very show, one of the best of its type. I am filled with the realization that I will be offered antiques of quality. I know a few very precious antiques will show up here for the first time, pulled out of some dealer's hidey-hole to be offered to panting collectors at just this right moment. In other words, at the cerebral level I know this is an exciting special opportunity. Naturally the understanding energizes me and disposes me to seek and buy. Just knowing what major dealers will be there and studying the advertisements for pieces on sale adds to the excitement. Color photos of booths from the previous year's show have the same effect. Collectors are being groomed by these and other stimuli to yearn, to lust, and to buy.

Have I ever bought something at a crowded show with mobs of people around? I have. Sumpter Priddy's book, *American Fancy: Exuberance in the Arts 1790-1840* (2004) had been on the market for a while and when I read it and it validated my interest in painted furniture and other pieces. At a show I saw a painted Vermont trunk and liked it. The dealer was willing to deal. I bought it on the spot.

An Exercise in Style and Connoisseurship

At first look, one sees a rather plain wooden trunk with rounded top. The attraction of the piece is all from its paint – movement, flow, swirls, and design. It looks alive. The trunk is larger than many painted Vermont boxes. Difficult to put on a table or highboy because of its size, it sits on the floor under a window in our home. Texture is smooth.

The color has softened over time. It is not nearly as vivid as the like-new painted Vermont box I saw in 2016, though they are both from the same era. A trunk is a trunk. I assume it is well made. These pieces were not signed and getting a history of ownership is rare. The trunk shows wear near the hasp, has a few cracks on the top, and has expected signs of paint wear on the top. The fact it is also painted on the back is more unusual and speaks in its favor. It looks pretty, a typical Vermont painted object.

It is not rare. Despite the "pop" of Vermont paint, it fits comfortably with other objects in our collection (we have color everywhere). I found it reflected *American Fancy* well. It costs more when bought than it would today. The dealer rated it a 7 on a 1 to 10 scale, and I agree.

Compromises. I made several compromises. Size is one. I preferred a somewhat smaller painted box but none was available. Condition was another issue but its less-than-perfect surfaces lowered the price enough that I could afford it. We are not passionate about nor collectors of Vermont painted boxes. If we were, upgrading now would be possible, but we have decided to live with the trunk and enjoy it.

℃

In brief, how we perceive a situation (taking into account all the various stimuli I have looked at – anticipation, our expectations, the crowd, and so forth) translates into energy. No wonder that it is so important at rock concerts, athletic events, and yes, antique shows and auctions.

The doors will open on the second day of the New Hampshire Dealers Show in about five minutes. Three or four collectors and I mill around. In 2018 a record second day crowd, 25 people, waited for the show to begin, so the small numbers here now are not out of order. Yesterday was exhausting for both dealers and collectors, partly because of the sheer size of the invasion. The day was long but for many, fulfilling. Today everything is different. The floor is almost empty. Many dealers are not in their booths yet. I see a number of pieces that I missed seeing yesterday because of the crowds. The air is almost somnolent. The pace is slow. As usual, walking about, I am surprised antiques I loved a day before were still there, unsold. A few will sell today but there is no energy in the room. As Dinah Washington sang: *What a difference a day makes, twenty-four little hours.*

Waiting to enter on the second day of the New Hampshire Dealer's show (and yes there is a third day I have never attended) there are no buyers to "mirror" excitement. To be blunt, a lack of energy is bad news. Here is a dealer talking about a show:

> But of more interest was the sensation that there was no real desire on the part of buyers to make purchase. Here was no opening door frenzy – no buzz – no excitement on their faces. Customers appeared to stroll rather than walk with eager anticipation toward appealing items. (*Maine Antique Digest*, December 2017, p. 9-C)

Serious, clever collectors find great buys on the second or third day of an antique show when the arena is quiet and largely empty. Their inner aesthetic compass and sense of purpose guide them. At times they are to be envied, for persistence if nothing else. But the first day, with the air crackling with excitement sure is fun.

An excess of energy can lead to long waits, pushy and noisy crowds, and a more intense pressure to buy. Still there is nothing quite like it. We collectors live for and love the feeling. Energy and passion go hand in hand, and having real, deep passion is one of the critical attributes of true collectors. If you are new at collecting and first feel yourself being swept up in the moment, this may be the gateway to a lifetime commitment. Without energy and passion my life as a collector life would be desolate or at least far less enjoyable. After all, "passion will move men beyond themselves, beyond their shortcomings, beyond their failures" (Joseph Campbell).

Chapter 19

č

From the Collection of . . .
Thoughts on Human Nature

Late 18th century walnut candle box. 3"w, 7½"l, 3¼"h. Sliding top, dovetail construction, old or original finish.

You see it written on item descriptions at antique shows, in print ads and auction catalogues, and on dealers' websites – 'from the collection of . . .' or '*ex* (insert name of collector or famous dealer here).' Sometimes the item cited appeared in a beautifully printed book that displays someone's treasures. Collectors seem to find an object compellingly attractive and precious if it has resided in a renowned collection. Pieces purchased from legendary dealers, especially if deceased, seem to carry the same cachet. It set me wondering, What are the reasons for this?, What is the psychology of it all?, Why value by association?, Why is a dead antique dealer better than a live one? I abandoned the last because it led me toward all sorts of lawyer jokes.

A dealer with whom I spoke pointed out one sound reason for valuing pieces from treasured collections: Famous collectors from yesteryear had nearly everything available to them and seemingly unlimited funds. Most of the really great pieces had not yet fallen into the hands of other collectors or been cloistered in museums or been hidden away never again to see the light of day. Wealthy collectors could choose from the best art, jewelry, furniture, silver, folk art, or statuary, pieces we now find breathtaking and immensely desirable. Anything from those bygone collections should be wonderful, though some buyers (accumulators) – like William Randolph Hearst – were indiscriminate, to say the least, buying up entire castles and villas, then throwing their contents into storage for indefinite periods.

Collectors like Bertram K. and Nina Fletcher Little, Edgar William, Bernice Chrysler Garbisch, and Abbey Aldrich Rockefeller built magnificent collections. When they began buying American folk art and antiques, few people thought them worth much. These pioneers established the legitimacy of the genre, effectively creating a new collecting category. If Colonial Williamsburg were to de-accession some of Abbey's folk art collection, having a great piece from it would be an extraordinary and (possibly) stunningly costly privilege.

From a rational perspective, pieces held in these well-known early collections are unlikely to be fakes or have their surfaces enhanced, though such corruptions are not unknown. Someone buying a piece from these and similar collections can be almost certain the piece is precisely as described. Yet back in the day, even the wealthiest collectors were fooled once in a while. *Treasures on Trial: The Art and Science of Detecting Fakes (*an exhibit at Winterthur for most of 2017 and ending in early 2018) was great fun, and educational. (H. F. DuPont inherited Winterthur Farms when his father died in 1926. He established a museum and was one of the foremost early collectors in American antiques. The museum's current collection features 90,000 decorative and fine arts piece produced in America up to 1860 – furniture, paintings, prints, metalwork, glass, textiles and the like). The museum displays and extols the virtues of pieces in this marvelous collection, the exhibit some of the somewhat less credible treasures. It is our good fortune that nowadays a careful antique collector usually gets the real thing and peace of mind most of the time, but *caution* still has to be the byword.

Attending *Treasures on Trial*, we ask ourselves: Would I have been taken in by the deliberate deceptions? Keep in mind the scholarship and scientific tools for assessing antiques we now take for granted were hardly conceived when DuPont was out in the largely unexplored collector's wilderness finding what would become his treasures. Yes, some pieces were, and are, too good to be true. Still, collections begun later are even more problematic and susceptible to tinkering. Antiques generally became pricier than when the market was first developing, offering the unscrupulous more money to be made by trickery and deception. Fakes tend to play upon human desire and as more people became collectors the intensity of the pursuit for specific genres or objects intensified, and so did prices. And our world is now flat: American fakes no longer have to originate here, because other countries house talented artisans and avaricious marketers.

Other than the peace of mind generated by purchasing pieces from established collections, another valid and altruistic reason for giving credence to items from such treasure troves is that many collectors see themselves as conservators. We imagine it is our destiny and calling to protect Americana and give our heritage a good home before it vanishes. We want to give our antiques' next caretakers some sense of their history. In written documents validating our antiques (*e.g.*, appraisal lists) or through small descriptions placed discretely on them we help establish or update the pieces' provenance and attributions (who created the piece, or in what workshop or artist's studio). We produce a record that helps prove their legitimacy and even desirability. Pieces from well-known collections seem tailor-made for such devotion, though no one should dismiss the possibility of undiscovered treasures appearing, even at this late date. They do so regularly.

Provenance (generally defined as "a record of ownership of a work of art or an antique, used as a guide to authenticity or quality") has its place: Sound documentation can prove that a set of chairs as made for X by the Y shop in Philadelphia (attribution) passed through his heirs to the present owner. Such a history makes the current possessor a custodian, helps place the chairs in the context of American taste and craftsmanship, and substantially increases their value. Take this as a single but hardly unusual example: A prominent New England auction house had a Philadelphia Chippendale walnut dressing table on the block (*Maine Antique Digest*, January 2018), having a long drawer over three drawers, the center of which was carved elaborately, and ball and claw feet. Estimated in the high four figures, it sold for six times that amount. Why? Because both the successful bidder and the underbidder researched and discovered the maker's identity. Surely something so seemingly insignificant shouldn't, have such a dramatic effect, right? When a collector knows the master's hand, the item gains tremendous significance (witness the worth of a painting by Brueghel contrasted to one "from the school of").

Still, provenance and attribution are not the end-all some think. In *Provenance: How a Con Man and a Forger Rewrote the History of Modern Art* (2010) Salisbury and Sujo ask, "What makes a great piece of art?" It clearly is not always the piece itself: Picasso and Leonardo had bad days as well as good ones, some cubist paintings are more hangover than talent, at times the chisel slipped. The attribution of the work to a particular artist (though as many as 40 percent of these are in error) and its provenance (who bought, hid or stole it from whom) play a huge role in how the artwork is appreciated, discussed, and valued both monetarily and artistically. If the provenance turns out to be faked and the piece itself a fabrication, it may no longer even look or feel the same to us. Our psychology is so interesting in this regard; we confuse what we think is crucial, the source and history of things, with what they are worth.

Collectors face a danger dating back to the Middle Ages: The collectors' willingness to believe what is said or written (perhaps I should say *alleged*) opens the vista of value-by-repute, the same phenomenon that persuaded lords and emperors to pay high prices for objects because they were brought from the Middle East at great peril, a circumstance which supposedly guaranteed their provenance (a sobering fact to encourage skepticism: Constantinople had not one but two heads of John the Baptist, one brought back to Europe at great risk and incredibly valued).

> It has been . . . estimated that the great monastic houses of England were so busy forging writs in the century after the Norman Conquest that over half the surviving charters of Edward the Confessor may be spurious. No one can be sure because their forgeries are so clever . . . (Jones, M. *Why Fakes?* In S. M. Pearce, Ed., *Interpreting Objects and Collections*. [1994]. p. 93)

There is something ineffable, some aura of origin or ownership that constitutes (as immeasurable as it may be) "value." I once had a reporter in the antique world who was well versed in silver tell me that coveted Paul Revere spoons were overvalued. She would never purchase one. Instead she would purchase silver that was more finely crafted, better made. As for me, I must have a bit of the crass in me. I would love to own a Revere spoon with his engraved initials. Nonetheless, collectors often are taken in by names. Grampp (*Pricing the Priceless*, 1989) defines *aesthetics* as the qualities of an object that make it desirable to someone. Paul Revere spoons have a cachet that would be desirable to me, but there exists silver with better form, even though it may lack the requisite historical association.

No one ever seemed to ask the question: Does this thing have any intrinsic merit, apart from its alleged origin? That is the lesson the silver-knowledgeable reporter was trying to teach me. What is the piece's merit? Collectors pay premiums to own a piece from a famous collector or maker. But should a painting fetch a high price simply because a noted collector or dealer owned it? I argue, only if it is good and believe I am in the majority. Regrettably, the vote will not be unanimous.

I believe an antique's worth is part, but not all, of what we turn over, look at, and touch. What we lend to the object, emotionally and rationally, is critical. Provenance and attribution help establish the intrinsic value of the piece. But what if the history is incomplete, or forged? In the case of the chairs mentioned above, no matter their appearance or condition, flaws in their purported history would lessen their desirability. Why should this be so? The answer, in part, is that the qualities of a fine antique or piece of art do not constitute its total value. Our own reactions to the object count, sometimes a great deal. What see when we look at a piece and what we know about it, determine our feelings and thoughts as to its worth. As an aside, Renoir agreed with Grampp that whomever pays the highest price for a work or art (or antique) values the object the most.

Psychologically, an object is not what it looks like or who owned it. The patina, form, or brushstrokes are only one part of its truth. A painting "from the school of" may be equal to or better than the founder's work, but it is not the real thing. A piece of furniture undergoes wood analysis and it turns out to be British. The would-be buyer is disappointed; she wanted an American piece. No matter how it appears it is not American. The final arbiter of value is our perception of the piece that well may be based on its aesthetics. Yet it is the meaning we give to an antique that ultimately determines its desirability to us.

Then there is human nature to account for. Let me offer myself as an illustration of the subjectivity of value. In an antique world where there are C dealers, B dealers, and the *crème de la crème*, an object sold by and purchased from someone occupying the apex of the milk bottle is often considered more precious than the same piece purchased from Mr. Two Percent. Deep down, I have persuaded myself that a couple of pieces I purchased from now-deceased, well-known, "high level" dealers or that were found by widely respected pickers are somehow better than they may truly be. I still struggle to explain why I think that way: snobbery? foolishness? Also, despite knowing that even good dealers sometimes do not inspect each antique they sell in detail, I sometimes find myself trusting the "rightness" of these pieces because they came from so-and-so's atelier. I know I should depend on my own judgment. Surely misplaced confidence, even cockiness, is doubly likely if the object of one's passion came from a noted collection and was sold by a noted dealer. What I am talking about is what is called the Halo Effect: The owner's rep and credibility is transferred to the object.

We need to acknowledge that there is a difference between antique collections and "antique collections." When auction house catalogs devote abundant space to biographies of a collector and the collection's history or offer special viewings and talks regarding the pieces, they are trying to build a Halo Effect: They are trying to brand the collection as desirable, while establishing a respectable provenance. If we accept that hagiography (ahem! Literally, adulatory writing about another person), we may be biased. We may see most or all pieces in the collection as wonderful and not give them the scrutiny they deserve. Yes, some collections are iconic, their collectors famous for establishing worth and substance when none existed before. Still, the meritorious guy or gal who accumulated these pieces may not necessarily have personally possessed impeccable taste in every piece purchased. In our hearts we know that not all collected antiques can be the best of the best. Yet we often covet them anyway, at times ending up ruing our credulity. Is it that simple? If we lust after one of the average pieces, but believe it to be a gem, it may be because the notorious Halo Effect is at play. Do we lovers of the old and well-made find peace of mind, despite the shrinkage of our pocketbooks, from buying from a noted collection?

Peace of mind may at times be justified. But . . . there is also the "By-Association Effect." Each of us has a bit of the snob inside. Proudly

200

we aver that this antique came from "so and so." By asserting this we are attaching ourselves to this allegedly famous artisan (say, Paul Revere), seller (Christy's), or person (Rockefeller) in whose collection it was found. Second – or even third-hand, we take on the mantle of awe or reverence others have for them, their elevated taste, their bottomless pocketbook or their notoriety. Everyday articles from Presidents or famous movie stars can cost a fortune and that is the reason why – the right association.

We own a little candle box that illustrates the power of the By-Association Effect. We purchased it from Donald Sack of the famous Israel Sack family. Its small size and walnut construction drew me to it. Yet knowing I own something sold by one of the Sacks makes me smile to this day. I apologized when I bought it (so little!) and Mr. Sack was most gracious; my purchase would cover his motel room for the night. It sits to this day in our living room. Yes, we use it to store candles.

℃

An Exercise in Style and Connoisseurship

A candle box is just what it appears to be, a rather humble if old container that once had a day-to-day use and value. This one has a great story, a good size, and a nice old finish. It shows some wear. The walnut's patina gives it depth. Rectangular, it demands little space. It has no ornamentation and is not painted. Its dovetails are well crafted and robust.

Candle boxes were not labeled. For such a common object, finding a history of ownership would be surprising. This one is smaller than typical. Its size is harder to find but not rare, per se. We consider it a nice accessory. Despite its low-ish price and value it is special to us because of from whom we purchased it, since it provides a wonderful story. It offers a good example of how the By-Association Effect of even a utilitarian object adds to a collection's charm. And the power of stories in collecting.

Compromises. None.

In our minds something carried by the piece rubs off and implies that we share the refined tastes, life style, and character of a region, an era or someone (craftsman, artist, collector, seller, VIP). Mutter *Winterthur* in the right context and suddenly that Windsor chair is extraordinary. Say *Paul Revere* to the right collector (bashful smile; I?) and that spoon is transformed into the Holy Grail. Some years ago I remember inquiring about a tavern table from a respected dealer. I asked what would make the table a *10*? He bristled: Who was I to question the thing, for it came from a well-known collection and, of course, from him. That seemed to finish the matter. I ended up purchasing what to my eye was a better table. In that case I trusted my own judgment. I withstood the By-Association Effect. Of course this was made somewhat easier by the fact I had never heard of the "eminent" collector cited.

Yet another reason why "from the collection of . . ." has significance may be that it communicates that we are in the know, we are one of the *cognoscenti*. I think most collectors want to feel and be recognized as deeply knowledgeable about their hobby. For some collectors, artworks or antiques from noted collections may be attractive because they inspire others to recognize their taste and expertise.

One of this book's major themes: Human nature is complex. Perhaps all these motives, associations and temptations are no more than a part of our makeup. Confidence in a piece's authenticity, respect for its maker, admiration of its owner(s), trust in the seller are all good reasons for purchasing an antique. Still, we have to realize that our own psychological needs may materially warp our decisions regarding value or beauty. At times our confidence and trust may be misplaced. Our discerning eye may have a mote in it. Because of all these factors we may invest the object we want with more value than it actually has or deserves. Antique collectors – like the rest of mankind – are not rational beings at all times.

In the last analysis, the worth of an antique lies less in what it brings to us than in what we bring to it.

Chapter 20

ॡ

Red Tag or Dot Means Sold

Circa 1740-1760 pair Queen Anne push-up candlesticks, brass, English, 8¾"h. No repairs.

You've seen them hundreds of times at antique or art shows, in art galleries too – the red "sold" tag stuck in the corner of painting, half visible inside a drawer, stuffed into a crevice on a weathervane. More subtle and some might argue classier is the red dot. The hope of many antique dealers is that the good old days return and sales take off, with red dots and tags multiplying like Tribbles in "Star Trek." But have you ever thought about what happens to behaviors and attitudes when the sold signs appear. What is the psychological consequence of knowing something has been sold? How does it affect the antique, the dealer, and the collector?

Marketers and those in retail sales have used colors as signals for a long, long time. The color red transmits energy and passion, signals danger, tells us to stop. Everyone can see a little red dot and every collector knows what it means. It does not necessarily suggest you should stop shopping. Rather, the sales sticker tries to give you the message, "pay attention," or "stop and admire," or "stop and think that you could have owned me."

The red sold tag or dot in a dealer's booth reinforces the notion that an antique has been put out by someone who has a refined eye, good taste, and fair pricing. Yes, those are a lot of message for one little pieces of cardboard or vinyl to bear, but the whispers are in our heads and hearts;

we have been trained over time to jump to exactly those conclusions. Somehow we come to imagine that the item and maybe the ones around it deserve closer attention. A little field of red dots in a booth may attract a group of collectors looking for competitive prices and ready to bargain. It also signals that people are buying, so if you see something you like you had better consider acquiring it before it, too, is decorated with a red dot.

Apparently in the art world having the red dot mark an item as sold has a long history. It has been used in galleries for decades, perhaps more than 75 years past. Obviously and for good reason no one has yet written a history of such use, though rumors of some sort of conventional color system abound: It is said yellow dot means "hold," just as in the art world it marks the piece as on reserve for 24 hours. In all my years at shows and auctions I have never encountered one of these mythic daisies, though that does not mean they are delusional.

The red tag or dot is rarely of a size or in a location to call too much attention to itself. You can still view the piece that sold. I had one dealer tell me that some collectors become angry if an item is not clearly marked as having been sold because they resent being emotionally drawn to an antique before finding they cannot purchase it. There are limits: A conspicuous red tag is tacky and borders on shameful braggadocio. A tasteful little red dot sends the need message while blaring that you missed out on a fine collectible. If the dealer is working with a partner, the dot keeps him from a fatal gaffe: persuading an eager collector to buy a piece that, alas, someone else already owns, a blunder that smirches reputation and engenders ire at the same time.

Experienced collectors read the sheer number of red dots as a measure of how healthy or slow the market is and how well a particular show is doing. If you had walked the entire show and several pieces of painted tin had red dots (I am looking a few years back) you knew the genre was selling well. Knowledgeable readers of a show's entrails – er . . . dots and tags – can even spot trends, or so they claim.

So you are attending a prestigious antique show in Connecticut. Being a fanatic, you have waited in line for hours and are near the door when it opens. Now you walk in and there is a dealer's booth, 10 minutes after the show's opening, already sporting a rash of red dots. His success could be no more than the result of a collector or two who knew what the dealer was bringing in advance and who were familiar with his wares and prices immediately snatching up the best pieces or the biggest bargains, maybe both. Lots of collectors do know dealers' specialties and the veterans have some idea of the quality of the items likely to be in the dealer's collection. Gravitating to one or two sites as soon as the show in hopes of beating the competition to the hardware is both wise and common. When I attend a show, like other collectors, I have sussed out where the booths I want to visit are located and made a calculated decision on where to look first.

It could also be that the dealer let possible buyers know what he was bringing either by word of mouth or in a supplement in one of the widely read antique publications. Now and then a dealer may have saved items for the show but told privileged customers about them. A buyer may have said, "I'll take it" days or weeks before the show opened. Sales such as this may not be fair and even break rules set by the show's promoter. But they not only have the virtue of a guaranteed sale, they let the seller start the day with a red tag in sight: free advertising. Hopefully such chicanery is rare. At times, collectors are exposed to items the dealer is saving for the show but has advertised, at which point he tells them; "Truth in advertising will not let me sell this piece before the show's opening bell. First to the booth can purchase what he wants." Again, the dealer gets a quick, sure-fire sale but maybe a little more ethically.

If a red dot is affixed to a piece you have been lusting after for some time your reaction may be disappointment, depression, anger, and having a heart-to-heart talk with the antique god or goddess of your choice. If the sold sticker is not on an item you love and absolutely must have, I advise you to stifle your behavior. Still, the sold marker always makes me pause, even when I am following on-line auctions of antiques. I play a game with sold items. I ask myself a variety of questions: If I had unlimited funds, would I have purchased it? Can I understand why someone purchased it at all – what do they collect? Would I have purchased the piece years ago? What must the home of the person who bought it look like? I almost always conclude that antique collectors are as diverse as snowflakes. In more fatigued or cynical moments I might add, "There's no accounting for taste."

Red dots also help me empathize with the travails of dealers. If there are few or no red dots and a booth does not look rearranged I sometimes feel sorry for the dealer. Why? Because if pieces are moving (being sold, sometimes literally taken off the floor), in the marketplace a dealer may shift what is left, giving prominence to one or another piece, hoping that will enhance the attractiveness of the whole display. At other time the lack of sold items makes me fret for fate of my hobby. When dealers at first-rank shows look as if they are barely covering costs, I worry about the future of the avocation I have enjoyed for so long. (Despite the lamentations that there are too few new collectors, when I look at the number of auctions of American antiques and the percentage of items sold I ask myself, where is all that stuff going? and I wonder whether the critics are not excessively pessimistic. But I digress).

Of course not all items that sell at an antique show have the red sold tag or dot. I know a dealer who has at least one customer who insists any item he buys immediately be hidden from view (thank goodness this picky person collects smalls). Does he fear someone else will offer more, even though a deal has been made, or that it will be stolen? Or does the buyer believe the item is somehow "fresher" and more desirable if kept out of sight? Other customers want to possess the antiques they buy immediately. They take them away, perhaps to touch, hug, love and cherish, immediately toss it in their vehicle, or perhaps to bring to the show's shipper.

Once in a while, collectors buy an antique only to see a better example at another booth or conclude they have acted rashly, so they return and ask if they can un-buy the piece. "Will you take the red dot off of it? I am so very sorry, I feel so badly, but I have decided it is not for me." It should be transparent that any such take-back is definitely not required, although the dealers I know typically do so. Whether or not such a plea succeeds depends on the good will of the seller, and most dealers have a copious amount. From the dealers' point of view, good will notwithstanding, this sort of item swapping carries a faint odor of questionable behavior on the buyer's part.

Let us assume your collection is a nice one that you like. To top it off, you are in your unbiased opinion a mature, levelheaded, tasteful shopper. You find something you really want at a show and purchase it. As you write out your check or wait for your receipt, the red dot is there to tell passing collectors the piece you bought is a good one (at least to you). Others in the area pause to compliment the piece. How do you respond? I can tell you how I reacted recently. I had just purchased a pair of Queen Anne candlesticks that I thought really popped. I was immensely pleased that other collectors looked at and liked them and figured that they probably could have sold a couple more times had I not wisely snapped them up. I was fascinated by the fact that they were pushups (had ejection devices). While I did not need validation from others the compliments felt good and I accepted the plaudits with becoming modesty. On the inside I was aglow with my triumph, outwardly cool and modest. Could anything be better? As I have said in the past, we collectors are complex.

℃

An Exercise in Style and Connoisseurship

These brass candlesticks (call them sticks) are of a good height and in excellent condition (they need a polishing now, but it is impossible to keep them shiny). They have a ruffled hexagonal base. The bobeche (candle socket where the candles sit in the stick) also has a ruffled base. Together with the stem with its turnings, the eye sees curves and motion. The base is proportional to their height.

Such candlesticks were cast using molds. Molten metal was poured into the form. Once cooled and hard, the casting was removed and the brass given a final finish by hand. Their three parts (base, each half of the stem, and socket) required soldering. On this pair the soldering is done so well that you cannot see seams on the stem.

The ejection mechanism, used to push out the stub of tallow, is located on the side. The previous candle stub had to be ejected before a new candle could be inserted. The mechanism is rudimentary, practical and straightforward. I like the side pushup's appearance and deliberately sought a set with this mechanism.

Queen Anne candlesticks are less angular – one might say softer in appearance – than Victorian ones and dress up a collection. Few are marked or documented. Brass (formed of copper and zinc) is a serviceable alloy – easy to work with, beautiful when polished. While some brass candlesticks were American made, most originated in England – Birmingham had a cadre of specialized tradesmen to make them. Then they were important in everyday life but few collectors use them for lighting. Still, once in a while Sandy and I illuminate the house with candles; then the antiques look different in a very pleasant way.

As the picture shows, the sticks have a softened appearance. When polished they look almost new. Our overall evaluation focused on their bases and ejection mechanisms. Their height fits a candle stand well (we would want taller ones for a large dining room table). They cost less now than what we paid. Purchasing them was an easy decision.

Compromises. None. Good scale. The ejection mechanism makes them a bit unusual and they are in excellent condition.

There are occasions when someone sees an item with a sold tag on it and asks the dealer if the person who bought it would be willing to sell the piece (at a profit of course). While this has never happened to me, I wonder how I would respond. It never hurts to ask the dealer if the new owner might consider selling. How much more would it take for me or other collectors to sell something they liked enough to buy? If the item is common it might be an easy decision. But what if it is hard to find in that condition, with that surface, in those dimensions? Someone else would have to love it a great deal (and pay a lot more) to make selling worthwhile.

The goal in the antique world is a win-win. A red sold tag or dot confirms that the dealer's eye was good, that the risks the dealers took in purchasing the piece have been validated. A collector valued the piece enough to purchase it. The red sold tag or dot is not only an indicator of income for the dealer and a piece being added to a collection, it symbolizes success for both. It is the elementary school gold star, the mark of a job well done!

So there you have it: the psychology, power, and nuance of that red marker on an antique. It is visible but subtle. Their number and when they appear can send many messages. Your reaction to a red tag or dot may be dejection; lack of one can lead to glee. If you buy something and leave it in the dealer's booth, it is informative and educational to monitor the reactions of fellow enthusiasts and your emotional response. Now and then, you may even find another collector who wants to purchase an item you just have just bought, giving you a profit. May that red dot in the future result from your buying an antique you have searched for and long coveted.

Chapter 21

ç

The Devil's Dictionary of American Antiques

*Hepplewhite birch one drawer stand, circa 1790-1800. 18¾"w,
17¾"d, 29"h New England. Tapered legs, beaded drawer, signs of
early red wash. Old brass pull.*

*Federal cherry 2 drawer drop leaf table, circa 1810-1825. 18¼"w
x 15¾"d top, 8¾" leaves, top extended is 33¼" x 18¼", 29"h.
Refinished with nice dark appearance.*

The dictionary words you find below all define aspects of Americana.
If you are a collector in other areas, I hope what follows gets you thinking
about the foreign (to others) lexicon you take for granted. The truth:
Every specialty has its own private language – business, law, politics,
the sciences, antiques. Sometimes the intricacies of a profession demand
words not in common use. Scientists mutter about "cosines," attorneys
about resolutions settled "with prejudice," actors about "panning shots."
And this argot is all but demanded by the individual's field. Words become
a way of asserting membership in a group, a way of belonging.

Language in the form of jargon provides inclusivity. "I know and
you do not." It forms a barrier between those who are "in" and those who
are "out" between the washed and unwashed (originally a theological
distinction, not a sanitary one.) See how specialization can spill over into
everyday conversations.

We who practice the American antiques' collecting hobby, custodians for the old and precious (at least to us) are no exception. Our language helps define us as members of the *cognoscenti* and may justify the sums we pay for antiques. Speaking plainly has no place here. In the world of antiques, collectors sometimes have to fight through the terminology to get to the truth. "Damn It! Is the piece any good or not? Answer the question!" Nonetheless, do not assume that the specialized terms of antique collectors have the same meaning, user to user. Sometimes accidentally (and, unhappily, sometimes not) seemingly common terms can be used deceptively.

So what is the vocabulary of the antique world? And what do all these fancy terms mean, literally and figuratively? To a neophyte in the antique world they start as gibberish and sometimes even the amply informed end up feeling a bit baffled.

What follows attempts to answer those existential questions (the language of auctions is another world entirely. Perhaps another time). If any of the terms defined herein do not call up a clear picture for you, simply Google the word or phrase and you will find pictures aplenty.

As an aside, at a time when the collecting population for Americana is shrinking, the very particularity of our appreciation, as reflected in terminology, may be one reason a younger audience avoids the hobby. Witness the extraordinarily popular *Antiques Road Show*'s unceasing chant about "patina." Yes, great Granny's Windsor chair could have been worth thousands but some hack refinished it, leaving its value a lump of half-dissolved milk paint on a patch of newspaper. Have you watched the "what the hell" look on the faces of the owners? "You mean getting rid of the dirt, the rust, the corrosion robbed me of my inheritance?" Well, yeah. "So old grungy stuff is precious?" That's a more difficult question to answer. Leave the "it depends" to someone with more foot speed than you or I have.

Meanwhile, let's look at some of our jargon. I borrow from the satirical thesaurus, *The Devil's Dictionary*, originally published in 1906 as *The Cynic's Wordbook*, written by Ambrose Bierce, an American author and journalist. The dictionary contains Bierce's witty and satirical spins on many common English words. Let's give it a try for the antique world. Have fun.

A Find – Most people think of "find" as a verb – to locate, discover, notice, or learn. But in antiques a find is a noun. It is a piece that is especially valuable to the collector, or an item located in an unexpected place, or a valuable piece that is priced as if it is much more common. A find can be an antique that a collector has been seeking for years, or a piece that completes or is the crown jewel in a collection. It could be an antique in a group shop that sells mostly dross, where no one had any right to expect it to be. It also can be an antique that is signed and rarely found, or signed and that enables the attribution of other, unsigned works to a painter or craftsman, often after they have existed in anonymity for some time. So a find is special, but in many different ways. Dealers and collectors are excited about finds, both intellectually if it furthers research or fills in a blank (now we know who made those clocks), and emotionally. "My goodness, I have looked for years for this Windsor bench in a small size, and this one is in great shape with original surface. To heck with the cost." A find equates to Archimedes' *Eureka* (when he discovered how to tell his king whether the crown was made of gold or baser metals) but few antique dealers or collectors run naked through the agora when they discover a find. But you are welcome to do so.

A Good Buy – This term is included because it is so very tricky. For once it means what it does everywhere else. The fact it has no obscure attributions or usages makes it easy to search for hidden meaning. A good buy may be a find. After years of looking you finally found the last piece in a group of painted tin made by a known shop in Maine. The price may be high but not exorbitant. Write the check, higher price be darned. It is worth it to you. Lust and form make the price a good fiscal deal.

Most of the time a good buy means what that you purchased something for a fair price, perhaps under what is considered market value. In other words, you were shrewd, or lucky, or haggled the dealer to within an inch of his death. When dealers speak of "buying well," such as "I bought well at the auction" I understand that to mean that they acquired merchandise they have a good chance of making a decent profit on. The goods were cheap or reasonable. So in this case, perhaps a good buy was a nice chest of drawers (a case piece) you got reasonably indeed.

Antique – "You're kidding me," you're thinking. Everyone knows what an "antique" is. It's an object more than 100 years old. It's an object found at antique shows or in dealers' shops. It's a collectible object with value because of its age. Tell that to collectors of late who buy high and seem to sell low. Yet even if the trinket sold low it has some value, simply less than when originally purchased.

Some hold that antiques must be made prior to 1830, when the age of mass production began. It's an heirloom. It certainly is not something outdated. Many Windsor chairs beat Ikea hands down for comfort. And many Windsors were made and still exist. They vary in surface, form, rarity, place of manufacture, and the like. But they are all antiques. But antiques cannot be too old or they become "antiquities," made and found in ancient times. So if you say that your granny had an antique potato masher (and you are technically correct) you are saying it is at least 100 years old. But what most folks mean is that granny used it when they spent time in her kitchen when little. And it often has emotional value to them because of the memories it evokes.

Some people would argue that an antique is an object that is not too common. The key is the definition of "common." Go to a series of antique shows and you will probably begin to beg to differ with this characterization – painted boxes everywhere, for example. Some items seem all too common, at least when aggregated with other antiques. And even if an antique is common it may still have some value, financially, emotionally, and historically. According to the "not too common" school of thought an antique is something your grandparents had that was passed down to your folks and you (if you wanted it). Perhaps an antique is what a vetting committee at a show says it is. It's . . . oh you get the point. Complicated, isn't it?

Antiques have value to someone. They may not be rare. They may not be lovely. They may have little if any utility nowadays. But someone prizes them, treasures them, has researched them, and wants to own them. I think of painted tin. Not terribly useful today, but it was in its day. It became "hot," desired, and then integral to many antique collections. The research began and we learned the styles that identified what shops made and painted them and where the shops were located. Painted tin was now established in the antique world. And if we are talking about language, the black background on painted tin is called *asphaltum* because it is derived from asphalt. Sheesh.

Collectibles become antiques when they age enough. But there are genres that are not 100 years old (so we cannot call them antiques, can we?) that have great value. Mid-Century modern furniture comes to mind although I recently read its value is declining. So perhaps collectibles are objects that are somewhat old but more expensive in cost than others of like kind their same age. There are even "tomorrow's antiques." Wrap your head around that phrase. And the "New Masters" (artists).

Another operational definition. An antique is an object that appears on the television show, *Antique Road Show*. This of course means 1930s jewelry, 1950s paintings, toys from the 1920s, and the obligatory piece of pottery. Perhaps they need to rename the show.

The United States Supreme Court once struggled to define pornography but one judge famously said he would know what it was when he saw it. *Voila*! You know something is an antique when you see it, hold it, and decide it is so. Of course lots of people think of old objects as junk. Antique collectors take great umbrage and point to new objects as junk. The junk war is never ending.

Beaded or Beading – such as a beaded drawer front or a beaded door. I have also seen the term *cock beading*. No trick here. Beads are round so this jargon must have something to do with incised or carved round "something." Right? Wrong! Or sort of. A drawer with a pull can provide little depth or interest to the front of a chest of drawers or table. Gluing a piece of wood around the drawer, protruding slightly with a rounded edge, gives it depth. It looks as if the drawer front was rounded or actually carved to create the depth if one did not know that the cock beading was attached. The bead is mitered on all sides and glued onto the drawer. The drawer ends up with a rounded edge on all four sides. The flat drawer surface is a bit recessed. A nice look. Instead of glue a craftsman can incise a groove to give the appearance of depth (see the photograph of the one-drawer stand in this chapter).

A bead is a visual detail. But if the drawer front is veneer it also serves to protect the veneer. Beading is a sign of craftsmanship and is not necessary, but it can protect the integrity of the flat surface. In essence, cock beading is a piece of molding on the drawer. You will sometimes find cockbeading surrounding the flat inserts on a paneled door. Thus a bead in carpentry or joinery is so molded or applied as to project beyond

217

a surface. As best as I can determine "cock" means, "to stick up," perhaps the erect feature of a cock's comb. But how we get from barnyard animals to drawer fronts is beyond me. Kind of sexual too. I was unable to find the etymology of either the term "bead" or "cock beading" that makes sense when applied to our discussion. The term *bead* dates to the 1590s, a drop of liquid but ultimately from prayer (the beads [bid] of a rosary) But imagine feeling like you are "in" if you were at an antique show and turned to someone accompanying you and asked them to take a closer look at the beading on the drawer. Nice feeling to be "in."

I hope you are sticking with the special language of antique collectors, or at least some of it. Remember, it serves two purposes: First, it allows traits of collected materials to be quickly and accurately identified. Second, it serves as a badge of membership in the broad club of experts. Let's look at some more terms.

Bowfat – *Maine Antique Digest* had pictures from an antique show of a South Carolina cupboard or "Bowfat." I had never heard the term before. I learned that in the book, *The Churchill Family in America*, there is reference to a bowfat cupboard. Bowfat is derived from the English *buffet* or *buffit*, and is a corruption them; it refers to cupboards of various styles including dining room "buffets" and corner cupboards. It may be a built-in or a freestanding sideboard and is used for the display of china and plate. You may have grown up with or are now living with a bowfat cupboard and have never known it. Now you know.

Brown Furniture – Such a simple term, and so deceptive. Hey, we all have seen and owned brown furniture: varnish- and stain-glazed pieces, dining room tables, commodes, chairs. But the brown cannot be due to paint or a wash (jargon again, diluted paint). As they age varnish, shellac, or wax surface of unpainted or unwashed furniture becomes a rich dark brown, usually but not always. The top of an unpainted piece may have been scrubbed over and over, making this surface quite pale, even whitish. And some woods bleach in the sun and actually lighten. Poplar wood when refinished has a greenish tinge, unless of course you use oxalic acid or a similar compound to prevent the green when refinishing it. But collectors talk not of tan furniture, nor greenish. Well, most brown furniture looks brown.

ℰ

An Exercise in Style and Connoisseurship

Here are two pieces of brown furniture. The one-drawer stand has remnants of red wash still visible. Other examples of brown furniture are pictured throughout the book. I chose these pieces because they are so different, one to the other, and because both are average, at best, in aesthetics and quality. The birch table has good proportion with its tapered legs. At least it is birch (a step up from pine). The beaded drawer (notice the incised line in the top also) is a nice touch of craftsmanship. The brass pull looks nice but may not be original. The top just sits there, nothing special about it. Traces of red wash enhance a worn piece but if the red wash really "popped" it would improve markedly. It shows wear. Not rare or beautiful. A collector would not expect history of ownership or a craftsman signature on either table.

This is a simple table with nothing special to call attention to it. At least it is not shiny (my wife and I do not like shiny surfaces, whether new or refinished). We bought it a long time ago and have never been motivated to upgrade. I do not know why. The table today would cost next to nothing. This is a good example of collectors living with what they have.

Compromises. Most red wash gone, pull, craftsmanship, and patina.

The second table in cherry is a bit later (Federal period), refinished with a dark appearance but shiny. Removing the shine would benefit the table markedly in our opinion. Nice grain on the top and drawer fronts. Drawer pulls fit the piece (are they original?). Turned legs on a better example would taper more and probably have sharper and more bulbous forms. It might accurately be called functional, but again there is nothing special about it. Nice but that is all. We purchased it when we needed bedside tables. Again, we have simply lived with it.

Compromises. No paint or ornamentation, a finish not to our taste, not top quality. It has an equal or somewhat nicer appearance than the birch table, the finish notwithstanding. Another good example of collector inertia. It has no compelling story or history. I do not believe we even notice it anymore.

Bulbous – In the world outside antiques "bulbous" means something fat, swollen, bulging, round or rotund, such as a bulbous nose. To call something bulbous is not to point to a positive attribute, since visions of overweight and bloated things come to mind. The term originates in something growing from a bulb and bulbs are round or rotund typically. Think of W. C. Fields' nose, not a pretty sight.

But if someone tells you that they want to show you a Windsor chair with great bulbous turnings you are probably about to see a really good example of the genre. Bulbous in the antique world, especially as applied to Windsor furniture, means robust. The legs are not sticks, or sticks with small, insignificant "reels" between rounded parts of a leg. Whether "ball," "ball and ring," "bamboo," or "baluster" I think of bulbous as meaning sharply defined, vigorous and typically showing rings that are crisp. Tracy, a well-known Windsor craftsman from the 18th century, is known for the sharp appearance of his chair legs and wonderful bulbous turnings. (See the Tracy Windsor chair legs shown in Chapter 3.) The turnings not only are swollen but they appear so because the reels (narrow parts of the leg) are smaller and the rings are finely executed. They exist in perfect harmony. "Bulbous" is positive, so there. The bannister back chairs pictured in Chapter 17 have bulbous front stretchers.

Bullet-Shaped – Shapes are tricky. People think in modern terms. So "bullet-shaped" conjures up pictures in the mind's eye of bullet-shaped trains for example – fast, aerodynamic, very modern. Everyone knows a bullet is cylindrical with a tapering end, dangerous too. But we are talking antiques. Stop and think. What shape did bullets used to be? Ah, correct: round. Bullet-shaped – such in a bullet-shaped teapot – is spherical like an old lead bullet. Many silver teapots are bullet-shaped. Know things like this and you are on the inside of the antique world, not outside looking in.

Cabriole Leg – A leg on a piece of furniture that usually (but not always) has the following attributes. The leg is shaped in two curves; the upper arc is convex, while lower is concave; the upper curve always bows outward, while the lower curve bows inward; with the axes of the two curves in the same plane. Whew! To simplify one would say that the knee curves outward and the ankle turns inward – a doubly curved leg. Yes, furniture legs have "ankles" and "knees" so the cabriole leg is another example where lingo describes lingo. It rolls off your tongue and identifies you as someone who is an antique collector, or at least knows the nomenclature for furniture. There is a great deal to learn. But notice if you know what a cabriole leg is, you can accurately picture one in your mind's eye. The walnut table pictured in Chapter 13 has cabriole legs.

Based in antiquity the cabriole leg emerged in 18th century European and American furniture. My understanding is that the term was originally used to describe the legs of four footed (and therefore, four legged) mammals, especially ungulates, such as goats. It derives from the French *cabriolet*, to leap like a goat. In America it is found on Queen Anne furniture, originally imitating the English Queen Anne style. Now if you know your history you know that Queen Anne ruled from 1702-1760, so the style became popular during her reign but continued after her death. There is early and late Queen Anne furniture, for example. It is most often associated with the Queen Anne pad foot, a nice thick pad being most desirable (not worn down, it gives the piece that little extra lift). To be perfectly honest, such a pad also is found on Chippendale furniture while the Queen Anne foot now often lacks a pad and instead sports a ball and claw. Of course cabriole legs vary in thickness and grace. They are fashioned from a solid piece of wood, no laminates for them.

Crackle Finish – Most people know that "crackle" is the noise a fire makes as wood pops and expands. In that context to crackle is a cognate for sputter, hiss, or sizzle – short, dry, sharp sounds. Crackle has another definition, however. It is a finish of cracks in painted, varnished or glazed surfaces – wood, ceramics, or glass. A crackle finish is very desirable on wooden surfaces such as tables or tall case clocks. It is easy to get a reproduction with a smooth, new finish but what is the point of that if one is an antique collector? I think of a crackle finish as a hallmark of high country (defined below) furniture, for example. There is a wealth of videos and descriptions of how to put a crackle finish on new furniture to make it look old. And how to put it on old furniture to perhaps replace a "less desirable" finish, and, therefore, decrease its value, if the replaced finish was original. There we go, the world of copying the antique look or faking it. I find a crackle finish, if not too far gone, to be inviting and I can only imagine that a 200 or 250-year-old piece of furniture must be pleased as to how it looks. Once one knows the language of antiques, one does not gasp and shake one's head in dismay at a piece with a crackle finish. One oftentimes is delighted and labels it for what it is. You are "in."

Ephemera – This definition is well placed in the dictionary since "foxing" follows. You will understand soon enough. I saw a definition of ephemera once: objects that are used or last for only a short time. Actually, ephemera is the plural of "ephemeron." (I have never seen the word used in the singular in the antique world, but I digress.) You could become a member of the Ephemera Society of America. Ephemeron literally refers to something that lasts only a day, such as an insect with a short lifespan. On its website the Society states that ephemera "refers to minor transient documents of everyday life," ones that were expected to be discarded. But the definition has been refined over time; "transient" has been deleted from the definition and paper has ascended as a crucial element. After all, a map can be 150 or 200 years old. If it is printed, and even if it was meant to last, it is ephemera. What is now collected has not lasted a short time at all. Banknotes are ephemera. Even they were not printed to be saved or preserved for any great length of time. They were to be used and what happened to them after that, happened.

But the definition is tricky. Books are printed on paper, and not necessarily meant to last for decades. But books are not considered ephemera. They are considered – ready for this? – "books." But items smaller than books such as pamphlets, leaflets, and brochures, are ephemera.

The correct question is, "What is a short time?" The answer: "longer than you think." One generally thinks of paper as having a limited lifetime. Ephemera are typically written or printed – think broadsides, sheet music, greeting cards, maps, movie posters, magazine covers, postage stamps, ticket stubs, party invitations, package labels, and postcards. If you have now concluded that antique collectors are crazy folks who will collect anything and everything under the sun, you are correct.

Foxing – Well, it must be a verb, like running or walking. Antiques with fox hunt scenes painted on them? Foxes are known to be sly so perhaps a good deal or faking something. To fox is to baffle or deceive. Or something to do with animals and antiques. These suppositions are perfectly logical and almost entirely wrong. Foxing is not a verb. Foxing is a blemish, or more accurately a bunch of blemishes, on paper, part of the deterioration of old paper such so that it gets spots on it and browns. Ephemera get foxing, books too. Paintings on paper, also. The spots are typically round, the edges of the spots blurred.

The stains sometimes have a reddish-brown-orange color, so perhaps the term is related to the color of a fox. The basis for the term is difficult to pin down. It certainly and negatively affects the value of any antique made of paper. Fascinatingly, foxing does not affect the integrity of the paper itself. While there are theories as to the cause of foxing, as best as I could figure out there is no definitive cause. A fungal growth or perhaps the paper reacting to iron oxide or copper in the pulp or rag from which the paper was made may cause foxing. High humidity also has been implicated. The consensus seems to be that foxing is a form of mold, so store your old books in a cool, dry location. If you have ever seen a painting or piece of paper with foxing, you know it is unsightly. It can be remedied, but the success of such efforts is not guaranteed. Restoration can damage the paper, ink, or paint.

At this point you may know more than you wanted. But if you are not an antique collector you can certainly fake your way into most inner circles. Still, there is more we need to know before you pull off the ruse of the century by pretending to be a long-time collector.

Highboy – A "boy" is not specifically an antique term (it is roughly related to the French *bois,* meaning wood) so a highboy is literally "tall wood." A highboy is a tall chest of drawers on four legs if Queen Anne or Chippendale. Some highboys that are William and Mary have six legs. The presence of legs is the key; a highboy does not sit on a base. So a highboy would not have a bracket base (more jargon here), or an ogee bracket base (even more lingo) nor would it be a chest of drawers that sits directly on the floor. In addition, a highway is not a chest of drawers perched on a frame, even if it has legs.

The Brits might call a highboy a "tallboy." Highboys usually come in two sections: a set of drawers is set on a lower section that if made without the top half would be called a dressing table or lowboy. The base section's top is not finished as it was built to have a set of drawers sitting directly on and above it. Cumulatively, a highboy is a wooden tall chest of drawers, usually in two parts, standing on legs. A chest on chest sits on its base with minimal space underneath, at the most a few inches. A highboy is open at the bottom, lots of room to vacuum or mop the dust that has accumulated underneath. It is lofty enough to display another object underneath – a hatbox, small blanket chest, or a wooden box.

The apex of a highboy can take many forms. Many of them have little more than a finished flat surface. On some it is elaborate, peaked, perhaps with finials or even a sculpted bust in the center. Highboys may have a fan carved in the bottom section, the top section, or both. A highboy always carries several long drawers on its upper section. It may have a center drawer with fan and a smaller drawer to either side. Sometimes there are two small drawers at the top left and right. Highboys can be an acquired taste, like single malt Scotch. I find them pretty.

High Country – Interesting term. There are no "low country" antiques even though there is low country in the likes of South Carolina. And fancier antiques are not called "high city" or even "city." These are "formal." The term "high country antiques" refers to furniture that was not made in areas following the latest fashion and style the way Baltimore, Boston, New York, Philadelphia, or Newport artisans copied trends from across the ocean or originated their own. In this case "high" indicates exceeding the common degree or measure – in other words, superior or distinguished in quality. Perhaps the antique is a perfectly formed simple piece. Think of a craftsman's attempt to replicate formal furniture or to dress up country pieces by making them from more desirable woods, with more detail. No worm holes, not beaten to death (they are not "primitives"). The best of design finish and form. High country is dressier and more formal than country but not formal per se. At the same time high country can be equally creative and as beautiful as formal pieces. Those who know, smile – they know exactly what I am talking about. This is a look and style very much worth collectors' consideration. The Queen Anne walnut table pictured in Chapter 13, the Queen Anne tiger maple candlestand in Chapter 14, and the Queen Anne desk on frame pictured in Chapter 23 are all high country pieces.

Hollowware – Well, it is hollow and it is ware, a specific type or something for sale. What is the specific type? I will use redware as an example. One form of redware is plates and chargers. The plates vary from small to large, chargers larger yet. And of course there are redware jars, pitchers, cups, banks, sugar bowls, and so forth. You would think those labels would be clear and they certainly seem that way to me. But how to readily identify that one collects, researches or has redware for sale that have depth and volume? One calls them hollowware, which has various spellings (e.g., hollowware or hollow-ware). The term provides a great example of the language of antiques, of an argot that only an insider would understand. And the term also applies to metal items that went with dishes on a table.

Lopers – This is a great term known only by experienced collectors. Lopers are the two pieces of wood one on either side of a drop-front desk that support the lid when it is lowered. Often you will find the hinges on these lids have been replaced. Someone forget to pull out the lopers and the top fell and pulled the hinges with it. If you want to give an antique dealer heart failure, start lowering the lid of a drop front desk without first pulling out the lopers.

A loper, obviously, is a person or animal that lopes or runs. That definition has nothing to do with the use of the term in the antique world. Lopers get between the desk lid (writing surface) and disaster. We all know that an interloper is a busybody or someone who interferes, a meddler, someone who intrudes. Perhaps that meaning is the basis for the term "loper." "Sliders" would seem an apt term for them but they are not called sliders. They also may be called drawer runners or drawer slips, although I have no idea as to why. Perhaps there is some physical similarity between them and the runners that support drawers. They typically have a small brass knob to hold onto when you pull them out. On a few great desks this knob can be more decorative. You can see lopers in the photographs of desks shown in Chapter 2 and 23.

To conclude, I cannot find an origin of the term loper as used in the antique world, but if you know the word and use it correctly, you are certainly in the know. An insider and special, privy to the secret language of antiques.

Marriage – You are looking at a chest on a frame, chest on a chest, secretary desk, or a highboy and it is described as a "marriage." You might initially believe this is good – to death do we part, a union made in heaven. But when one thinks of a marriage there is another component, two unrelated (well, most of the time) people coming together. And that is what a marriage is for a piece of furniture. Two pieces, usually a top and bottom that started life separately and now form a union. The wood of both parts may mesh perfectly but telltale signs such as dovetails, backboards, construction of the joints, plane marks, wood that is dark as if it has aged but not consistently so, and wood that is lighter in color where it should be dark from aging, tell an experienced dealer or collector this piece is a combination of two disparate pieces. A marriage may look fantastic and genuine, but its value is much lower than a piece that has been unified from the outset. I think of a marriage as two old pieces joined together (but not in holy antique matrimony). Some include a new piece joined to an old one.

Noggin – Pitchers of various sizes and shapes have existed for a long time, millennia. And wooden pitchers have a long history. So you would think that a wooden pitcher would be called a wooden pitcher, or perhaps a "treen" pitcher (treen is defined below). Ah, sorry, it's just not so. A wooden pitcher is a noggin. A noggin also is a small cup or mug, and a small (think a "gill") measure of drink – think a whiskey measure. Perhaps early cups were a quarter of a pint; I do not know. The term seemed to pop up in English in the late 16th century. When its use entered the antique world is unknown (at least to me). I have seen a glass whiskey noggin up for auction in Great Britain. But when I think of a noggin, I think of a wooden pitcher. There you have it. Drink anyone? Someone get a noggin. I'll get the whiskey.

Old Paint – For those of you who are Oater aficionados, old paint is self-explanatory. Oaters are the old Western movies, turned out in droves, often shot in the same locations despite different heroes or the same heroes and different plots. How many times can the posse chase the desperados through the same canyon? A great many times it turns out. Old Paint was an affectionate name for many people's horses. But that definition certainly does not apply here.

Original paint on old furniture is desirable. A Windsor chair with great form and original green or white (the rarest color) is to die for. Many Windsors are advertised, displayed, explained and sold based on the merits of paint layers – black over a red over the original green. The layers are described as "old." Layers like that on Windsors showing appropriate wear give a beautiful look. The Windsor chairs pictured in Chapters 3 and 9 both wear original paint.

But the rub is, what does "old" mean? Old paint may be perfectly acceptable and add to the piece's history and appeal. Or it may be too new and detract from that Windsor chair or bench. For example, paint put on in the 1890s is certainly old, but much different than if the Windsor constructed in 1790 was repainted in 1810 or 1820. The former detracts from the piece whereas the latter is more acceptable. Of course in Great Britain "old" can mean 1650 or even earlier. Never assume you know what old paint means unless you know the history of the antique you are looking at. Time to go repaint my side porch – hasn't been touched in a few years and the weather and sun have made a hash of it. Now that is "old" paint. My wife and I had an "arrow back" Windsor bench that had been stripped (taken down to the bare wood). We painted it 35 years ago. That paint is "old" but is not "old paint."

Piggin – A small wooden pail, can, tub, or ladle. And not just any small wooden pail but one where a stave is extended as a handle so it can be used as a scoop. You could dip into grain with it, scatter seed, slop the hogs, or use it as a cream pail. It's a "lading-can" but calling it that gets you no more understanding from those outside the antique world than calling it a piggin. The piggin was an all-purpose Swiss army knife of its time. Don't blame the current antique world for the word. Piggin may derive from the Middle English *pygyn* in the 14th century. Or perhaps it is Scottish, Gaelic (*pigean*), Irish or Welsh. I have heard that *pig*, *pigg*, and *pipkin* are synonyms for a piggin. The term originated somewhere in what we would call the United Kingdom that of course was far from united back then, and did not yet exist as a political entity. So it has a long period of use and describes a very specific object. Try bringing the term up in general conversation or after you and your friends have had a beer or two (wine will do). The response will be universal, a confused stare. And people may think you strange. You are not. You simply belong in the antique world. I guess you are somewhat strange after all.

What a wondrous language we use. And perhaps more technical and mysterious than we realize. Or perhaps simply pretentiously erudite. I shall let you decide. Let's finish our Devil's Dictionary.

Polychrome – This is one term that is relatively easy to parse. Poly means many and chrome (Chroma) indicates color. So why not call a carved piece of wood, colored? I guess that would indicate one color and perhaps not many colors. You could of course call something "many colored" but that is prosaic and not the stuff of jargon or exotic language. Of course there is Joseph and his Coat of Many Colors, or should we say his polychrome coat. You get the point.

Posnet – No one uses the word posnet anymore, well almost no one. The term is obsolete. A posnet is a little basin, a porringer, a skillet. Think of a small copper molded round cup on three legs with a handle, or a metal skillet. Both are posnets. The term comes from old French and while it may be obsolete if the term is old, why not use the original label for something in the antique world? Why not indeed?

Rare – Everyone knows what rare means – scarce, hard to find, infrequent, few and far between. But many outside of the antique world and even some within have a built-in notion that rare means valuable and thus expensive. Dealers and knowledgeable collectors know that is far from the case.

Why might an antique be rare? Well, it could be that a very expensive (and I mean expensive when it was constructed) set of eight dining chairs were ordered in Philadelphia in the later quarter of the 18th century. The patron or merchant wanted the latest design. And it turns out that the shop from which he ordered had a master carver (few and far between). That set of chairs would be rare in and of itself, and if one or two of the set of eight are missing and you find one – go buy a new automobile or add on to your house. Jackpot. It is rare and dearly priced because of its form, attribution, provenance, and beauty.

On the other hand, a piece can be unique or rare and not be worth a farthing (quarter of a penny, or one nine hundred and sixtieth of a pound sterling. Minted of bronze and first issued during the reign of Queen Victoria, it wasn't worth much, to say the least. But I am wandering again.) Rare could mean so unusually awkward or, if you excuse the term, ugly, few if any were made, and even fewer preserved. A case piece (of furniture) can be so wide, deep, or tall as to be ungainly and clearly unpleasing to the eye, but rare. I could go on but. . . a piece that is rare and worthy of stewardship will probably be a *10* in whatever genre it exists, and, therefore, beyond most collectors' pocketbooks.

Rhykenologist – Well, there is esoteric and then there is a rhykenologist. It is obvious, of course that a rhykenologist is someone who studies or collects "rhykens." You are not far from the truth. A rhykenologist collects wood working planes, the name taken from the ancient Greek *rukanĕ*, that is a wood working plane. The term certainly gives a large touch of class to the collectors who label themselves such. The fact that folks collect these planes is testimony to our interest in all facets of the antique world, including tools.

Sandpaper Painting – Well this one is easy, or it should be. It is painting painted on sandpaper, right? Nope. Nor is there abrasive from sandpaper in the paint. Sandpaper paintings are often Hudson Valley or Civil War renditions. Young ladies did much, but not all of this work, and the art form was taught in academies in the 1850s. A sandpaper painting is pictured in Chapter 1. Julia and Robert purchased it at auction.

I have read that marble particles were mixed in the paint to achieve the effect. Others describe the process as covering a drawing board with white paint and when it was not quite dry sifting pulverized marble through finely woven muslin onto the surface. Charcoal and rarer yet, pastel in stick or powdered form created the images' shapes. To achieve lighting and definition some of the board could be left untouched or the material could be rubbed away with an eraser of leather or a sharp knife. The end result is that the painting glows or shines.

Sandpaper paintings are more vital and mellow than "normal" paintings. By the mid-19th century they were sometimes called "Grecian" or "monochromatic" paintings. But as you by now have concluded, sandpaper is nowhere to be found.

Scrub Top – Surely this is a top of something that has been scrubbed. Exactly. You've defined it. Think of a tavern table used in the 18th century. It may have begun with a painted, shellacked, or otherwise finished surface. But such objects' surfaces are going to be cleaned repeatedly. What happens is that any surface disappears and the piece is left with a raw wood top. That is a scrub top. Some collectors prize a scrubbed top. It can really offset a painted or dark wood base. I for one do not like the look but appreciate what it represents, if genuine. It is easy to fake, obviously. New furniture is sold with a scrub top that is a natural wood appearance but has a finish applied to protect it.

Smalls – Smalls are antiques that will fit pretty much anywhere when one is filling a house or decorating. "But what they are cannot be as easy as that," you say, and you are correct. For example, small pieces of silver would be called "silver." And small framed silhouettes or paintings are called artwork, silhouettes or paintings. In one of Jonathan Gash's books about Lovejoy – one of the most beloved fictional antique dealers to ever exist – he calls a small a "finger," something small enough to be held in one's hand. I think of smalls as something you can buy at a dealer's shop or an antique show and easily carry away in a shopping bag or stick under your arm. Note the term easily. I am not sure that a small cannon ball that weighs a great deal would be considered a small, despite its size. Think something no bigger than a breadbox.

Smalls are not a smaller version of a "large." When looking at a child's Windsor chair one might say, "That's a really small Windsor." But that doesn't make it a small. A dwarf clock is sure smaller than a regular sized tall case one. The same is true for most salesmen's samples. Again, one knows a small when one sees one. Faberge eggs do not quality, nor does jewelry. Smalls can be truly expensive if they are wonderfully painted boxes, or firkins for example. A very expensive small box with original paint whose provenance or attribution is known can be identified becomes a "large" to some people.

Smalls typically are more modest in history and use – boxes of all shapes, kitchenware, and a thousand and one other objects that had a household (utilitarian) use long ago. Redware, spongeware, Rockingham and other small sized pottery would be defined as pottery or ceramics. On a drop front desk one might find a quill holder (one is pictured in Chapter 6), sander (used to blot the ink), a pipe tamper, and perhaps a painted tin box. They' be smalls. Are the brass candlesticks on the desk a small? Good question. Some folks would consider them brassware; just as I think as a small piece of glass as belong to the glass category, rather than a small. There is, of course, reason to differ on what one defines as a small. I would think a small toy is a toy. I would think a pincushion would be a small but perhaps to a diehard collector it falls in the sewing or textile realm. Of course this Devil's Dictionary is meant to be more fun than definitive. Attend an antique show and look at items in the cases in dealers' booths. Therein you will find many smalls. A dealer's website often calls smalls "accessories."

Smalls complete a room. A colonial room with a wooden floor, molding, and furniture would look bare without some smalls to round the edges and complete the setting. Many wonderful collections are marked as much by their smalls as by anything else. Smalls are important.

"Speaks, The Antique" – Ask a non-antique collector if antiques can talk and you will get looks as if you are out of your mind. "Of course antiques cannot talk. They are inanimate objects, after all." But collectors hear their voices. Antiques certainly speak. They tell you what was fashionable way back when, and how they evolved. A Windsor chair in the 1830s or 40s might have had dabs of gold paint (teardrops) put on its spindles, for example. (See the Windsor chairs pictured in Chapter 3.) Antiques tell you who was negligent of their needs (look for replaced hinges, replacement glass in cupboards, and so forth). They tell you how styles changed: a transitional Chippendale chair. If you listen they will remind you what marvels they are to have survived this long, and who doesn't get a ding or two along the way?

The truest sense of an antique speaking to you is one telling you, despite its size or how hidden it may be on a shelf of smalls or in a dealer's booth or shop, that "I am really good!" Once you know something about various forms and objects, aesthetics and style, the antique taps you on the shoulder. "Psst, over here." Stand in a dealer's booth at an antique show or in his shop, and feel the vibe. Eerie. Put your conscious mind aside for the moment. Observe which way you turn and what antique you walk towards. The antique most often is very good. It whispers or shouts to you.

Sure collectors at crowded shows often do a quick "walk through" or two, especially if they are looking for a piece they have been searching for forever. But I believe the bliss of being a collector is when the show thins out and you have the luxury of strolling – of simply standing, and listening. But of course, you have to be "in" to know to do that, and "in" to know what to call your behavior. As for the antique, it already knows it is speaking to you. The question is whether you hear it or not?

Tote – Most everyone is familiar with a tote bag, a bag with handles with which you carry things. They are ubiquitous at farmers' markets. But totes can be made from hardwoods, rosewood or other woods. We have moved beyond a bag I believe. A tote is the rear handle on a bench plane. Of course by now you know it cannot be called a "rear handle." There are tote screws, bolts and nuts to hold the tote to the plane. The best explanation I could find is that in 1883 a *toat* was defined as the joiners name for a handle on a plane. *Toat* is the English variation of tote and if you look at drawings of planes from the 1600s the handle is raised and looks like a carrying handle. They could be used for "toting" around the plane. We are back to tote bags.

Treen – One would think that small wooden objects, usually for domestic purposes – bowls, spoons – would be called woodenware, wooden utensils, domestic woodenware, or wooden "stuff." But no, technical language wins out. So it is called treen or "treen ware." Treen defines small domestic functional objects, made entirely of wood. Some hold the term applies only to antiques. So you would not call your new salad bowl treen ware if you belonged to this school of thought. (On the other hand, I guess you could it you wanted since there is reproduction treen ware for sale.) The term derives from the old English and modern English *tree*, think *tree-en*. My research showed that its use began about 1800. It consists of bowls, cups with stems, mortises and pestles, shoehorns, needle cases, snuffboxes, dough bowls, measuring cups, trenchers, trays, and spoons. The term does not apply to chests of drawers, tables and pieces of furniture. I have read the term does apply to agricultural wooden objects but I assume they must be small. A wooden plow would not be termed treen ware. Close-grained native trees were chosen for their wood, sycamore and beech for example. Treen is jargon personified.

Volute – A volute is a spiral scroll found in Ionic and later Corinthian columns. Now if a Windsor chair has an ear on each side of the top known as a "comb piece" or "crest rail" – a round piece of wood with a spiral carved into it – we call that a volute. The same is true for the arm of a Windsor chair ending in a carved scroll. The end of the arm is often called a "knuckle" and if the knuckle has a carved spiral incised in it that is the volute. Woodworkers have sets of tools for such carving and one can find *YouTube* videos depicting the crafting of volutes. One first has to draw where the carving will take place and then carefully carve the volute. I find it gives pieces a fancy look; I like volutes.

Phew, I'm tired and I imagine you, the reader, are also. We have come to the end of this edition of the Devil's Dictionary of American Antiques. By now you should be on your way to being an informed insider in the antique world, or at the least, far enough to not embarrass yourself. The former professor in me calls for a quiz at the end of our musings. But we will forsake one. The true measure of your learning lies in your knowing the paradoxes, and twists and turns the language of antiques takes as we discuss, define, and demonstrate that we know what we are talking about. We do, don't we?

I am certain there that I have omitted words in the antique world that are the equivalent of verbal secret handshakes. If you have some great words that belong in the Devil's Dictionary of American Antiques please let me know. It is time for me to rest.

Chapter 22

The Mystery of the Artist, Ship, and Location[1]

Circa 1855-1880 ship portrait, two-masted schooner, the 'E. A. Elliott.' American, possibly coastal New England. Unsigned, possibly attributed to William Stubbs. Oil on canvas, original frame. 23⅜" X 31⅜". Excellent condition, lightly cleaned, otherwise untouched.

As you have read, an intellectual side to collecting exists. Collectors often research what they own – where an object was made, how it was used, previous owners, craftsman or artist, other similar details. Dealers also often investigate pieces they have purchased to accurately label them, to establish their fiscal value before pricing them, or to determine the appropriate bidding level at auctions. Doing this, the dealer can provide purchasers not only an insight into the piece but a context that adds to the piece's appreciation. In this chapter I incorporate a second theme that supports the use of the intellect – giving of one's time to go (in this case sail) the extra mile. The antique I am focused on is a painting I purchased. As I looked into its origins and the nation's maritime past that inspired it, the seemingly simple picture took on a fresh life of its own.

The painting reminds me of a schooner ride my wife and I took out of Camden, Maine, while on vacation. That adventure started me researching

[1] All quotes are personal communication unless otherwise noted

the genre of coastal paintings. While this particular picture nicely comp-lements our collection, what I learned about the artistic genre has enriched my collecting life. And it still holds personal meaning recalling our time on the Maine coast. In this instance I have decided to describe the painting in the text rather than a separate "Style and Connoisseurship Exercise."

The ship (I suppose a Downeaster would say "boat;" technically she is a *coaster,* a vessel built to trade from port-to-port) is the "E. A. Elliott," a two-masted schooner. She is depicted oil on canvas, broadside, and I purchased the painting from a well-known dealer. As a teenager I read voraciously about seafaring and had fantasies of what such a life must have been like. When I first started going to art shows I was immediately drawn to paintings and prints of ships and docks. Yet until recently, in all of my years of collecting, I had somehow neglected maritime antiques. Not any longer.

The painting is a canvas size (23⅜" x 31⅜") common for the mid-to-late 1800s. Its condition is pristine, front and back. It had never been cleaned and the dealer had it lightly done after he purchased it. I learned that it has the bells and whistles associated with paintings of its genre – three flags including the American flag, several people (aboard the schooner) and detail in the background (an additional ship or two would make it perfect but it is still very nice). The perspective is excellent, the colors bright. The schooner has a sense of motion. She is a proud vessel with American spirit and she is treated as if she were a credit to all of the hard working schooners she represents. We made no compromises in purchasing her.

Of course in everyday use most coasters were not nearly so glorious – paintwork no longer bright, patched sails. And depending on cargo and caulking (how much water they took on) many rode low in the water.

But many questions about the "E. A. Elliott" were unanswered when she came into my possession. Who painted her? Who was she named for? What was her history? Where is the scene depicted in the painting? To get answers, numerous investigators were involved. Alas, no trench coats, good-looking dames, revolvers, or foggy nights. Their investigative methods included books, *New York Times'* information on ship traffic in the 19th century, the *New York Maritime Register*, data bases (e.g., Mystic Seaport's vessel registry [to locate captains, home ports, and owners and holdings]: *Connecticut Vessel*), other archives for vessel registry, local newspapers, the experts' years of experience researching paintings and maritime history, and their resolute dedication. One investigator passed me to the next. None asked for fees but I donated to their institutions – how could I not? Even at the end of their probing blind alleys and differences of opinion persist and the answers may not be as iron-clad as I would like. But we now know much more about the "Elliott" and its history than when we started. Marine paintings of this period, while appearing to be "folk art" or "primitive," were precise (but it is not uncommon to find them called "primitive" in style). Accuracy and detail were what counted.

Foremost it was an art of practicality and purpose – usually commissioned by an individual patron to record for posterity a specific vessel's likeness . . . The true ship portrait is to a vessel what a formal portrait is to a person . . . An accurate representation of a named vessel is the paramount concern . . . (Penobscot Marine Museum Seaport and The William A. Farnsworth Library and Art Museum. [1988]. *Goodly ships on painted seas: Ship portraiture*

by Penobscot Bay Artists William P. Stubbs, James G. Babbidge,
Percy A. Sanborn. Nimrod Press: Boston. p. 10, 11, 12)

These artists evinced "technical proficiency . . . a relentless adherence to the specifics of naval architecture . . ." (Granby, A., & Hyland, J., 2000). The artist who painted the "E. A. Elliott" possessed these observational and artistic skills, as did many who painted the sailing ships of that era. Hence, a definitive attribution to a particular artist is fraught with difficulty.

The difference(s) between paintings by Babbidge, Stubbs, Badger, Drew, and others can be very subtle especially when one [takes into account] . . . the range of the changes each artist evolves through within their respective careers as artists. (Alan Granby, Hyland Granby Antiques, June 19, 2016)

The dealer from whom I purchased the painting initially attributed the work to Stubbs; the brushwork, proportions and setting seemed like his. Such an attribution carried its own excitement, since Stubbs' work is not only famed but also highly valued by collectors. Many experts say he signed all his works and this painting was unsigned, seemingly putting paid to that prospect. However, David Kimball, former curator at *Mystic Seaport* and now owner of Stagecoach Gallery in Granby CT, stated that he has seen unsigned Stubbs' works and added:

Stubbs signed the majority of his work (usually in red). However, the ravages of time quite often take a toll on the condition of paintings. Signatures are rubbed off, cut off and over-painted through the years. (April 27, 2016)

Could this be an unsigned Stubbs' painting waiting to be confirmed as his work? I hoped to find out.

Two staff of the dealer who sold me the painting provided biographical information on William Stubbs (b. 1842). He was the son of a shipmaster and worked with his father before becoming a marine painter in Boston. Newman Galleries, via Roger King Fine Art, provided additional biographical information.

Born in Bucksport, Maine to a sea captain and shipmaster, William Pierce Stubbs became the master of his father's ship in 1863, a post he held for ten years. He was self-taught as an artist, painting his first ship portrait in 1871. By 1876 he was listed as a marine painter in the Boston city directory. He . . . had studios variously in Boston, East Boston, and Charlestown . . . His early paintings were genre scenes of seaside life in Bucksport, but he later became known for his ship paintings in the tradition of popular ship portraitists. Among his many early works were paintings of the whaling fleets of New Bedford and Nantucket. After 1887, Stubbs developed "melancholia," showing signs of manic-depression following the deaths of his wife and daughter. His work appeared at the International Maritime Exhibition in Boston in 1890, but in 1894 he was committed to the Worcester State Hospital. In 1899 he entered Medfield State Hospital, where he died ten years later. His works remain highly regarded today and are in the collections of many American museums.

Kelly Page (Registrar/Librarian) at the *Maine Maritime Museum* in Bath agreed that Stubbs signed all his works. She consulted a colleague with 45 years of experience who thought, "that there were some features that reminded him of Stubbs, but the style of the water was different and he had never heard of an unsigned Stubbs" (March 15, 2016). Catherine Robertson, a reference librarian, with the *Phillips Research Library* of the *Peabody Essex Museum* located in Salem, Massachusetts was a great help and compared the painting's background to the museum's signed Stubbs' work. She also opined that similarities existed but nothing definitive marked the work as a Stubbs.

Fred Murphy became the oldest investigator into the "E. A. Elliott" mystery (he is in his nineties and has been on the *Madison Historical Society* board in Madison, Connecticut since 1963). For the last several years he has worked as a volunteer in the office of Patricia Kane, Curator of American Decorative Arts, Yale Art Gallery. He offered the following:

In 19th century American maritime art, there is a specific genre called 'ship portraits' paintings' usually commissioned by builders and/or owners . . . and while much of this work is unsigned, as is your painting; there may be idiosyncrasies which point to an individual artist . . . (April 13, 2016)

Hope was still alive at this point. Nothing definitive pointed to Stubbs but here was just enough resemblance between his works and this one to keep people, even experts, guessing.

David Kimball thought the painting might have been done by Elisha Baker, (1827-1890), a Connecticut artist of the period. He worked at the same time as Stubbs and while they were not formal associates they did have contact. Baker did not sign many of his paintings. According to Antiques and Fine Arts.com:

> Though Elisha Baker's paintings are scarce, their great charm makes them highly desirable to collectors. Baker was born in New York City and grew up in Colchester, Connecticut. He went to sea in 1851. He worked as a painter from 1868 to 1880; a Marine [painter in New York], . . . he is known primarily for his paintings of ships, yachts, and steamboats. He traveled throughout New England, and is thought to have traveled to the British Isles in the 1880s. Baker died in 1890 in Orange, Connecticut . . . His works are in the collections of the New Bedford Whaling Museum and the Mariner's Museum, and the Mystic Seaport Museum. As late as 1979, only twenty-four paintings by Baker had been recorded; eleven others were subsequently attributed to him . . .

The "E. A. Elliott" painting is similar to one pictured alongside the Elisha Baker biography on AskArt. That ship's masts almost touch the top of the painting with substantial water at the bottom. His *Sloop Under Sail* and S*peranza* (Granby & Hyland, 2009, pp. 116-117) display the same feature. But are the composition, brush strokes and style of the "E. A. Elliott" those of Baker?

Pat Schaefer, Collections Access and Research, at *Mystic Seaport: The Museum of America and the Sea* compared the "E. A. Elliott" painting with two pictured in Brewington (D., 1982, MSM) and wrote:

The two paintings in our *Marine Paintings and Drawings of Mystic Seaport Museum* show lots of sky above, and no shore details at all . . . they are "attributed" to Baker. I would have to say the style does not look the same to me, but I am far from being an expert on art.

Then I heard from Alan Granby whom I had originally contacted (prior to the dealer who sold me the painting) to inquire about purchasing a different two-masted schooner painting (beyond my means as it turned out).

With some assurance I suggest that your painting is by the primitive American marine artist James Babbidge. In 1988 the Penobscot maritime launched an exhibition with a catalogue titled *Goodly Ships on Painted Seas: Ship Portraits by Penobscot Bay Artists* . . . The catalogue discusses a few of the American primitive ship portraits including Babbidge, has black and white illustrations, biographies, a list of known paintings by the artist... In 2009 Mystic seaport published a book written by my wife Janice and I called *Flying the Colors: The Unseen Treasures of Nineteenth-Century American Marine Artists*. Babbidge's painting of the three masted schooner the "Jamie Middleton" is illustrated full-page color on page 138. You will see many similarities to your picture . . . (June 19, 2016)

Relevant for our purposes is this:

The greenish-blue water and the bright blue skies with pink horizons are a trademark common to Babbidge's works. This somewhat primitive but pleasant rendering of the primary vessel and a smaller vessel in the foreground are also typical . . . . (June 19, 2016)

The "E. A. Elliott" painting has no ship in the foreground, I am uncertain about water and horizon colors and the painting is not signed or initialed. Yet paintings by James Gardner Babbidge (1844-1919) I viewed on-line often depict a shoreline. His paintings of the *Race Rock* (listed as in the manner of Babbidge) and *Frances Hatch,* for example, fly three pennants aloft in the same sequence and the black hull with gold stripe is similar to the "Elliott." Other paintings are attributed to him, so others must believe he painted without signing or initialing all of his works.

We have some biographical information for Babbidge from *Maine Antique Digest.*

Babbidge and his brothers, Frederick Warren and Alvin Judson . . . flourished into the 20th century painting the interiors and exteriors of houses and ships. . . . James Babbidge's forte was painting ship portraits. . .

The firm . . . would not only offer to paint the hull and cabins of the ship, but James would also offer to paint her portrait. The exact date of his first portrait is unknown, but we know that he first appeared, vaguely, in the 1868 directory as a 'painter of ships.'

[He] was born in Rockland, Maine, on September, 2, 1844 . . . [and] learned about the sea and ships working on the prosperous Rockland shipyards, serving for a time in the U. S. Navy during the Civil War, and later as a seaman.

He dated most of his paintings. The earliest is from 1876, *Lottie Ames* . . . the latest is from 1903. . . . [It] appears that . . . his artistic career was . . . relatively short . . .

His work is indistinguishable from his contemporaries. There are times when he evokes Stubbs. There are times when his treatment of water suggests the work of the master, Jacobsen. The fact that his style does not set him apart from his fellows, and that he frequently signed his work so diffidently, has contributed to his relative obscurity . . .

By the turn of the century, Marine maritime commerce had begun to slacken. . . . Babbidge became a postman! Then illness overtook him and for years he was unable to paint. Barely a month before he died, he was committed to the national Soldier's Home. On January 8, 1919 he died of a heart attack. (Peluso, A. J. Jr. [1986, January]. *The Other Ship Portrait Painters of Penobscot Bay.* p. 18D)

Why would this painting be unsigned? There is no definitive answer. It was not unusual for many maritime and folk art artists to leave their works unsigned. For example, in Brewington's *Marine Paintings and Drawings in Mystic Seaport Museum,* 93 Western (as opposed to Oriental) maritime paintings are from the hand of an unidentified artist.

There is a certain appealing logic to this anonymity: If the painter advertised, and some did, and the portrait was commissioned, why bother to sign? Family history would know the artist, at least for a generation or two but, more important it would have the painting itself.

As for the "Elliott," at least I ended up with a likely source. No, not Stubbs, as lovely as that would be. I have a work probably by Thomas Babbage, and I know enough about him to be pleased with the product, if not greatly impressed by his importance. And now I know something about the habits and traditions of those who painted ships' portraits.

Let us move on to another question: Who was E. A. Elliott? I thought that was a critical matter, a clue as to the ownership and origin of the schooner and its place in history. I immediately and falsely assumed that the E. A. Elliott was named after its owner. Pat Schaefer offered me this perspective after consulting with her colleague Maribeth Bielinski:

> Ships could be named for lots of people, including owners, wives of owners, other family members, etc. Or for mythical figures, places, famous people (Washington was popular), etc. . . . The Charles W. Morgan (our whaling barque) was named for one of the partners in the shipbuilding firm. So don't rule anything out. (April 21, 2016)

So the E. A. Elliott was a foundling of sorts, or so it would seem. Fred Murphy had more success in nailing down its namesake.

> I . . . Googled the name, and found nothing useful. Since most genealogy is based on wishful thinking, I narrowed the search to Connecticut and found the name Ely Augustus Elliott, born 1781 and died 1788, son of George and Hannah Ely Elliott. The surname Elliott is found very early in Killingworth (later Clinton), Connecticut and that town is immediately east of Madison, on the

shoreline of Long Island Sound. There is an Elliott house on East Main Street, parts of which date back to 1710.

I then, using the CLDS web site (Ancestry) researched George and Hannah, and found the Ely was their youngest child, and then researched George, Jr., their eldest child, who had married Patience Lane and found they had also named one of their sons, born in 1791, Ely Augustus. He died 1871, and it would appear that he is your man (April 16, 2016).

Not only mystery solved but also I was given some intriguing detail about the ship's likely namesake:

Ely Augustus Elliott is listed in the 1850 Federal census with his wife Susan in Killingworth (dwelling 50, family 62, aged 58, no occupation) owning real estate valued at $15,000, a very considerable amount for that time. In the 1870 census, he was listed with his wife . . . aged 78, occupation: retired merchant, owner of real estate valued at $70,000 and of personal property valued at $30,000, which made him a very wealthy man.

On top of all that, detective Murphy tagged the likely owner and even the mariner who had attended the Elliott's death throes:

Of the names listed as Masters, Chauncey Kelsey was also a Killingworth (Clinton) native; Sereno Scranton was a Madison native whose family was very involved in coastal shipping . . . and Hazard Marsh, also from Madison was perhaps master when this ship was wrecked in a storm in 1882. The Scranton family could well have been the owners. It is, I believe, unlikely that the owner would name the ship after himself, while (in this case) Sereno Scranton (or his father Jonathan, who was the real entrepreneur in that family's transportation business of that period), might name a ship for his friend and good customer. (April 16, 2016)

My proud vessel, it turns out, was firmly woven into the maritime history of New England, named for a cherished offshoot of an early American magnate, and doomed to be a victim of the weather gods.

The next question follows logically and you may already have guessed it. What was the sailing history of the "E. A. Elliott?" Kelly Page and Pat Schaefer found information indicating it was built in Madison, Connecticut. Rick Camp, President of the Madison Historical Society forwarded my research request to a small, independent not-for-profit organization – the *Charlotte L. Evarts Memorial Archives*. Nancy Bastian, its archivist, discovered a schooner built in Madison named the "Ely A. Elliott." Fred Murphy anted up additional information:

> [I] found the Mystic Ship Database information that probably led you to our Historical Society. As you know, it described the ship, date built (1855), dates registered (1855-1859), tonnage, physical characteristics and masters (or owners)
>
> [S]hipbuilding of vessels such as the 'E. A. Elliott' was the major industry here during the 19th century and there were at least eight yards at work during this period. The yard at East Wharf operated by Charles Miner was the largest, and the last one, and it burned in 1890. We have never been able to find a list of vessels built, or owners who contracted for them. (April 13, 2016)

As far as can be determined the "E. A. Elliott" was built in Madison and operated out of Nyack, New York and Boston for most of its days before wrecking in 1882. We know the coaster carried hay, potatoes and almost certainly other cargo. Its custom district was New Haven, Connecticut, using the customhouse there.

Coastal traders were incredibly numerous and sailed year-round, carrying cargoes from port to port from the Canadian Maritime Provinces along the US coast to the southern United States and as far as the West Indies. They were not meant to be deep-water vessels. Prior to the 1930s they provided many isolated towns east of Portland, Maine with a link to the world (Leavitt, 1970), mostly because roads were both poor and an inefficient means of moving bulk, low-value – though necessary goods. Actual coasters have passed into history, though several modern manufacturers of pleasure craft use the term for what they build. I, given my love of sailing ships, lament their passing.

The Connecticut Ship Database lists many of the "Elliott's" masters (captains) – Colson (1855-57), Chauncey S. Eilsey 1858), DeGroat, its builder (1866), Miller (1867), C. Baker (1868, 74-78), Spowl, Sereno H. Scranton, and Hazard Marsh. A ship's master is a professional seaman trained in and responsible for all operations of a ship at sea and in port – keeping the log, recording weather, navigation, loading and unloading, and the like.

The "E. A. Elliott" was 87 feet, three inches long, with a 27 foot, one inch beam. It was built as a two-masted schooner with a square stern, one deck, and a draft of 7 feet, seven inches. It is listed as having a billet head – a decorative piece of woodwork, the small, decorative rounded end of the prow. In many cases the billet was a figurehead or a bust. The painting has two gold dots on the bow that portray it. They are small and there is no discernible detail beyond that.

Tonnage is listed as 157 78/95, though David Kimball stated it was 121 tons. Fred Murphy wrote:

> Tonnage description . . . are based on cargo space volume and cargo weight limits and are used as a basis of in-port charges and duties. Since most coastal trade for Connecticut sailing shipping was agricultural products, this ship's tonnage figures would reflect that cargo weight and space. (April 13, 2016)

Kelly wrote that tonnage does not refer to weight but to volume, but it turns out there is gross tonnage; net tonnage, gross register tonnage and net register tonnage, which helps explain the lack of agreement among these experts. A comment by one of them summed up the muddlement when he wrote that tonnage was "a measurement based on an arbitrary formula, intended originally to be a rough measure of cargo capacity" (Leavitt, 1970, p 201). I am reluctant to pursue any more detail regarding these; sometimes curiosity results in too much detail.

Kelly also provided the obituary of William De Groat, the schooner's builder. It appeared in the "Rockland City Journal" and reads in part:

CAPT. DE GROAT'S DEATH.

HE PASSED AWAY ON SUNDAY MORNING. He Was President of Nyack for Three Years—A Well Known Navigator. Captain William DeGroat, one of Nyack's best known citizens, died at his home, corner of Broadway and First Avenue, on Sunday morning. He was in the eightieth year of his age. . . . His father was Capt. John DeGroat, owner of the Samsondale, the first market sloop which sailed between Haverstraw and New York. William sailed with his father until about 18 years old, when he came to Nyack and learned the carpenter's trade with Thomas Burd, then the only builder in this vicinity. After serving his time Mr. DeGroat embarked in business for himself. . . . When about 24 years old, Mr. DeGroat went boating, owning and running at different periods the sloop David D. Crane, the schooner Ringgold, the schooner Nye. with which he and the late Elisha Ruckman, of Tappan, conducted the oyster trade for a long time. He then built and commanded the schooner E. A. Elliott between the North and Southern ports. He afterward had the schooner Sunnyside and the schooner Geo. H. Hoyt. In 1867 Mr. DeGroat built the large three masted schooner Elias Moore, which he ran between New York, the West Indies and South America. . . . Capt. DeGroat was a man of integrity, of robust health, and had the respect of every one. . . .

Kelly advised me to be cautious in inferring that Captain DeGroat actually built the vessel despite what the obituary says. It is possible he ordered it built, not for himself but for someone else.

Kelly was also able to determine how the "E. A. Elliott" ended its days.

Dean, [his surname] of and from Winterport, ME, with hay bound for Boston went ashore on Cod Rock below Portsmouth, NH AM Mch 18 and became a total wreck. Crew saved. On Mch 20 about 300 bales of hay and a considerable quantity of wreck stuff were picked up by the residents along the shore. (New York Maritime Register, Schooners, March 22, 1882).

E. A. Elliott of and from Winterport, ME, for Boston, wrecked at Gerrish Island, has been sold to parties in Portsmouth and Boston for $228. Her cargo of hay most of which is scattered along the immediate shore was also sold (New York Maritime Register, Schooners, April 5, 1882).

As noted earlier, the painting not only showed the "Elliott," flags aflutter, but had a background I assumed was realistic, rather than just a fiction. If I could identify the setting, it might reveal more about both the artist and his practice. Considering how widely these practical boats ranged, it would be interesting to know when and where this "snapshot" was posed.

I learned in from books showing sailing vessel paintings that when the ship's location is known, it adds to the painting's history and desirability. Being a landlubber sent me down the wrong shipping lane. The "Elliott" is pictured as sailing to the right (east?) with a lighthouse to the left rear and land behind it. So if it is sailing towards the Atlantic why is a lighthouse pictured where it is. Had I a detailed map of Long Island Sound, for example, I might have learned of the many inlets and waterways feeding into it, some of which could need a lighthouse to signal danger and that could have helped me determine the exact location.

The antique dealer from whom I purchased the painting hypothesized this was a New England scene. Kelly wrote:

> Even with decades of experience, it is difficult to pinpoint the location of a port scene in a painting as there are many approaches to the same port and structures do not look the same from all angles ... In short, we can't say much beyond somewhere on the Atlantic coast. (April 5, 2016)

She also speculated that the Elliot might well have been sited elsewhere, interesting if the artist was New England local, as Babbidge was.

I don't have an eye for harbor view/landmark identifications, so I consulted the book *Stebbins Illustrated Coast Pilot*, to see what I could come up with. Don't take my opinion as authority here, but

I couldn't seem to come up with anything in the North East or Mid-Atlantic that looked like the lighthouse and fort-like structure in your painting. Since it was involved in trade in the South, perhaps it is a Southern scene? I conferred with my colleague (45 years on the job) and he didn't recognize the landmarks. (March 15, 2016)

Pat Schaefer at Mystic Seaport provided a different perspective:

There seem to be other land bodies in the background, which makes me think of offshore islands, and Long Island Sound. Around here (I'm thinking specifically Mystic, since that's where we keep our boat, but it works for most of the coast of CT), if you leave a river you can run east or west, but you're not out in the Atlantic. And if we turn to starboard when leaving the Mystic River, we're running west toward New Haven . . . I think you'd be better off trying to identify the lighthouse and that other building, to see where that puts you. . . (April 7, 2016)

She had stated earlier:

You could also try local newspapers (New Haven, if not Guilford or Madison), to see if there was an article about the launching. You might also see if they could give any information about the location of the painting. There are several paintings in the local county historical society of local vessels in their home Thames River (New London). Since there's a lighthouse in the painting, Madison would be able to tell you if it was a local lighthouse, or if you'll have to look farther afield. (March 25, 2016)

The Madison Historical Society did not have any local history on the location depicted in the painting, but Fred Murphy focused on a possible Connecticut location and hypothesized the background with lighthouse and fort (?) may be little more than an exercise of artistic license.

. . . you have to remember that a ship portrait of this sort is a form of advertising, and thus doesn't necessarily display the ship actually underway. In the same sense, the background could be actual or imagined.

Of the background, there was, in the middle of the 19th century, a lighthouse at the entrance to New Haven harbor, and another at Old Saybrook at the mouth of the Connecticut River. The only lighthouse between these two was (still is) the one at Faulkner's Island, three miles off Guilford. Yours may well be a figment of the artist's imagination, since at that time, there was no other way to capture a "live sitting" of this kind of subject. (April 13, 2016)

Nonetheless at least two paintings in Brewington's book and four Buttherworth paintings in Granby and Hyland (2009) depict similar buildings in the background. David Kimball posited that the ship is sailing west to east in Long Island Sound and wonders if the lighthouse depicted was destroyed in a hurricane in the late 1930s.

That leaves open two possibilities, the first of which I favor: (1) this is an actual scene, at hand, with similar buildings found in multiple locations, and therefore accessible to a number of painters or (2) a number of different artists adopted the same cliché, creating a setting that would serve for a variety of ships' portraits. The background detail – a large building several stories high, perhaps a fort with a lighthouse nearby – may assist someone in identifying its locale, unless, of course, the artist simply put in the background details to please the painting's consignor or his taste.

After all of that probing and speculating, mysteries remain. The schooner may be named for Ely Augustus Elliott, but we have no irrefutable proof of the connection. The tonnage figures remain muddled. The true location of the scene is unclear. The painting's artist – and that is not certain either – painted in the established maritime style of Stubbs, or Baker, or most likely Babbidge.

My research into this painting makes me wonder how many other American artists have vanished into obscurity. There are literally hundreds of 19th century maritime – and historical – paintings floating about. Additional research on the part of owners and dealers might give us a new perspective on these coasters and a deeper appreciation both of the bygone culture and its art. My experience with the painting made me sharply aware of the marvelous resources that are available to us collectors, and my generous correspondents provided me an exciting opportunity to become fully – well, mostly – familiar with an object I love. The work these museums' research staff and others did to provide me with answers to often ill-constructed questions impressed me greatly. I can only hope there was some fresh discovery for all of us who spent so much time trying to unravel one small mystery among the many offered by antique collecting.

Chapter 23

ℰ

The Virtue of Patience

Circa mid-18th Century, 1750-1760 Queen Anne cherry chest on frame; drop front desk with original pad feet. 32¾"w, 36"w at base, 43"h, 17½"d, 32" writing height. Eastern CT. The interior shell has a horizontal concave line at its base which is also found on at least two other Eastern CT case pieces. Desk is in its original first surface with craquelure. Old repair to lid, some repair to lid and some lip damage expected with long use and wear. Second set of 18th Century brasses with Connecticut pine treetops. Connecticut Tudor rose in the skirt and shell carved interior.

Remember the wisdom granny taught you: "He who hesitates is lost." "Strike while the iron is hot." "Look before you leap." "Good things come to those who wait." Rushing pell-mell into purchasing antiques can be fatal. Yet sometimes some of us who know better wait too long to pull the trigger, losing the opportunity to add a prime item to our collection. Patience may be a virtue, but it is one that has to be exercised with a degree of caution.

Let's define our terms: *patience* is the ability to abide delay, frustration, and troubles with equanimity. Flying commercially comes to mind: we enter a Zen-like state, knowing that the process of getting from point A to Point B is largely out of our control. The runway is under the command of the tower. The plane is under control of the pilot. The weather

253

. . . forget it. All we can do is sit back, sip our seven-buck Bud Lite and be hauled. Being upset by unexpected events will not change a thing. Feeling depressed or victimized has no effect. At times, patience is little more than despair wearing the cloak of virtue.

Undoubtedly, we all wish to be virtuous, even if it is mostly public display. Waiting, the refusal to be pushed to act precipitately, and hesitation can all be good things. On the other side of the line, being dilatory, indecisive and denying laudable impulses can be bad. The trick is to commit oneself to the side of the angels and avoid that of – dare I say it? – The Dark Side. Oh, and the real trick is telling the difference between the two. My concern is that there are merits on both side of the issue. Yes, the wise collector is cautious. But to collect well he also has to be decisive.

It seems appropriate that we ponder the various forms of patience collectors exercise as they go about amassing treasures they initially covet and then cherish. A dealer told me long ago never to lock in on any one type of antique when I visited a dealer's shop (there were more shops back then) or attended a show. She believed that doing so presented two risks. First missing other, better antiques because of my myopia. Second, buying what I sought even if it wasn't very good. A painted tin teapot I discuss in the chapter, *Memorable Moments*, comes to mind as an example.

Jonathan Clements' *How to Think About Money* (2016) urges us to "avoid being too focused on the short-term." Sometimes the urge to add to one's collection, fill a spot in your home or shelf or cupboard of antiques, or to be in the game is overwhelming. When American Express marketed its "Don't Leave Home Without It" campaign, it was meant to remind us of the value of the newly issued (1975) credit card and its traveler's checks . . . both big profit centers, by the way. What does this have to do with collecting antiques? A lot actually, if you substitute an antique at a show, auction, or dealer's shop for home ("don't leave without it"). The notion that one must buy now, regardless, infects many collectors, even those with decades of experience behind them. Needless to say, giving in to this mantra is both costly and ultimately unsatisfying.

Time for a story. I talk with a collector I have just met while we are waiting in line for an antique show to open. He is looking for a pie safe (a piece of kitchen or back porch furniture that keeps "pie safe," in case you were thinking of something made of cast iron and having a dial lock) in good condition with interesting designs on its tins. I clue him into a dealer's booth or two he might want to visit, and of another dealer not doing the show who may have one that is just what he is looking for. He goes his way and I go mine. After an hour or so we run into each other. He has found a pie safe that is exactly what he wanted. Would I look at it? He tells me why and how the pie safe is perfect for the uses and location he has in mind. He has purchased it: The red tag is on it. His feeling that he had found what he truly desired takes me off the hook as a critic, and I tell him the pie safe is nice indeed. What else can I say? My point is this: I saw several examples at other shows within a few weeks, and another two or three superior ones on dealers' websites (better condition, higher off the floor, nicer proportions, more interesting designs punched in the tins), all for about the same price he paid. Perhaps we had different criteria for style and aesthetics. Just as likely, with his goal so firmly in mind, he had convinced himself he could not leave the show without one.

All collectors need to learn that the best antique shows, visits to dealers' shops, or auctions are often ones where they purchase nothing. Doing so leaves money in your pocket for the next time. You demonstrate self-discipline. Clements writes exhaustively how building a nice-sized nest egg for retirement is a decades' long process. The same holds true for building an antique collection.

If you are a serious collector of antiques, just any old piece will not do. It may take years before we find exactly what we seek. Most of the time, death, divesting, divorce or debt eventually will bring out treasure onto the market. A good example is my lengthy search for a high country desk. I had seen several at shows that seemed contenders – until I lowered their lids. The interiors were only so-so. After a long dry spell, a dealer sent me photos of one being downsized from a solid collection. Had I not exercised patience I would have been forced to make do with a desk that, while serviceable, was less that spectacular. Paradoxically one of the ways I could afford this particular desk was to divest myself of two buying mistakes I had made much earlier, both due to lack of patience.

ℰ

An Exercise in Style and Connoisseurship

What a beauty: a fan, a Tudor rose (typically five-lobed figure of a rose used in architectural and other decoration in the Tudor period), original surface, great form. Width to height, and the writing height all are proportional. It rules but does not overwhelm its setting because of its size. The form is angular but the scalloped valences, curves on the brasses, ogeed cubbyhole dividers, fan and rose are decorative elements that capture and please the eye. They greatly enhance the desk and are well executed. The upper fan especially, for example, is well and graciously carved. Everything from its finish to its pad feed shout "original," and it even has even 18th century replacement brasses. The frame (base) is separate from the chest/desk that fits into it, an early design. Well constructed, it has one unusual design element: the horizontal concave line carved under the shell that tells us it is from eastern Connecticut. (An antique dealer told me he is aware of only a few other pieces of furniture with the same horizontal line, all from this region.)

Desks such as this one were rarely signed or labeled, and finding history of ownership is unusual unless it has stayed in one family over the decades. It was made as a desk with storage (hence the drawers). Its condition is excellent given its age and past problems (the lid had broken off at one point in time and was repaired), replacement yet early brasses, lip damage, and an ink stain. Taken together they give it character rather than detracting from its aesthetics and value. Some collectors love little things like the ink stain, a visible record of its use and history.

It is made of cherry wood (compare this desk's deep color with another cherry drop front desk pictured in Chapter Two). The desk on frame works well: It is both rare and beautiful, meeting my all of the aesthetic and style criteria with no apologies. While expensive, my wife and I jumped at it as worthy of purchase. Our patience was rewarded.

Compromises. None.

Collectors also need patience in the face of a variety of small irritants that truly challenge them. Stillinger's *The Antiquers* (1980) describes a well-known collector, Horace Eugene Bolles, who when searching for a rare New England table mentions using steam and electric cars as well as walking through the snow to a farmhouse, where he was allowed only 15 minutes to view the piece once he arrived. Up to that moment, his quest had been a history of "inconvenience, discomfort and delay." Recognizing the table's desirability he thought that he would be able to purchase it then and there. The owners were not in a compliant mood, perhaps noting his eagerness or the travails he had already put up with, and he had to make the same trek a second time to complete the transaction.

Even in the best of circumstances, collectors put up with a lot of trouble and bother. How is it many antique shows take place in venues where the restrooms were last remodeled when Washington was president? Think of the absence of good food. I think of the No Chair sign at the New Hampshire Dealers Show. I think of the rarity of small courtesies: liquids for those waiting in line, shelter for those standing in the rain. Since they are no more than a matter of course, why rush decisions or buy on impulse or compromise your standards?

To be patient in these conditions requires finding good things to offset the bad. If the line for a show is long, acquaint yourself with the people waiting near you; at least one, and probably more, is guaranteed to be a character or a raconteur. You never know what great stories you will hear and what wisdom you will gain. To avoid numbing boredom bring good coffee or tea to an auction and something to read, or good music to listen to. At an outdoor show have that rain jacket handy. All this will identify you as a serious, patient collector. In 10 hours, 10 days or 10 weeks you will have forgotten the discomforts and indignities you experienced. Knowing you will re-experience these indignities time and time again; patience truly is a virtue. It will keep your blood pressure down and a smile on your face. Your physician will commend you.

Collectors also need to learn to be patient with themselves, not just the uncontrolled others. Keep in mind that you *choose* to collect (although it may seem more like a compulsion). I chose the 5:30 a.m. flight to have a bit more time in New Hampshire. I chose to wait hours for a show's opening. Remind yourself that the positives (getting to the good stuff first) outweigh the negatives (yawn!). When they no longer do, it may be time to try another hobby.

The corollary of being patient with yourself is to learn to be patient with others. Since auction houses personnel are busy folks, your email inquiring about a piece or two at one of their many auctions does not top their priority list. At times their response can seem maddening slow and, when prompt, cavalier, clichéd or commonplace. Since I do concede I am not the center of the universe, I finally call as the auction grows closer if I have received no response, and I am most pleasant when I do so. Then I get the information I need. Patience pays.

The most difficult situation requiring my patience occurs when a dealer contacts me to say he is visiting a collector who might have a piece of interest to me or that he has heard about a piece I have coveted for some time. And then the curtain of silence descends and I wander about checking my phone, my computer, my phone. I feel like a child on Christmas Eve, sent to bed waiting for morning and his presents. Yet wait I must and I have come to finally accept the fact; Julian Gallo's "no wine before its time" applies equally to antique dealers dealing.

Developing patience often means stepping back from your avocation.

Habituation is a well-researched psychological process. We cease to sense any stimulus we are repeatedly exposed to. We simply do not respond to it anymore. Habituation's basis lies behind evolution and survival of the species: if we constantly attend to the common sight of waving grass or trees we will fail to notice the saber tooth tiger looking at us for lunch. Work in a shop that plays music all day and it does not take long before you do not notice it. Work in a leather store and you do not smell the leather goods. Wise, dedicated collectors therefore should take a sabbatical from the pursuit for a few days or weeks or longer every once in a while. Go for walks, smell the roses or watch for the presence of saber-toothed predators. Reinvigorate yourself. When you return, the antique world will seem fresher and more nuanced. You will notice things again; can pay them the close attention they deserve.

Collectors also need to learn to be patient with the "cussedness of collecting." Every collector should be familiar with the insight of John Milton, who wrote in *Paradise Lost*, "they also serve who only stand and wait." Give things time. Let them find their voice in your heart. It is not unusual to find collectors who began their accumulations committed to one narrow category – weather vanes or redware. Yet over time their passion widens and gains depth. Letting human nature take its course – as it most assuredly will – bears its own unpredictable rewards.

If a new collector asks me for advice one of the first pieces of counsel I give: Think of building a collection as a work for the ages (yours and the pieces'). Move too fast and you will quickly burn out. If you have truly caught the collecting bug, the affliction will last. Giving it time carries its own benefits. You may not know what makes you smile until you have been collecting for some years. Saving money to fund your collection can be done gradually and as a result you can obtain better pieces. Time will give that bachelor uncle who owned a million acre sheep farm in Australia a chance to die and name you his sole heir. Your children will build their *bona fides* for full college scholarships or find menial jobs. Over time, you will have a chance to find the venues and dealers that most meet your needs. In short, patience eventually proves to be its own reward.

In the last analysis, you cannot control who dies, gets divorced, or divests. You may be outbid on items at auction, be second person to put a hold on something at a show, dither over a buy and lose out. That's what

259

this hobby is about: Shake your head, mutter an expletive deleted or two, and move on. It really is a marathon. Keep telling yourself that.

Patience is a valuable currency. It is a virtue needed by all parties in the antique collecting world. Your spouse has to be patient with you – the catalogs and piles of books, time spent at the computer, time away from home. Your children also live in a house with all that "old stuff." Their friends may feel sorry for them. "Can't your parents afford nice things?" they ask. Dealers need patience with you – your questions, equivocating, asking for time to pay off that expensive thing, the "have you found one yet?" – and you with them. Patience greases the antique collecting engine.

Patience can have its own payoff. It will give you the time to be prepared and act wisely. Your mental health may be better. You will be ready to spend money on what you truly want, when you can find it. Patience is actually the prelude to striking when the iron is hot. When that piece you have been looking for becomes available, buy it. Buy the piece to cherish and take delight in. Be decisive.

Self-restraint runs counter to American society's pressure to buy, buy a lot, and buy now. Mantras help maintain self-control: "Not spending is magical and good." Or "I can live without it, I really can." Not rarely, at shows I attend the antiques I truly love are beyond my financial means but they challenge my patience: They become goals somewhere down the road. By being patient I can accrue enough purchasing power to buy one of them every now and then. Self-control allows me to have a few items that meet style and aesthetic criteria with few if any compromises. Sometimes a great antique comes along with our name on it. Patience (and preparation) wrote it there.

Chapter 24

୧

Evaluating Your Collection

Chippendale cherry Massachusetts or Connecticut six drawer high chest, circa 1770-1780. 36"w, 55"h, 18"d. Graduated drawers. Remnants of original red wash/paint enhanced with thin coat of red paint and over-varnished. Drawer guides replaced. Replaced brasses. One small replacement, left rear foot. High straight bracket base with excellent cutout. No lip replacement. Heavy cornice molding, "tray top."

Collecting and amassing are far different things. Some folks – accumulators – ignore style and connoisseurship and buy items just to own them. In contrast, collectors often purchase antiques that command their interest because of their aesthetic or historic qualities. You may find Louis XIV French clock here, a Paul Revere spoon there, but both somehow appealed to their owner's historic and artistic sensibilities. Other serious collectors will have pieces reflecting a theme and complementing one another. Their goal: to employ their prized possessions to create coherence (e.g., high country, painted surfaces, what you might find in a fine Newport mansion or a saltbox in the Connecticut River Valley). But whatever their goals, collectors make their buying decisions based on their personal style, expertise and preferences.

A beginning or inexperienced collector might readily be satisfied with something that falls short of the first water (as jewelers say about the clarity of gems) but a sophisticated one is drawn to objects that have all the earmarks of artistry, rarity (usually) and even brashness (That might seem an odd use of the term, but there are creations bold enough to break away from tradition and set a new direction – Brancusi's in art, Wright's in architecture for instance).

Preparation

Every so often prudent antique collectors have to evaluate their collection and the degree to which it meets their goals and tastes. Before they add to it, they need to know what they own, how good the pieces are, and how they fit together; what is jarring should be shed and what is strikingly absent should be pursued. While the rule sounds simple, obeying it is anything but.

Culling and improving any collection starts with performing a critical and honest evaluation. If you find yourself dissatisfied with one or several pieces you own, look inward. Why are you unhappy with the antique? In my case, the dismay has something to do with superior items I have found since my initial purchase. At times I erred in buying the piece to begin with, in others my taste has matured and insight has grown.

You should add to your collection when some pieces could be upgraded, there are lacunae you want to fill or you discover an item that is simply irresistible. As I wrote in Chapter 3 it is your collection. If a dealer tells you, "your collection must have a dressing table", or, "every good collection of Americana has a highboy," should you pursue one? Only if you covet such a piece. Marketing and the collecting environment pressure us to spend money on things that are supposedly fresh and better. Beware of what I call the "stainless appliances and granite countertop phenomenon." Not all kitchens gain grace by their inclusion, and likely your precious collection of antiques will not automatically be improved by adding a bracket clock, jardinière or Tiffany lamp, no matter how expensive or high quality.

I have never seen any writing saying how collectors can assure unwavering satisfaction with their antiques. The frenzy of antiques' events in NYC in January, Philadelphia in April, Manchester, New Hampshire in August; wonderful auction catalogs, the onslaught of auctions on what seems a weekly basis, and the occasional nudge by a dealer, spouse, or fellow collector make it difficult to stay true to our taste and to buy only that which will make our treasures complete or at least bring us nearer that lofty goal. As I said, a thorough assessment of where we stand ought to precede hauling out our checkbook or credit card.

So how do go about taking such an inventory? Asked about their collections, buyers often say, "I know what I like." True enough as far as it goes. But is what you like an adequate benchmarks against which compare what you own? At the other end of the scale, comparing just about anything to its equivalent in famed collections will produce nothing but dejection. These apples-to-oranges contests may help you refine your taste and materially increase your knowledge but they won't give you much in the way of guidelines for refining you collection. Almost everyone lacks the money and the opportunity to purchase such refined antiques. No collector should commit to the goal of owning only *10s* unless he is content to own only one piece . . . or maybe none, depending on what he collects.

We all have to face the fact we cannot possess perfect antiques, sometimes because they really never existed and when they do because the ideal costs too damned much. We need to realists, asking instead whether the pieces we do have reflect our notions of quality and taste. The key questions: "Do we like living with them?" "Do they make us smile?" If we accept compromises (and we often have to), we better know how many and much we can put up with. Flawed paint? A minor crack? Veneer that has been re-glued? Antiques test our tolerance and we need to know the limits on what we will tolerate before nodding or shaking our heads. As we grow, our tolerance changes, often getting narrower. What was a livable antique some years ago may now be an item we would gladly pack away or consign for resale. That is one reason to do periodic assessments, for they not only tell you what you think of what you have but they help you understand how you have grown.

If you are beginning to build a collection or furnish a home, take an honest look at the antiques you already own. Do you like them? Do you like how they make you feel? Ask whether you should continue buying pieces in that particular genre (primitive, country from the mid-1800s, earlier American, Mid-Century modern, English) or whether you can be a bit more eclectic. What will you pursue next? Don't forget to take into account your basic needs. If you are tired of eating off of crates then get a kitchen or dining room table and chairs. Rather than that slick Formica piece at the local store, here's a chance to find something really good that fits with your other treasures.

Then become familiar with what is available. One of the most satisfying aspects of antique collecting is that it gives you a chance to research and to learn. Collecting is not a passive activity. Find what dealers and auction houses are the ones you simply have to keep a close eye on. What shows should you attend on a regular basis? If you allow yourself to be exposed to a great number of antiques, you will start to see the gaps in your collection; then you can decide what items at what level of aesthetics, history, location, and price point are right for you.

Keep in mind even a "consolation" (an item requiring slightly compromising style and connoisseurship because of the size of your wallet) can be a wonderful purchase. At the same time, as I have said, be honest about how much falling short of the ideal you can handle.

There are always objective considerations we must take into account. Certainly there are questions regarding the worth of any given collectible – what an antique costs and can be sold for. "If I trade this item in or put it up for auction, what will it bring?" "Does that gain me enough money to buy a piece that is better?" "What would it cost to upgrade my dining room table?" Market exposure will help you make good financial decisions, at least at the point where you must work within limits. Knowing all the parameters – cost, market value, personal satisfaction, etc. – makes it easier to answer the question, "How should I proceed?"

To evaluate your collection, you also need to know yourself. This may be the biggest trick of all, for who among us can accurately explain or predict our aesthetic impulses? The very fact that we are faced with so many choices arises from two facts: (1) there are many who, like us, find beautiful old things irresistible, and (2) our preferences have been molded by a lifetime of unacknowledged – and perhaps unknown – forces. Since we are first and foremost human beings our individual tastes differ. There are also some preferences that different people share. That is why we find cliques that collect early silver or jewelry or furniture. The perfectly proportioned Pennsylvania desk that crowns your collection suits your taste for the same reason those John Lobb wingtips do; they are part of your aesthetic . . . and maybe that of a few hundred other tasteful dudes.

Why? The answer resides somewhere in how you define terms like *grace*, *craftsmanship*, *aesthetics*, *style*, and *culture*.

Knowing yourself results in preferences. That is why some collectors will only own Americana. I lean in that direction but as you noticed in this book I do present a pair of British candlesticks and a World War I British poster. I am not a purist. In fact, I find myself liking antiques more for their individual virtues than their origin. Many of the non-American pieces in our collection are the result of emotional forces, as you shall see. Our British silver teapot raises warm feelings about of our first trip to England when Harrods had its Silver Room. A French small redware pitcher resulted from a trip to New England of all places. Our candlesticks are wonderful regardless of where they were made. The British poster just could not be resisted for my wife's collection.

Value and Emotional Attachment Considerations

When you assess your collection you also have to think about another sort of worth, beyond what you paid or could sell it for — what the piece means to you beyond its fiscal implications. If your grandmother's Bible is worth $600, you will take care of it and keep it in a safe place. But your memories of sitting on her lap and eating fresh chocolate chip cookies probably far outweigh its market value. Anyone who has watched *Antiques Roadshow* has encountered someone who dragged in a seeming piece of trash that was assigned an astronomical price. At some point, Jane or John sighs, "This belonged to my great grandpa and I wouldn't sell it for a million dollars." That may be an exaggeration but we all seem to recognize the feeling. (As an aside, that is why people are told that the replacement value of special pieces may always fall short. Another Bible would lack family history and emotional specialness.) One reason I can sympathize with cherished goods is that I have one at hand: The bowl and pitcher I gave to my wife as a wedding gift no longer fits in our collection and has very little monetary worth yet its value is immeasurable.

You should not be surprised to find as much emotional impetus as rationality behind the things you wanted for your collection. As we have built our holdings, emotions may have bent our preferences and desires. Sometimes we keep things that don't quite work or fit because of the stories they carry with them. They remind us of that time when . . . We hang on to them even if better examples enter the marketplace. I own an eagle weathervane I have considered replacing but I hold on to it because I was with my elder son when we purchased it. There is no way I could sell it, and the power of remembering his being with me (and being the one who spotted it in a shop) is priceless. My younger son has a WWII poster I purchased for him via telephone at an auction. Though it went for less than we expected, we have never run across another. While he has put other posters away this one remains out for viewing. The story behind its discovery is just too good.

As an example, one special class of antiques Sandy and I struggle to upgrade is made up of some of the first pieces we purchased. A couple pieces were the first my wife bought and she will not let them go because of their history in our family (watching the children grow up, reminding us when we were young). I have no say in the matter. I am no different, choosing to keep at least one or two pieces from the dealers we became friends with years ago (Bernice and Jim Miller) who are now deceased. I tend to think Bernice is smiling when I touch the small walnut drop-leaf table she sold us, described and pictured in Chapter 13. Emotional attachment is a funny thing. The last time I did a walk-through of our collection I lingered by a five-drawer chest purchased from the Millers years and years ago. I noticed that the feet probably need a bit more height for really good proportions. I had never noticed that feature before.

An Exercise in Style and Connoisseurship

Basically a chest is a rectangular box. This one's bold cornice, strong "spurs" on the bracket base and the cutouts on the side add curves and soften it. The chest's width (36 inches) is proportional to its height. There is no ornamentation. It has a smooth finish, enhanced with a thin newer red wash and over-varnish. Though it is made of cherry, the red wash hides the wood's true color, yet its wood's pattern is visible. A tad more height to the bracket base would raise it more and improve its scale (am I being too much of a perfectionist? Do you find it fine the way it is?). Still, it is constructed well, and sports an alluring tray top (molding surrounds the front and sides and the top is set down into it).

Made to hold clothes, one would not expect the country piece to bear an attribution or history of ownership. It shows its age, despite the added red wash and replacement brasses and has some repairs.

Overall appearance is of a proud, good-looking chest of drawers with some strong components. We purchased the chest before our style and aesthetic criteria emphasized surfaces as much as they do now, and we did not hesitate to buy it. Fairly priced when we bought it, it would bring less in the marketplace today.

Compromises. This is a good example of how changing collector tastes affect how pieces purchased long ago are perceived: We would not buy this chest today because of its surface. Even with a better surface we might wait for one with a taller base, a more perfect chest.

The Process of "Really Seeing" What is in Your Collection

Assuming you have done your preparation, what remains in assessing your collection? Let me tell you how I do it, since experience offers the best advice. On a quiet Sunday morning or weekday afternoon I slowly walk my home, mug of tea in hand. I approach individual pieces in my collection; I touch them; I pick the smaller ones up; I may hold or stare at a piece for some minutes, sometimes longer.

I live with my antiques every day. I walk past, sit in, and eat off them, and I listen to their ticks and chimes each hour. Therein lies a problem. In the preceding chapters I describe the psychological process of habituation, the process that makes the familiar disappear. When we live with our antiques, after a while we cease seeing them.

Seeing our pieces has a darned serious purpose, of course. It may make us appreciate them more, but I can tell you from personal experience that is not always the case. Knowing the truth of what we own helps us decide what to look for and purchase next. If you have a wide variety of smalls in a cupboard, when is the last time you really looked at them? By focusing on and touching them, you gain a new appreciation for and understanding of them. While going through my collection in detail I assess my feelings. If the house caught on fire, would I grab for it quickly? Is there no point in replacing that chair or piece of redware? Sometimes I hear myself saying: "Time for something with original surface." "You know you're tired of it." "You'd really miss it if it went away."

Another strategy is to enlist the help of someone else. This person could be a spouse, fellow collector, a dealer with whom you work. But if you do so I offer several caveats. Be sure to tell your co-conspirator to be candid and honest about pieces you may want to consider upgrading. Tell her that honesty will not hurt your feelings, even if it will. Someone looking objectively may suggest upgrading pieces you love, that you believed were really nice. The view is worth pondering, even if you end up knowing it is not what you believe. At the end of the process, you may end up feeling your collection is not as good as you thought. But you need the opinions of others. Ask them to consider other locations for your pieces. Some pieces look fresh and even better in different light, or a different room, or even a different place in a cupboard. Lastly, share with them what is on your "to buy list." Ask them what they would rank as first or second in priority.

Reproductions

Collectors in various genres have to decide on how original their collection and its setting needs to be. Many parts for classic cars from the 1960s are identical to what was manufactured back then, but are not original. Sometimes a "survivor" brings high prices in the classic car market, unrestored and never repainted for example. But its new owner may still upgrade it with new old parts.

Collectors of antiques vary in their need for the purity of their collection and home. Some toy collectors value originality above everything, even if it means flaked paint or scratched surfaces. Others will accept restorative touches here and there. When it comes to American antiques some collectors also are purists. Jim and Bernice Miller were such collectors. The stereo for Jim's beloved jazz sat hidden in a closet, never to contradict the ambience of their antique collection. The sofa in the keeping room was a country example, circa 1825. The woodwork and brick in the kitchen were brought from New England and correct for the period of their home and collection. That is the way the Miller's wanted to live but not everyone wants to or can afford to do so.

When I evaluate my collection I give attention to the reproductions we live with. Let me talk about some of the reproductions we own and the reason we have not upgraded to "genuine antiques." Since I have never seen this matter discussed maybe these comments will give you permission to have a "repro" here and there, or to feel better about the ones you own. Admittedly, some of the reproductions we have linger in our home for inexplicable reasons, although inertia plays a part.

In the living room we have a reproduction Camelback sofa, Chippendale in style. It looks period. Our two wingback chairs also were purchased new decades ago. They are high quality and have never been recovered. If we lived in the East where it was easier to find originals I believe we might have done so. But they are comfortable and we like them. The chandelier in the dining room is a brass reproduction with bulbs shaped like candles. I know some collectors who go so far as to light with antique chandeliers using candles, a bridge too far for Sandy and me and a bit perilous. Several of our seemingly antique lamps are newer stoneware, not old jugs drilled for the cord and bulb. Throw pillows have new fabric that fits our décor.

Our kitchen is a hodgepodge, a compromise between our differing tastes. Appliances are not hidden behind wood panels, which suits us both fine. The crackled finish red stained shelves (a reproduction) carry both period redware and some reproductions; my wife likes the reproduction redware because it is food safe and one or two plates bring back memories of visits to historic museums with our kids. The television in the den sits on a new stand (horrors!). We could find an antique to put it on, I suppose, but have never bothered; thinking the mixture of antique and tech might inadvertently prove ironic. In our downstairs bathroom is a (reproduction) cantback cupboard that we purchased from the Millers decades ago. Bernice thought that for the price (it is handmade and painted in green) this cupboard made more sense than paying much more for an original. Upstairs antique rope beds with antique trundle beds underneath sit in our two sons' bedrooms. (The term "sleep tight" came from sleeping on a rope bed that was taut). But the queen-sized bed in our bedroom with tester is a reproduction (go find an antique queen or king sized bed. I dare you). That sounds like a lot of reproductions, and perhaps it is. But there really are a lot of antiques also.

There you have it. If you started as someone just buying antiques and ended up a collector, I hope these ideas help you in continuing to the endless process of winnowing and sifting. When you got to the end of the third grade, you may remember how often the teacher said, "now let's review." Reassessing your collection is no different: it improves your grasp, refines your appreciation and gives you a guide for coming actions.

Chapter 25

౿

Memorable Moments: The Cherished
and the Missteps

Circa 1780-1790 Lehigh Valley poplar blanket chest. 39¼w" x 24½"h x 22"d. Cleaned to original blue with salmon moldings, Ogee bracket base. Original lock, strap, escutcheon, hinges and till.

Every collecting odyssey has its highs and lows, and mine is no exception. I occasionally am forced to recall blunders that even years later make me shake my head and wonder what I was thinking. I considered showing you, the reader, antiques I mistakenly purchased, but fortunately most of the ones that are not disposed of are hidden away. I do not need them reminding of my foolishness day after day.

If we are to learn anything from our mistakes, they need to be memorable, personally significant, and painful. All collectors know those of like persuasion have made these blunders (themselves excepted, of course) and appear to take considerable satisfaction when someone publicly admits being a sinner. Here is their chance to grin. As a good psychologist I have spent some hours on my own couch maundering to myself about my miscues. I am consoled by the comment made by Joahann Wolfgang von Goethe: "By seeking and blundering we learn."

When dealers make mistakes they often end up living with them, for the market can be a cruel taskmaster. Antique collectors may pay a different but no less painful price, the mumble of a little interior voice that keeps saying, "you goofed."

We collectors find it much easier to talk about our triumphs. A collector of pewter and I renew our acquaintance in line each year while we are waiting to go antique hunting. I remember how excited he was one time, ebullient even. He had snatched up a pewter tankard, had a noted expert look at it, and was told his buy was a bargain. The thing was not worth thousands but it would fetch more than he had paid. It was all he could talk about, and chatter he did enthusiastically. Had the case been different (oops, missed that little "made in occupied Japan" on the base) he would have been as still as the Sybil on a bad day.

I must admit that I am being selective in examining my mistakes. The number of them is not important (I will admit it is larger than I would like); the lessons learned count for more than their quantity. To say that collecting failures are unavoidable is neither a rationalization nor a defense. At times, my human impulses overwhelmed my rationality. Now and then my judgment failed. And time, which is alleged to heal all wounds, does not guarantee that you will never again make a bad deal, chase a so-so antique or pay too much for something simply because you love it. You shall see.

Painted tin (*toleware*) was all the rage at one time and I was on a mission looking for a teapot. As I said in Chapter 23 ("The Virtue of Patience"), missions are perilous for collectors. I thought I simply had to own a painted tin teapot though I do not know why this one. Working on this chapter, I dug it out of its dark corner on a kitchen shelf, shook my head and keened, "I should have known better." Its condition is only fair. One side looks nice but on the other the paint is largely gone. The top is ugly and crusty. It would look like a street urchin among sophisticates if I gave it prominence in our house. Regret struck almost instantly and to this day it is a cautionary tale.

My Mistake. I was too hasty. I did not consider my own collecting criteria and the pieces we already had. Patience flew out the window and I bought an item that simply did not deserve a place with our other possessions. Because I was all fired up looking for a teapot I let myself get caught up in the show's energy. My mission was to buy, dang it, not to deliberate the teapot's style and aesthetic qualities. As a consequence

I got exactly what I now have displayed (why I do not know), but not prominently, that and a sense of shame for not heeding my own good advice.

Right now I own seven tin bird decoys, all in good condition, each one mounted on a stick sitting on a piece of cork. When I accumulated them, I thought the grouping would be pretty. Somehow I overlooked the fact that I have no place to display them all together at the same time. So three keep each other company and the other four sit on a closet shelf. They are attractive. They are of good quality. But their orphaned status raises a nagging prospect: I need a bigger house.

My Mistake. I did not consider where I could display them; the artiste in me was infatuated with the idea of a grouping.

Then there are the two very average Windsor chairs we bought and then moved to less conspicuous locations when we found really good ones with fine paint and better form. This was not merely a case of collectors upgrading; we could have bought better pieces to begin with, had we more knowledge of the genre. The resolution to the proliferation of Windsors in the house (yes, England had that problem too) was to market the lesser two chairs and, no, I will not mention ugly words like "profit" and "loss".

Our Mistake. Lack of preparation. We failed to examine and study in enough depth the characteristics of desirable Windsor chairs and what is would cost to purchase better ones to begin with. We also failed to understand our tastes would improve. (I am not clear this is a mistake *per se* but there is some value in having a handle on your ability to and inclination to grow, change and adapt.)

Then there is perplexing purchase, seven pewter French spoons. They sit upright in a pitcher next a clutch of coin silver American ones in yet another ewer. Why did I buy them? The spoons are soft and their silver becomes even more malleable when dipped in a hot soup. Still we keep them; our mistake sitting in plain sight may lend us humility and help us make better decisions in the future.

My Mistake. I listened too attentively to the dealer who was selling them rather than to my own inner voice – or Sandy, who never wanted them (they are too large to be soup spoons). I failed to adequately consider how they could be displayed (they do not look that wonderful) and how they fit into our collection: we own only one other French piece, a small redware pitcher, and that fits because I collect redware, not its origin.

Uncertainty can make collecting exciting. Benjamin Franklin in a letter to Jean-Baptiste LeRoy (1789) summed up the matter nicely: "Our new Constitution is now established, and has an appearance that promises permanency; but in this world nothing can be said to be certain, except death and taxes." His pithy, widely quoted comment about the uncertainty of the world preceded Ben's delivery of the *mot*. Alas, he did not coin it. Being uncertain about the piece, its origins, its price and a host of other variables is a sure-fire invitation to make a mistake when collecting antiques. Sometimes you can beat the odds. So let us step off the booby-trapped path briefly to look at an instance when we (maybe) did everything right.

Sandy and I were looking for a World War II Tuskegee Airman poster. As noted, Sandy likes Black Americana; we both are interested in aviation. Over the years, we had met many of the surviving Tuskegee Airmen at the annual Experimental Aircraft Association Convention held in Oshkosh and their personalities and life experiences just sharpened our interest. After a lengthy wait (years) not just one but two such posters came on the market at the same time. "Of course they would," I grumped. One was up for auction in B+ condition I believe. The other was for sale by a dealer, I think rated an A-. The dealer's copy was priced higher than the auction poster's estimate. The difference between B+ and A- was insignificant and hardly noticeable. We purchased from the dealer, figuring it was a bird in the hand. What was going to happen at the auction was fraught with uncertainty and surely beyond control. As it turned out, we made the right choice: The auctioned poster sold well beyond its estimated price and we ended up with a bargain.

Uncertainty is a major pitfall for the collector. In the instance just preceding, two comparable items were on the market at the same time, one with a defined though higher price, the other subject to the vagaries of the auction. Choosing either one lined us up for disappointment but there was no alternative. In that case, Sandy and I gambled and won.

Even a good dose of common sense not enough to insulate us from errors. As Voltaire noted, "common sense is not so common." We tend to overvalue the quality of our decision-making. The painted tin teapot is a good example of my losing sight of my common sense. I am sure Sandy believes I lose it much more often than I know. In addition to blunders of commission – doing the wrong thing at the wrong time – there are those of omission – the piece we didn't purchase, the cherished treasures that lose their charm and belied their provenance.

A common form of uncertainty leading the collector astray is to buy a piece he has not inspected in person. How a piece is described may be accidentally or deliberately inaccurate or incomplete. The virtues attributed to it by the auction catalog, dealer or fellow collector may be illusory or mere hype. Once I sought a chest of drawers with a center drop, a look I liked. I found one advertised in an antiques' publication, requested and received a pile of photos, and decided to purchase it. The piece was good - nice scale, acceptable finish (old varnish), and from the hand of a known craftsman. For some inexplicable reason it failed to stir my affection. I ran my hand over it in the bedroom where it stood and felt nothing. It was precisely what I thought I wanted but it was a dud (to me). Still it sold rather quickly when a dealer brokered it for me. My loss (oh that word!) was another collector's gain. The chest's appeal or lack thereof can be accounted for by differences in aesthetics and taste. The error was mine and readily identifiable.

My Mistake. Once again I was too impatient. Worse yet I did not do enough research to appreciate chests with center drops regularly come on the market and existed in a wide variety of style, finishes and shapes. Now

I realize I should have reached out to several trusted dealers and asked them to look for one I might like. Had I been wise I would have headed east to personally view the chest before making up my mind. I now knew that when it comes to furniture touching and seeing in person is paramount for me.

Years ago, Max Hamrick, the former weaver at Colonial Williamsburg (and now a dear friend) sent color pictures of a blanket he was willing to weave for us. Its colors did not seem "true" and my wife asked if he could change them. He was willing to do so, to craft a blanket in yellow and gold in the same pattern. We had the good fortune to visit the blanket when it was on the loom, and provenance just does not get any more immediate than that. Max took us to the Colonial Williamsburg archives. We signed the logbook, put on protective gloves and walked to the bin where the original blanket was stored. It was gorgeous! Max offered to weave us another in its colors, reds and blues and I ended up preferring the second one to its one in yellow-and-gold mate. Had we not seen the original, we would have missed out on a real beauty. I should have known better when I purchased the chest of drawers but I had forgotten the blanket's lesson: Nothing trumps seeing and touching a piece before deciding.

Our Mistake. We should have been more ready to trust Max that the blanket in its original colors was beautiful. We should have used personally viewing the original as a reason to visit him at Colonial Williamsburg before committing. "But," I hear you say, "You trusted the dealer about the French pewter spoons and they proved a mistake." True enough. But something intervened between my lobes then, even though I was staring at their weaknesses. Sandy saw immediately that they were a poor choice, so why didn't I? In this case, we had both the maker and the object, right at hand. No one was selling us (me) anything; we were making the best choice we could. And it still could have been a blunder, but happily was not.

Here is yet another tale, this one more upbeat. Don't worry; I have not yet given up on cataloguing my goofs. A spot in our dining room seemed to be crying out for a card table. Bernice Miller had one of birch with a red stain we liked. Rather than selling it to us, she – like the mentor she was – said we needed to see more options. She brought back from New England a pine version with original brasses, its grain painted to look like a fancier wood. When we chose this table Bernice was delighted: It was the better of the two in her judgment. Her willingness to educate our taste has a lot to do with the pleasure we now take in the antique and in the antique collecting in general.

Then again, long ago I was at my first Northeast Auctions sale prior to Antiques Week, waved my card and ended up owning a basket. Auctions have an odd effect on buyers; having someone giving the nod to you makes you think you won some sort of prize. Here I had seen the basket but I found it was not as good as I initially thought.

My Mistake. When you are buying a piece such as the basket there are always going to be others, often better, to be purchased. The energy in the room goaded me to bid on something that was not all that inspiring. Deep down I wanted to buy something at a well-known auction and my common sense took a nap. The biggest error was failing to appreciate that winning at this auction was important to me. The price I paid was small, the lesson learned important.

The next tale is one of generosity and serendipity. We were on vacation in Maine a few years ago staying at a B&B. In talking with the proprietors my wife mentioned she liked Black memorabilia. The owners said they had something that might interest her. They were not antiques but would she like to see them? An antique dealer in the 1970s made a number of three-dimensional oven mitts of black faces. Over the years various dealers and auction houses have offered them as post-civil war, circa 1930s or 1950s, or contemporary. Sandy instantly loved the ones they showed us and for a nominal amount they were ours. Months later, while searching the Internet, I found a single mitt, obviously made by the same hand, priced dearly. It was advertised as almost new and similar but not identical to the pair we owned. That exact same mitt showed up in an on-line auction the next year because its owner was divesting many antiques. I purchased it for my wife for a very reasonable price. The perfect black caricature complements the two we already have that my wife uses regularly. In both cases, the purchases were serendipitous. Good collecting and sheer luck are not opposite forces.

Regrets are nothing original to collectors, but sins of omission can be as painful as missteps. In the heads of most of us are lists of antiques we could have, should have and didn't. The robin's egg blue blanket chest I mentioned awhile back still sticks in my craw. The litany is endless. I should have bought a pine chimney cupboard with great patina for storing and displaying our blankets. I should have bought a one-of-a-kind weathervane of an airplane. I should have bought a fabulous shirred rug picturing a vase of flowers. I should have bought a set of yellow chairs. I should have bought a Queen Anne drop-leaf table for our kitchen. I should have bought a small painting of a young Black woman. These hindsight grievances lead to consumption of single malt scotch to ease the pain of the keepers that got away. I'm glad I write in the morning when I don't drink. The consolation is that all of those objects are still out there in one form or another and somehow, someday I'll stumble across one and pounce on it, finally feeling vindicated.

Collectors sometimes are protected from such painful miscues.

We saw a blanket chest years ago at the Riverside Antique Show in Manchester, NH (since discontinued, much to our dismay). We liked it but it was would have stretched our budget uncomfortably. Then we saw it again the next day, still for sale. We thought it would have sold to a more prestigious dealer and moved up the food – and economy – chain. Still we equivocated. The next day the Riverside show was over and the dealer was assisting a colleague in his booth at another show. We asked if she still had the blanket chest. It was in her truck ready to be transported back to her shop. We finally purchased it. The luck that it was still available made up for some of the downright dumb decisions I have made.

℮

An Exercise in Style and Connoisseurship

This is a late 18th century chest that likely came from the Lehigh Valley in Pennsylvania. I never asked if the dealer from whom we purchased it knew its provenance. One dealer told me the style of ogee feet could be Pennsylvanian and another dealer said definitely Pennsylvania based on the mid-molding, feet, the proportions, and the wood.

The blanket chest is angular and has no painted design to soften its profile. Its proportion is good. It is high enough that a full-width drawer (common in Pennsylvania chests) could have been inserted below where the front molding attaches. The molding and salmon trim provide a counterpoint to its dark blue hue. The color is not soft. Its paint improves the chest and is well executed, as is the ogee bracket base. The base and salmon trim color work together to "make" the chest. The finish is smooth to the eye and touch.

Overall it looks to be a solid, functional box with a few nice touches. It was over-painted and at some point later was scraped back to the original colors (perhaps resulting in the blue paint appearance). It has aged well and has all original parts. Usually, blanket chests were not labeled or signed and this one is not. History of ownership for blanket chests is unusual.

An overall evaluation would rank this blanket chest as a step above the ordinary. While not rare it is good looking, not because of the rectangular box but due to its paint, base, and molding. Chests with much fancier paint exist. I rank this chest a *7* or *8*.

Compromises. We made few compromises to our ideal and settled for a less than truly great blanket chest. We chose not to pursue a chest with decorative design of hearts, flowers, dots, or swirls. We did not want one with a drawer(s) nor were we seeking a vivid or certain color. After equivocating for two days we found it worthy of purchase.

Even when you see an item in person it can deceive, of course. When the antique holds center stage in a dealer's shop or is nicely lighted at a show it can look quite different from the way it will appear in your living room. Collectors are always well advised to ask the dealer whether the piece can be seen in natural light. But that is not the only pitfall. It is challenging to determine the size and proportions of a larger piece when it is staged in isolation. It may be visually a bit too large or small for the spot you had picked out for it even if you measured both the piece and place for it more than once. Perhaps it is a matter of color, how it complements or clashes with antiques you already own.

Have I ever made the mistake of liking something in its setting but regretting the purchase once I took it home? Of course. A gamecock weathervane with a black surface seemed a worthy complement to other ones we own. Once unpacked and displayed it did not please me at all.

Sitting on a pedestal in the dealer's booth it seemed okay. Sitting at home on a chest it looked wrong it. It is now gone.

My Mistake. I overvalued the form and ignored the vane's surface. I should have placed it next to other vanes in the dealer's booth to see how it would look.

A basic tenet of collecting antiques is to look closely. That is why serious collectors carry lights and magnifying glasses. In the last five or six years, early in the New Hampshire Dealer's Show, I twice saw a piece of furniture upside down with a dealer and collector studying it closely. To heck with the buying frenzy in the first hour or two that is the norm for this show. The buyer was going to be certain the case piece was right. I respect such obsessed sorts for their diligence and sense.

Have I ever done anything like that? Yes, and it confirmed that several pieces of furniture seemed true to their representation. I also have failed to look closely. We own a blanket chest from the late 18th century in the original red. It pleased me, but after I brought it home I noticed small nail holes. A piece of decorative trim was missing. With knowledge of the missing trim pieces would we have purchased it? I do not know. Certainly I would value it differently if I knew it was complete, but it still has given us pleasure over the years.

My Mistake. I did not spend enough looking at the chest closely. Add to that a failure to study: I did not know the genre well enough to know trim would have been a decorative element.

Yet moments occur when inadequate preparation means you will be caught on your back foot. We owned a simple Queen Anne maple candle stand with no, what Kirk (1977) calls "strangeness" to it, or so I thought. When having our collection appraised some time ago the appraiser looked at the stand – old cleat, old screws affixing the top to the bottom, original feet, old finish. Old, old, old should mean good, right? The expert concluded it was a marriage. He showed me how the color of the maple and the surface finish was slightly different top to base. I never noticed the subtle shift in hue when I inspected it.

My Mistake. I was looking but I didn't know what I was looking for. Even after the appraiser showed me the color change that led to his opinion, it seemed okay to me. There is such a thing as a trained eye linked to great experience, but it does not come to us collectors (or anyone) readily, meaning mistakes like this are unavoidable.

One temptation almost every collector indulges is overpaying for something, and that surely qualifies as an error. My overpaying is usually the consequence of unbridled enthusiasm, leaving me feeling foolish. A red basket I bought comes to mind.

My Mistake. I had driven several hours to a show and wanted something to bring home. The basket was nice but I became caught up in the "don't leave home without it syndrome." I dragged out my American Express card and grabbed it for more than it really was worth. Again, the desire to buy something – justifying my time spent on the road – overcame my rational side.

The edge of the collecting cliff is never too far off, and jumping on the fad bandwagon assures a lengthy, breathless fall. If I counted each different type of object that arises in ads from antique publications, auction catalogs and the sort for one or two years over the previous five decades I would find periods when certain genres predominate. Things like Beanie Babies were briefly *in vogue* and then faded away. Looking 20-year-old photos of dealers' booths leads me to wonder, does anyone even purchase bowl and pitcher sets anymore? Once they were a must have. Beware of the falling into the mindset that every good collection must have a certain widget or that trendy item such as Victorian fish forks.

I have jumped on the fad bandwagon but not too terribly often. I own one-third of a stack of painted boxes. We (OK, I) purchased a horse and sulky weathervane when they were the bee's knees, fab, whatever.

My Mistake. Stacks of boxes still look nice to me in dealer's booth and shops but we lack a good place one in our home. As noted earlier, I should have thought where this collection would fit in and did not. I like the weathervane, but I should have waited and studied the form in more depth. I could have found a better one.

Going against the prevailing trend can be rewarding, too. If you do not learn about new categories, you may miss out on wonderful opportunities. (Even if you do not buy a piece, you will become more knowledgeable.) I now own one maritime painting, the schooner I talk about in Chapter 22 and it opened up new horizons, as you can tell from the research that has gone into getting to know it. And recently I have become interested in coin silver from North Carolina where one of our sons lives.

The strumpet call of rarity lures many collectors. I touched on the topic in Chapter 14, "Collectors and Their Money." Someone seriously into antiques learns early on that "rare" is not the same as "desirable." A piece may be rare because few were made (no one wanted them back then), its dimensions or materials were odd, or the originals were so ugly, useless or shoddy that they were swiftly disposed of over the decades. A collector who does not know what is available in the marketplace may mistakenly believe something he is buying is rare. Our French pewter spoons are a good example. We had never seen any when we purchased ours but later learned they are readily and widely available.

The "death grip" is another trap collectors face. Unless certain pieces have great sentimental value, holding on to them for their own sake is probably a mistake. As your tastes mature and change, consign pieces that no longer charm you to a dealer or group shop, put them in an auction, or see if one of your kids want them. You'd be surprised how often that old piece is exactly what a son or daughter has been hoping for (or how little interest they have in antiques). Our first two dining room tables are now happily living with our sons. Failing to build on what you have can impede the development of a nice collection and affect your happiness.

One final mistake and I am giving up the confessional. Years and years ago I spoke with a dealer at a show about a desk he had for sale. It cost a pretty penny. He did not know me, what I collected or could afford to buy. He suggested I talk to a fellow dealer who also had a desk in his booth, though of lower price and quality. I had already seen that specimen. The pricey dealer was, in my judgment, cavalier and I was chagrined, feeling as if I had been dismissed. I should have returned to the first dealer when the initial rush of collectors had abated, when he was perhaps more patient and talked with him about the qualities of the antique. Instead I gave his wares a cold shoulder for years, this despite the fact he was described to me by more than one person as a typical grouchy New Englander. I missed the chance to build a good relationship with a dealer who carried antiques I liked and that probably cost our collection a nice piece or two.

My Mistake. The cliché: "Pride goeth before a fall." The dealer was true to who he was, a grouch sometimes, but well intentioned and very knowledgeable. I was not true to myself, inquisitive, thoughtful and just plain nice.

I end with a positive memorable moment. I hope by now you have grown tired with the mistakes but my hypothesis is that you have not. It was (again) antiques week in Manchester and the second day of the fairly new Antique Collector's Fair. It was mid-afternoon and dealers had time on their hands. A dealer I know and had done business with (it was his tiger maple candlestand described earlier in the chapter, *Collectors and Their Money*) sat by himself in his booth. I asked if I could join him. One of the downsides of antiquing by myself (my wife stayed home that week since she has recently completed 10 days of grueling volunteer work and is glad to have me out of the house), is that there are few folks with whom to talk and compare notes − making sense of what I have seen, the state of the market, and so forth. The dealer and I had never really spent any time together. Yet there we sat for nearly an hour talking about everything "antique" under the sun. He will never know how grateful I was of his company and good conversation. Random acts of kindness are powerful.

Oscar Wilde wrote, "Experience is simply the name we give our mistakes." The fatal blunder is not learning from them. I have lots and lots of experience, as you have seen, much of it painfully gained.

I cannot end this disquisition without warning you that this lengthy catalogue of misapprehensions, misunderstanding, failures of scholarship and the sort has not in the least dimmed my enthusiasm for antique collecting. Just as openness to new experiences is the groundwork for liveliness, risking mistakes – and avoiding them, when possible – makes that life interesting. And my positive experiences as an antiques' collector far outweigh the missteps.

Chapter 26

ℭ

Reflections on Collecting Antiques

Hoadley and Thomas wooden works tall case clock, circa 1810-
1813. 18⅜"w (bonnet), 10⅜"d, 86½"h to top of finial. Case has
the original red-grained paint in excellent condition and has been
restored only where improper replacement hinges were removed
from the base and bonnet doors. There is a chalk signature on
the backboard of the case. The fretwork on the bonnet is original.
The finials and the knobs on the case door and bonnet door are
replacements. The movement is in working condition. The original
dial is decorated with a partridge in a pear tree and is signed.
The back of the dial has several repair signatures and dates from
the mid-1800s. The hands are proper replacement Hoadley-type
hands; the pendulum rod is replaced; the bob and weights are old.
Originally sold by well-known pickers in New Hampshire.

My musings regarding collecting are finished, at least for the moment. It feels good to bid the subject *adieu*. I have a more coherent sense of collectors of antiques and other things – coins, cars, bottle caps – and their world. Philosophers claim that the highest form of deliberation is puzzling about thinking. Finding ways to pass on what we do and don't know is no less challenging and no less noble. That opinion may come from decades of being a college professor.

You remember that we started with the basic elements of style and connoisseurship. I end with the "essentials" of the collecting spirit. Think of collecting as a complex geometric figure made up understandings, insights and presumptions – a sort of intellectual mandala. Little wonder my hours of musing so often yielded mixed results. I regularly found myself writing "maybe-this" and "maybe-that" and "people are complex." To be honest, this is not the sort of three-dimensional puzzle that will yield a singular conclusion, no matter how hard we work on it. Not every collector does the same things or seeks the same outcomes. I imagine you and other collectors will not nod affirmatively at every conclusion I have drawn.

But to the essentials. What exactly does it mean, 'to collect?' Joseph Alsop provides a whimsical and believable, yet incomplete definition.

> To collect is to gather objects belonging to a particular category the collector happens to fancy, as magpies fancy things that are shiny, and a collection is what has been gathered. (*The Rare Art Traditions,* 1982)

Now I have nothing against the mythic acquisitiveness of this avian species, but Alsop's *mot* has the same defect the allegation magpies pick up shiny trinkets does: It is not true. Yes, we collect what attracts us but there is an irrefutable element of rationality behind what antique collectors pursue and possess. The sheer range and variety of collections can be accounted for by an individual's obsessive interest in our history, legends, fads and trends, country tastes and city preferences and a hundred other elements, each one interesting in itself . . . if not to everyone.

We collect the remnants of everyday life from long ago as evidenced in the warm paint or toning on drawer pulls, dings in brass candlesticks, rings on desktops or tavern tables. Some of these objects antique collectors continue to use, some they simply protect and appreciate. Collectors dig up the significance of long-gone craftsmen and how they practiced their artistry. True meaning for a collector is wrapped in the history and significance an antique communicates. I am not trying to minimize the notion antique collectors are attracted to the objects they pursue; of course they want to find these objects beautiful, but "beauty" has its own, highly variable definition. A hard-used highboy with dull brasses and a scarred top most likely is not aesthetically attractive but if it was built by John Goddard (1723/4-1785, apprentice of Job Townsend) it has a sort of historic halo around it. Defects are trivial, provenance in this case everything. Collectors treasure what someone made by hand, designed from her imagination, labored to make as perfect as possible. These are the sorts of things that make collecting antiques alive and vibrant.

In the process of collecting we study of maps Connecticut, Lehigh, or Hudson Valleys to understand sources, artisans and eras. As my "Devil's Dictionary" describes, collecting lets us learn and then become fluent in a strange lexicon. We marvel that objects survive as long as they do and that at least for the moment, we choose to be their proud caretaker. Do magpies, enjoy the objects they pick up and collect? I do not know but the primary reason I collect is because I delight in the activity as well as the objects.

The definition of *taste* changes – sometimes the victim of learned analyses, more often an offshoot of the *zeitgeist* – so in a way what we gather is shackled by our particular place and time. Some collectors embrace the identity being contrarians, rejecting received opinion and fashionable taste, now and then being different for the sake of attention. For the future, will what we collect still be held in esteem years from now? Will people laugh at us? No sure answers to such questions appear evident, but even if the answer is a despairing "no" and the second an abashed "yes," for the collector what has meaning right now and right here justifies the act.

To offer some perspective on the promise and perils of forecasting, it is valuable to remember the first museum exhibitions for American decorative arts took place not much more than 100 years ago. Yet well before that, descendants tucked away grandpa's kilt, grandma's lace collar, the earl's sword, later to be pulled out now and then and cherished or passed on. In more modern times, we have been exposed to antique collections of classic cars, barbed wire, Coca Cola wares, Star Wars memorabilia, cartoons, ceramics, watches. Hype, showmanship, promotion, style and a few agreed upon elements of taste – as well as a mighty dose of guile – contribute to the collector's world, what we come to value in and how much we pay for objects. As new categories and tastes emerge, so do rarities to found, traded and purchased.

Relationships bond collectors to their community. Henry Wood Erving, a founding member of the Walpole Society, the first club of Americana for collectors, wrote of " . . . congenial and new friendships and the cementing of the old" (Stillinger, *The Antiquers*, p. 167).

Without other collectors and dealers in our lives, what would we do and who would we be? They provide us with a society in which we can share our passion, energy, laughter, knowledge, and appreciation. They mentor tyros to the passion, giving support and encouragement. They model a cherished way of life and what it means to be serious about collecting. They respect what the objects collected mean, why they have import, what they communicate. Collectors and dealers strive to be trustworthy, courteous, and respectful, and they actively seek regard and respect. They help us marvel at the complexity and variety of the antique collecting universe, not lament its decline. Collectors are a community – an odd one, at times, like most communities from ice curlers to marching-band enthusiasts – but a body of friends, too.

Collecting antiques demands faith, the "substance of things hoped for and the evidence of things not seen." Belief in the discipline produces resilience, for a collector's success and certainty never last for very long (or at least mine do not).

Serious collectors realize that amongst them hide scoundrels, reprobates, loafers, and self-centered, ambitious poseurs. The antique world, like other universes of those we meet, attracts its share of dolts, timeservers, slackers, whiners, martinets, sea-lawyers, and snobs. Some folks gather prestige and attention however they can. They claim expertise they do not really possess – big hat and no cattle types. Even if we do not walk the path of the "cult of personality" we can appreciate the need in others, and smile at it. This means that the society they live in is not all that much different from what all of us encounter day to day. When they are at their very best those who collect enjoy the humanity and foibles of those wending their way toward the ideal. An old story tells of a professor whose uncle was electrocuted in Reno for having murdered the local barber. In the uncle's obituary, the prof noted that: "At the time of his death, George occupied the chair of applied electricity at a major Western institution." As much as self-aggrandizement belies the way you live, you have to laugh.

Some dealers may drop the chain of reasoning about provenance with a resounding and indifferent "clang." Admittedly, our own approach to collecting antiques may put others off. It all comes down to that bastardized Latin phrase we bandied about as school kids: *llegitimi non carborundum est* (don't let the bastards wear you down). Carry your dignity, worth and grace with you.

Collecting antiques allows a peaceable life at times. Contentment and serenity cloak me when, a cup of tea in hand, I view auction catalogs, websites, or print magazines. I set aside time to look at the pieces I have already collected and think about them seriously. Quiet nourished me as a collector and in my life. Collecting insists that I lend my hobby moments of contemplation, thank goodness.

Those who live in the antique world can never shake their sense of awe. Collectors seek what is aesthetically and intellectually enticing and let themselves appreciate its beauty, significance, and presence. They hope to find an antique in a dealer's shop or booth that is too good to be true yet is "right" by any definition. At this moment, a tall case clock whose makers were only in business together for three short years demands my attention. Someone bought it brand new. It is now over 200 years old.

ễ

An Exercise in Style and Connoisseurship

The Thomas and Hoadley tall case clock is a marvelous example of a country piece in good condition. The case beautifully proportioned (many suffer from being too narrow or tall), its angular lines offsetting some of its loftiness. The dial has wonderful color and execution, and is decorated with a partridge in a pear tree and flowers (that look surprisingly delicate). It includes whimsical painted representations of the holes through which one would insert a key to wind the clock for time and strike. The dial's ornamentation and the case's grain painting (not exuberant but well done) soften and offset its angularity. Some of the more wildly painted cases to be found in this genre enter the world of folk art; this one is more subdued. The addition of a second hand on the clock's face gives it a touch of sophistication. It keeps good time.

The dial's surface is original, the case largely so. While smooth to the touch, the eye gets a sense of texture. The wooden dial shows some minor loss of paint, making it a bit uneven and irregular. The clock's craftsmen

292

used common materials, something to be expected for the clock's time and place. Its case is pine; the 30-hour works wood rather than brass. Despite the painted keyholes on its face, you wind it by opening the door and pulling on the bob attached to weights for both the hour strike and time. A picker discovered the clock in a barn replete with a mouse hole chewed in the case. The colors are vivid even after all these years, especially those of the bird, the gold pears, and the flowers on the face.

Overall the clock's appearance pleases. A knowledgeable collector will never mistake it for a formal piece. High-level craftsmanship on the case, dial, and in the works give it character. Whoever painted the dial excelled at her craft. Notice that the craftsmen made the two pieces of fretwork on the bonnet slightly different shapes, a wonderful idiosyncrasy.

Thomas and Hoadley worked together only from July 7, 1810 to December 9, 1813 (page 32 in *Eli Terry and The Connecticut Shelf Clock*, by Kenneth Roberts) and many of their dials are signed, as this one is. Their clocks occasionally come on the market and are relatively affordable. I have never seen another clock bearing this particular dial and finding any clock with a "good" dial (flowers, birds, a house) is increasingly difficult. My overall evaluation: The clock is a "keeper." It rates an *8* or *9* because of the dial's subject matter, superb execution, affordability and its condition. I expected it would have had minor replacements over the years and that is precisely what I have found.

Compromises. Finding a clock with a more pristine dial and case and more originality struck us as a fool's errand. If one came on the market we would not replace this clock but add the new one to our collection.

What is it like to live with an antique collection? That object in your living room has been around since before the colonies ratified the United States' Constitution. People broke bread at your dining room table for 250 years. God knows what topics patrons discussed over ale and dice or cards, or other games, at your tavern table – the mundane, memorable, and momentous. Oh, if the painting on your wall could tell you of all it has heard and seen. Antiques create a world of their own, more wonderful when you understand them, their story, their creator, their significance.

Antique collectors cherish and preserve knowledge. The *Perfesser* (antique collector) might have played a piano in a whorehouse, but he (Perfessers were always *he*) lived above and apart from the general run of louts. He brought the saloon not only the superficial arts of the day but reminded them that pokin' cattle was not all life was about; there was something more melodic, graceful and gratifying than Gert upstairs or Old Paint at the hitching rack. Collectors seek to understand our modern world by peering through the prism of the past. In our more elevated or delusional moments we may even claim to pursue truth free from equivocation, the demands of expediency, and the desire to spin make what we have something that benefits us as collectors.

Collecting antiques may not always be linear, or successful, or come easily. But once you have joined the club buckle up for a hell of a ride. The act defines, affects and shapes us.

But now that I am off the couch, how to bid it *adieu*? I settled on a single question: "What does it mean to collect antiques?" I answer: "What does it mean to live one's life?" I hope that the understandings at which I arrived in *Come Collect with Me* resonate with you. For in the end, collectors collect. I hope you heard in what I wrote the subtle echo of happiness. I hope you heard the music of elation and jubilation. I hope you learned. Rising from the couch is not the same as fleeing from my life-long hobby. Sometimes it is enough to let it be and indulgently bathe in what it does to and for me. It can do the same for you.

Chapter 27

ૐ

A Proposed "Collector Code of Conduct"

I think every dealer hopes for knowledgeable collectors who look for a win-win (the dealer makes some money and the collector is happy with his purchase), and have the means to follow through. However, anyone who deals with retail finds most of the people desirable to deal with, yet there is a segment that makes it so hard that we have to ask ourselves sometimes what the heck we are doing. (Well-known American Antiques dealer)

This "Collector Code of Conduct" was motivated by my work as an academic and clinical psychologist. More recently themes in Towles' *A Gentleman in Moscow* struck home: We are obliged to take the high road and live a life with grace. Put simply, this is my attempt to help collectors engage in morally good and correct behavior.

Dare I say it? Collectors are born to *kvetch*. We grumble at length about the auctioneer who missed our bid, the item misrepresented in the auction catalogue, the dealer who failed to respond to our inquiries, and the general injustices that befall us. We bemoan the bad-egg dealer, despite knowing there are many honest ones: it fills our time and seems more fun. We seldom inspect our own behavior or criticize ourselves that closely. Would that we did have some innate sense of rightness, ethics and good behavior: the world – even the collector's world – would be a far more tolerable place.

Fetching for a way to examine proper conduct without sounding like Miss Grundy, I decided using an imaginary conversation. In a sense, it completes the circle, for we saw a similar dialogue in the first chapter on auctions and another between a prof and a student not long after.

Let us go back in time 18 months. Two men walk into a bar — yes, all stories start that way but really. I was one of the duo. "Some of the people at the antique show today seemed to have mistaken me for . . . I don't know, a waiter? The shoeshine boy?" the tall dealer, Bill, growled. "They wave imperiously at some piece and ask things like 'how much for that?' In their 'that' I can hear they are thinking 'trash.' I've been in this business for years and I know good antiques. I also know quality. That's what I deal in. That's what my reputation is built on. I love talking with collectors who want to learn. I love educating them. But this?" I smiled, maybe a bit wanly; there may have been times when I was less than gracious in my interactions with dealers. "But as you said you've been doing this for a long time" I sipped my beer. "Why the frustration now? Jerks like that are rare, right?" I knew the answer but had to ask, out of sympathy if nothing else.

"Got to me today. And they're not as rare as I wish," he shot back. "They come to shows thinking an attitude is a golden key to bargaining. As if! I'm less likely to dicker and far more reluctant to explain the merits of a piece to a snob who shows no respect for the antique or me. Some kind of caretaker for the past they'll be."

"Hey, bargaining is tough work," I said, "although it took me some time to learn how to do it, and even more time to be comfortable haggling."

"Yeah, so is collecting, and being a dealer is even more difficult. If you stay in this business there has to be some joy in it. My fun comes from people treating one another with respect. That's all I want: a chance to be a human being. I think I – dealers – have a right to respect. Rudeness isn't a hallmark of personality and culture has nothing to with it, despite all the clichés. Sure, some New Englanders are gruff. But even the ones who are work with me mostly and some are not only good customers but good friends."

"You know" I remarked, "I was at a big antique show sitting in a chair at the edge of a well-known dealer's booth. Someone he knew was talking with him and simply would not let him go to work with buyers clearly interested in a piece he offered. In a case like that, dealers must have the patience of a saint. So you're saying not just honor thy father and mother? Honor thy dealer?"

Bill laughed and raised his glass. "Works for me." He paused. "It can work for collectors, too. They may complain about the unethical dealer, the dealer who misrepresents what he is sells, the huckster. They demand dealer's be ethical (everything should be vetted, everything should be exactly as represented, a dealer should take back an item no questions asked, and so forth *ad nauseam*). They should look at themselves. This business is certainly less fun with the bad apple collectors out there."

"There's a need for a collector code of conduct?"

"Yup, it would help the entire enterprise if more collectors could be taught how to behave or follow a collector code of conduct. Wonder how that would work? Imagine," he said, "show managers could have copies of the code near the front door where they put the usual stacks of antique publications. Dealers could have copies in their booths and shops. Workshops could be offered to educate collectors." He was getting carried away, even ignoring the Blatz on the table in front of him.

"I think I know what you are saying. There are hundreds of unwritten guidelines behind the collecting hobby. That very complication may have a lot to do with the shrinking number of new collectors. The code could be simple and out in the open. No secrets, just sound advice."

Bill nodded enthusiastically, sipping. "But it would have to come from collectors, not dealers. Otherwise people would see it is as self-serving."

I thought about that. Yep, if dealers proposed the idea, collectors would probably see it as another way for them to gain an advantage, to tilt the 18th century Queen Anne table even more their way. "Well, maybe tomorrow will be better," I offered. "May the jerks be few in number, may the sales be good, and may the wind be at your back."

"Thanks," Bill replied. "So how come you didn't buy that chest of drawers I have on the floor?"

"Hard to put into words," I said. "But the best I can say is that I don't love it."

"Understand," Bill said quietly. "Understand. So what about that code of conduct?"

"Let me think on it," I said. "Would be a lot of work, but might be fun."

As I said at the outset, I taught in college for decades. Successful teaching involves a heck of a lot more than blackboard discipline (OK, it was a while ago) and articulating ideas clearly and precisely. Behind everything teachers do lies a code of conduct and it varies by specialization and even whether you teach at an all-women's college or a sectarian university. There simply are some things that are beyond the pale (not that some people don't violate those boundaries but almost all of them unwillingly leave eventually with the encouragement of their colleagues and superiors). As a clinical psychologist I also did private consulting: psychotherapy, assessments, supervising mental health professionals. The only required discipline to be mastered, year after year, in my continuing education to retain my license was ethics. That is the foundation for what follows: Those ethical readings put into practice applied to collecting antiques. The code does not exist, at least yet, but I wish it did.

A Collectors' Code of Conduct

The guiding principle: An ethical collector embraces the good, the right, and the virtuous. Treat others in ways you would like to be treated.

- **Be respectful of dealers, auction staff and others making a living in the field.** Recognize that they are fellow human beings and treat them with courtesy. No matter how upset you may be – and passions can run hot in the antique world – do not swear, or rant and rave. Your language is a reflection of your character. Avoid disparaging epithets. Do not intimidate or be offensive. Be considerate, patient, and civil. Avoid loud or rude behaviors.
- **Let the dealer and others do their jobs.** Do not monopolize a dealer's time or attention. Be sensitive to other collectors in a dealer's booth. Avoid insensitive and self-centered behavior.
- **Be respectful of other collectors.** If someone is looking at a piece you may want, let the dealer know you are interested, too. Do not sharpen your elbows before a show opens so you can better push other collectors out of the way. Do not intimidate other collectors so you can purchase a piece you want.
- **Avoid disparaging gossip.** Admittedly, gossip is one of the coins of the realm in the antique world. Do not subvert dealers, auctioneers

298

and others based on second- or third-hand information. Give credit to those with whom you have had good experiences and whom you trust. Take the high road whenever possible. There are always two sides to a story and sometimes more.

- *Be knowledgeable*. Learn as much as you can about the genre you collect. Give dealers an informed starting point so they can move you along to even greater understanding. The extent of your knowledge and willingness to learn show you are a serous collector. Signs of a healthy curiosity are attractive to many in the American antique collecting field. Ask dealers if you can come back and talk in more depth when the show quiets down, or before or after auctions. When you are serious about learning, dealers may have the time and the inclination to help educate you.

- *Ask questions before you buy*. For example, ask if a piece can be returned if it does not meet your expectations once home. Ask how long you have to decide whether to purchase it. Ask a dealer how he or she would rate a piece. Why is it a *7*? What would make it a *10*? Comparison shop. Ask auction house staff about condition, return policies, shipping, and the like.

- *Be truthful*. Be honest with those with whom you deal. Display integrity. Do not return an item under the pretense that it is broken or the dealer or auctioneer misrepresented it. If you love a piece but cannot afford it, tell the dealer. Ask if he or she will entertain a payment plan. Live up to your obligations. Enter agreements in good faith, and pay your bills when they are due. If you cannot, inform the dealer and explain why. If you put a hold on a piece and change your mind, let the dealer know. Others may be in line waiting to purchase it and he dealer has every right to be able to sell the piece. Who's to say the same dealer will not have even more interesting finds in the future. Don't burn your bridges.

- *Act your age*. Be sensible. Don't make unreasonable demands. Never expect to get something for nothing. Understand dealers may not compromise on price beyond a certain point. Allow sellers to make a living. As self-employed business people, antique dealers have many expenses; don't be obnoxious in trying to drive the price down, and then down more.

- **Be kind**. If warranted, compliment a dealer's booth or a piece or two you really like. After talking with a dealer, especially if during a show's quiet time, offer to get them a bottle or water or something to nosh on.

So there you have it. Yes, there are dealer-curmudgeons and collector-curmudgeons. Some sellers are less than honest, as are some collectors. But for the sake all of the *mensches* who sell, auction, and collect, be kind, be honest, and enjoy.

Recommended Readings

A new or experienced collector of Americana need not own all of the books listed but each is worth looking at. (And others no doubt exist of which I am unaware.) My interests lie in certain genre of American decorative arts and the readings are weaker in other areas (e.g., stoneware, glass). The nice thing about books about antiques is that they retain valuable information for the collector regardless of when they were published. Resources worthy of your attention exist beyond books and the reader is urged to look at *The Magazine Antiques*, *Maine Antique* Digest, *Antiques and the Arts Weekly* (the *Bee)*, *Antiques and Fine Art,* dealers' websites, and auction catalogs and auctions. And attend antique shows, lots of them. Such learning also is invaluable for the experienced collector looking to move into new genres or upgrade a collection.

Architecture/Homes

Colonial Williamsburg Foundation. (1971). *Legacy From the Past: A Portfolio of Eighty-Eight Original Williamsburg Buildings.* Williamsburg, VA: Author.
Considering building or buying a colonial-style home. Wonderful color photos.

Garrett, W. (1995). *American Colonial: Puritan Simplicity to Georgian Grace*. NY: Monacelli Press.
The Americana I collect existed primarily in homes. Wonderful color photos and equally good text. Fascinating read.

Pomada, E., & Larsen, M. (1987). *Daughters of Painted Ladies: America's Resplendent Victorians.* NY: Dutton.
Not everyone wants a colonial style home. Feast your eyes on these painted ladies.

Pomada, E., & Larsen, M. (1992). *America's Painted Ladies: The Ultimate Celebration of Our Victorians.* NY: Dutton.
More painted ladies. Oh the cost of having a house's exterior painted nowadays.

Whiffe, M. (1960). *The Eighteenth-Century Houses of Williamsburg Rev. Ed.* Williamsburg, VA: Colonial Williamsburg Foundation.
Many Americana collectors live in early American homes (new or reproduction) or love colonial architecture both outside and inside. A good description of architectural styles, the craftsmen, tools and how such houses were constructed. A visit to Colonial Williamsburg for a collector of Americana is required.

Candlesticks

Burks, J. M. (1986). *Birmingham Brass Candlesticks.* Charlottesville, VA: University Press of Virginia.
Many homes with American antiques have brass candlesticks as an accessory. This book has good history and even better black and white photos of sticks.

Michaelis, R. F. (1978). *Old Domestic Base-Metal Candlesticks.* Suffolk, England: Antique Collectors' Club Ltd.
More black and white photos and information on sticks.

Clocks

Distin, W. H., & Bishop, R. (1976). *The American clock: A Comprehensive Pictorial Survey 1723-1900 with a Listing of 6153 Clockmakers.* NY: Dutton.
All varieties of American clocks.

Morris, P. E., Jr. (2011). *American Wooden Movement Tall Clocks 1712-1835.* Hoover, Al: Heritage Park Publishing.
Meticulous scholarship. Color photos galore. Owning three such clocks makes this book a bible for me.

Roberts, D. (2010). *A Life with Antique Clocks*. Atglen, PA: Schiffer.
Perspective and stories of an English clock dealer. Color photos and interesting stories. I have never read about robberies and thefts from a dealer before. An interesting chapter on collectors and another on dealer buying.

Roberts, K. D. (1973). *Eli Terry and the Connecticut Shelf Clock*. Bristol, CT: Ken Roberts Publishing.
Black and white photos with excellent history and text.

Zea, P., & Cheney, R. C. (1992). *Clock Making in New England. 1725-1825: An Interpretation of the Old Sturbridge Village Collection*. Sturbridge, MA: Old Sturbridge Village.
Primarily black and white photos. Excellent history and description.

Collections (All have a wonderful array of photographs and text to train and delight the eye).

Hollander, S. C. (2001). *American Radiance: The Ralph Esmerian Gift to the American Folk Art Museum*. NY: Harry N. Abrams.
This book could just as easily be listed under Folk Art. Luscious color photos, page after page of beautiful folk art. Complete descriptions of the objects depicted.

Katcher, J., Schorsch, D. A., & Wolfe, R. (Eds.). *Expressions of Innocence and Eloquence: Selections from the Jane Katcher Collection of Americana*. Seattle: Marquand Books.
Some unusually good essays and vivid color photographs. A treat for the eye.

Cadou, C. B. (2006). *The George Washington Collection: Fine and Decorative Arts at Mount Vernon*. Manchester, NY: Hudson Hills Press.
Bravo to the Mount Vernon Ladies Association for saving and preserving this national treasure. Marvelous color photographs and even better history and stories.

Folk Art including Paintings

Bishop, R. (1979). *Folk Painters of America.* NY: Dutton.
Black and white and color photographs. Arranged by geographic region.

D'Ambrosio, P. S., & Emans, C. (1987). *Folk Art's Many Faces: Portraits in the New York State Historical Association.* Cooperstown, NY: New York State Historical Association.
Color and black and white photos of paintings. A good array of artists.

Ericson, J. T. (1979). *Folk Art in America: Painting and Sculpture.* NY: Mayflower Books.
All photos in black and white. Nice section on folk art in general Covers 12 artists and 8 types of sculpture.

Hofer, M. K., & Olson, R. J. M. (2015). *Making it Modern: The Folk Art Collection of Elie and Viola Nadelman.* London: Giles.
I like this book not because it has numerous photos but because of the old black and white photos and the text describing various folk art genres. Some of the best item descriptions I have ever read.

Johnson, B. (1976). *American Cat-alogue: The Cat in American Folk Art.* NY: Hearst Corporation.
A few color, mostly black and white photos. Any cat lover who wants to add cat-related folk art to her collection will find this book invaluable.

Kallir, O. (1973). *Grandma Moses.* NY: Harry N. Abrams.
Biography and black and white, and color photos. Oh to be able to afford one of her winter scenes.

Furniture

Comstock, H. (1962). *American Furniture: Seventeenth, Eighteenth, and Nineteenth Century Styles.* Exton, PA: Schiffer.
Almost all black and white (700) photographs. See what you like.

Evans, H. G. (1996). *American Windsor Chairs. NY: Hudson Hills Press.*
In-depth scholarship, lots of it. I like this book more for its array of photos of Windsor chairs. After you learn what styles you like, you can then read about their history and craftsmen.

Evans, N. G. (1997). *American Windsor Furniture Specialized Forms.* NY: Hudson Hills Press.
Wonderful photos and text. Some chairs but also children's furniture, miniatures, stools, stands and so forth. Once again, feast your eye.

Fales, D. A. Jr. (1981). *The Furniture of Historic Deerfield. NY: Dutton.*
Color and black and white photos, superb content. A visit to Historic Deerfield is a must if you have not yet done so.

Kirk, J. T. (1977). *The impecunious Collector's Guide to American Antiques.* NY: Knopf.
Important content on how to look, knowledge, and quality of design.

Lyon, I. W. *The Colonial Furniture of New England: A Study of the Domestic Furniture in Use in the Seventeenth and Eighteenth Centuries.* NY: Dutton.
Early meticulous scholarship on American furniture.

Nutting, W. (1931). *Furniture of the Pilgrim Century 1620-1720 Including Colonial Utensils and Hardware.* NY: Bonanza Books.
Tons of photographs with excellent item descriptions.

Nutting, W. (1948). *Furniture Treasury (Mostly of American Origin) – All Periods of American Furniture with Some Foreign Examples in America. Also American Hardware and Household Utensils.* Volumes I & 2. New York: Macmillan.
Wonderful black and white photos. Fun to page through.

Nutting. W. (1973). *A Windsor Handbook.* Rutland, VT: Charles E. Tuttle.

A small book with black and white photos comprising illustrations and descriptions of Windsor furniture of all periods.

Sack, A. (1960). *Fine Points of Furniture – Early American.* NY: Crown.
The original *Good, Better,* Best, and the finest book I know of to help a collector train his eye for furniture. A must have. Republished several times.

Sack, A. (1993). *The New Fine Points of Furniture: Early America – Good, Better, Best, Superior, Masterpiece.* NY: Crown.
The title says it all. A must have addition to the original 1960 *Good, Better, Best.*

Santore, C. (1992). *The Windsor Style in American: Volumes I and II.* Philadelphia, PA: Running Press.
For anyone interested in Windsor chairs and other furniture. One of the *must have* books.

Schaffner, C. V. A., & Klein, S. (1997). *American Painted Furniture.* NY: Clarkson Potter/Publishers.
Delightful color photos of high-style and country furniture.

Trent, R. F. (1977). *Hearts & Crowns.* New Haven, CT: New Haven Colony Historical Society.
Classic on the heart and crown chair-making tradition. Black and white photographs.

Paint

Fales, D. A. Jr. (1979). *American Painted Furniture 1660-1880. NY: Dutton.*
Both black and white and color plates. A strong motivation to add color to one's collection.

Priddy, S. (2004). *American Fancy: Exuberance in the Arts 1790-*

1840. Milwaukee, WI: Chipstone Foundation.

If this book doesn't motivate you to add color to your American decorative arts collection, nothing will. Wonderful photos and excellent text.

Paintings/Prints

American Historical Print Collectors Society. (1991). *Currier & Ives: The New Best 50*. Milwaukee, WI: Author.
Color prints of the top 50. Pick your favorites.

Brewington, D. E. R. (1982). *Marine Paintings and Drawings in Mystic Seaport Museum*. Mystic, CT: Mystic Seaport Museum, Inc.
Western and oriental artists. A thick book with color and black and white photos, and detailed descriptions.

Christie's. (2004). *The Magnificent Sachsen-Meiningen Set of Audubon's The Birds of America*. NY: Author.
An auction catalog with color photos throughout.

Christie's. (2012). *John James Audubon's The Birds of America: The Duke of Portland Set*. NY: Author.
A second auction catalog from Christie's with color photos.

Conningham, F. A. (1970). *Currier & Ives Prints:* An Illustrated Check List. *NY: Crown Publishers.*
A complete listing. Not many photos but nice content on suggestions for collectors and quality guidelines for the prints. Also lists the Best Fifty.

Granby, A. (2004). *A Yachtsman's Eye: The Glen S. Foster Collection of Marine Paintings*. NY: Norton.
Magnificent color plates with even better description of the paintings. Foster certainly knew the best and his collection reflects this taste and his *Yachtsman's Eye.*

Granby, A., & Hyland, J. (2009). *Flying the Color: The Unseen Treasures of Nineteenth-Century American Marine Art*. Mystic, CT: Mystic Seaport.
A marvelous book for training one's eye for 19th Century American marine art. Lots of color plates. I covet more than a few of the paintings herein.

Howat, J. K. (1972). *The Hudson River and Its Painters.* Middlesex, England: Penguin Books.
Color and black and white photos. I would love to grace my home's walls with these paintings.

Holdridge, B. C., & Holdridge, L. B. (1969). *Amni Phillips: Portrait Painter 1788-1865*. NY: Clarkson N. Potter.
I consider Phillips to be one of the premier American folk art limners. Excellent history. Primarily small black and white photos of paintings with three full page color plates.

Lane, C. W. (undated). *A Guide to Collecting Antique Historical Prints*. Philadelphia, PA: The Philadelphia Print Shop.
A small but valuable publication with content on what constitutes an original print, reproductions, restrikes, where prints come from, how prints are described (size, condition, states, editions, proofs, and what is involved in collecting prints (themes, condition, knowledge, preservation) and reasons for collecting historical prints.

Miles, E. (Eds.). (1977). *Portrait Painting in America*. NY: Main Street Press/Universe Books.
Primarily black and white plates of American portrait paintings by both trained and folk art artists.

Penobscot Marine Museum. (1988). *Goodly Ships on Painted Seas: Ship Portraiture by Penobscot Bay Artists*. Searsport, ME: Author.
Primarily black and white photos. Emphasis on William P. Stubbs James G. Babbidge, and Percy A. Sanborn. Excellent content and resource.

Tillou, P. (1973). *Nineteenth-Century Folk Painting: Our Spirited National Heritage.* Marshfield, CT: The William Benton Museum of Art.
A nice book of folk art paintings from the collection of Mr. and Mrs. Peter Tillou.

People, Objects, and Collecting

Freund, T. (1993). *Objects of Desire: The Lives of Antiques and Those Who Pursue Them.* NY: Pantheon Books.
Enthralling stories about three American antiques all for sale in New York during Americana week in 1991 and the dealers and collectors through whose hands they passed. Of the three – Chippendale card table (Philadelphia 1759), Federal sofa table, and a robin's egg blue pine blanket chest – there is no contest. The latter is to die for. A fascinating book well worth the read.

Keno, L., & Keno, L. (2000). *Hidden Treasures: Searching for Masterpieces of American Furniture.* NY: Warner Books.
Great stories and beautiful photographs. Insight into how dealers and auction houses find the treasures they do.

Sack, H. (1986). *American Treasure Hunt: The Legacy of Israel Sack.* Boston: Little, Brown, & Co.
A testimony to his father and a history of the Sack firm that established American antique furniture; the quest for the best furniture never ceased. An enthralling history of American antique collecting in the twentieth century.

Stillinger, E. (1980). *The Antiquers – The Lives and Careers, the Deals, the Finds, the Collections of the Men and Women Who were Responsible for the Changing Taste in American Antiques, 1850—1930.* NY: Knopf.
Great stories about these early collectors and the placement of American antiques into both collecting and the American consciousness.

Periodicals (All have websites)

Antiques and the Arts Weekly. Published weekly (an amazing feat). Reports on auctions and shows, has interviews and articles of interest. Contains ads for upcoming shows and auctions. A complete array of antiques. Called the *Bee* (Bee Publishing Company).

Antiques and Fine Art Magazine. Published four times/year. Like *The Magazine Antiques* a glossy publication with scholarly articles and wonderful color photos. Probably for the more advanced collector.

Maine Antique Digest. Published monthly. Reports on auctions and shows, reviews books. Dealers' ads, lists upcoming auctions, informative articles. Covers much more than New England antiques.

The Magazine Antiques. Published 6 times/year. A glossy and more "upscale" magazine. Known for its scholarly articles. Beautiful color ads. Probably for the more advanced collector.

Quilts

Kiracofe, R. (1993). *The American Quilt: A History of Cloth and Comfort 1750-1950.* NY: Clarkson Potter.
Lovely color photos and excellent descriptions.

Ramsey, B., & Waldvogel, M. (1998). *Southern Quilts: Surviving Relics of The Civil War.* Nashville, TN: Rutledge Hill.
Color photos.

Tobin, J. L., & Dobard, R. G. (1999). *Hidden in Plain View: A Secret Story of Quilts and the Underground Railroad.* NY: Doubleday.
Some color photos, a fascinating story (if true), and nice drawings of the quilts' code patterns.

Tinware

Devoe, S. S. (1981). *The Art of the Tinsmith: English and American.* Exton, PA: Schiffer.
Black and white photos, good history.

Martin, G., & Tucker, L. (1997, 2000, 2004, 2007). *American Painted Tinware: A Guide to Its Identification (Volumes I, II, III, IV). NY: Historical Society of Early American Decoration.*
If you are interested in painted tinware these are the books to educate you. Color photos.

Weathervanes

Bishop, R., & Coblentz, P. (1981). *A Gallery of American Weathervanes and Whirligigs.* NY: Dutton.

Kaye, M. (1975). *Yankee Weathervanes.* NY: Dutton.
Good history and pen and ink drawings.

Klamkin, C. (1973). *Weathervanes.* NY: Hawthorn Books.

Miller, S. (1984). *The Art of the Weathervane.* Box. E. Exton, PA: Schiffer.

Bishop, Klamkin, and Miller all have history on and photos of weathervanes made by the major United States manufacturers. What I always wished for was a book written for collectors. Such a book would show the same vane in several surfaces talking about the pluses and minuses of each surface and value of each vane. Alas, such a book does not exist.

Other

Campbell, R. (2007). *No Longer Hidden: An Exhibit of Black Cloth Dolls 1870-1930.* Still River, MA: Harvard Historical Society.
Catalog of an exhibit of dolls from the collection of Pat Hatch. Great

color photos. A must for my wife who has only found three she can love in the last 30 years.

Eversmann, P. K. (2001). *The Winterthur Gide to Recognizing Styles: American Decorative Arts from the 17th Through 19ᵗʰ Centuries.* Winterthur, DE: Henry Francis Du Pont Winterthur Museum.
One of the best primers I have read on the major style categories complete with color photos. The book defines what style is, learning to look, ornamentation, line, color, how each style became popular, and how the objects were lived with.

Gash, J. Fiction. *Lovejoy series.* Lovejoy is an English antique dealer, rogue, and divvy. Descriptions of his love for and what he feels around a genuine antique put into words what a collector experiences. The descriptions of fakes or Lovejoy faking antiques should send chills down the spine of anyone who collects antiques.

Kitzmiller, D., & Bish, C. (1992). *Figural Bottle Openers Identification Guide.* Mechanicsville, PA: Collector's Companion.
Page after page of color photos. Each opener is rated on its rarity.

Lanmon, D. P. (1999). *Evaluating Your Collection: The 14 Points of Connoisseurship.* Winterthur, DE: Henry Francis Du Pont Winterthur Museum.
Fourteen criteria on which to assess an antique. Color photos for each. chapter with each criterion "in practice." One of the best I have read.

Leavitt, J. F. (1970). *Wake of the Coasters.* Middletown, CT: Wesleyan University Press.
Coasters were schooners and in researching the schooner painting I own this book provided invaluable history. A bygone era I wish I had experienced.

Lindenberger, J. (1999). *Black Memorabilia for the Kitchen: A Handbook and Price Guide.* Atglen, PA: Schiffer.
The price guide is obviously dated. Almost all color photos of objects.

Little, N. F. (2001). *Neat & Tidy: Boxes and Their Contents Used in Early American Households*. Hanover, NH: Society for the Preservation of New England Antiquities.
Black and white photos with text of boxes of all shapes and sizes.

McConnell, K. (1990). *Spongeware and Spatterware*. West Chester, PA: Schiffer.
Good color photos. Some good content on pricing and terminology.

Montgomery, C. F. (1973). *A History of American Pewter*. NY: Weathervane Books.
A nice beginning point to learn about pewter. I especially enjoyed the history of its use in America, the photos and learning about its rivals (wood and pottery). Includes elements of connoisseurship.

Szurovy, G. (2002). *The Art of the Airways*. Minneapolis, MN: Zenith Press.
See why my wife and I like posters with airplanes. Lots of color photos. My favorite: American Airlines: West With the Night. I have never seen one on the market.

Index

About the Author

Baron Perlman is a long-time collector of American decorative arts. His childhood and teen focus on stamps, comic books, and baseball cards was supplanted by American antiques. He was born to collect.

Born in Chicago Perlman attended Lawrence University (Appleton, WI) and then Michigan State University where he earned his master's and doctorate in clinical psychology. He served in the U.S. Army, including a tour in Viet Nam.

Most of his professional life was spent in the Department of Psychology at the University of Wisconsin Oshkosh and in consulting. His applied work as a clinical psychologist including just plain listening and trying to "make sense of" serves him well as a collector. He is now joyfully retired.

His interests in collecting and writing have led to numerous columns that continue to be published in Maine Antique Digest. He also pens a monthly column for the local newspaper, the Oshkosh Northwestern, about local, state and national matters – involving the interactions of three people in a bar (about as Wisconsin as one can get).

Married almost 50 years, his wife Sandy joins him in collecting. They have lived in Oshkosh, Wisconsin for a long time and have two sons and three cats. Neither son is as consumed with collecting as their dad is. Nor are the cats.

ℭ

Connect with Baron at comecollectwithme.com, facebook.com/baron.perlman

If you have enjoyed this book, reviews are greatly appreciated!

CPSIA information can be obtained
at www.ICGtesting.com
Printed in the USA
LVHW070333021120
670430LV00017B/57/J